Running for Judge

Running for Judge

The Rising Political, Financial, and
Legal Stakes of Judicial Elections

EDITED BY

Matthew J. Streb

New York University Press

NEW YORK AND LONDON

NEW YORK UNIVERSITY PRESS
New York and London
www.nyupress.org

Library of Congress Cataloging-in-Publication Data
Running for judge : the rising political, financial, and legal stakes of judicial
elections / edited by Matthew J. Streb.
p.   cm.
Includes bibliographical references and index.
ISBN-13: 978-0-8147-4034-7 (cloth : alk. paper)
ISBN-10: 0-8147-4034-0 (cloth : alk. paper)
1. Judges—United States—States—Election.   I. Streb, Matthew J.
(Matthew Justin), 1974–
KF8785.A7R86   2007
347.73'14—dc22   2006033781

New York University Press books are printed on acid-free paper,
and their binding materials are chosen for strength and durability.

Manufactured in the United States of America
10 9 8 7 6 5 4 3 2 1

For Logan, who always reminds me that
work can be put off to play catch

Contents

List of Tables

List of Figures

Chapter 1

The Study of Judicial Elections

Matthew J. Streb

In a 2004 election, Lloyd Karmeier and Gordon Maag spent a combined total of approximately $10 million. The Democratic and Republican Parties accounted for roughly half of that money, and Political Action Committees donated much of the rest. Candidates, political parties, and interest groups spent more than $5 million on television advertisements alone. The tone of the race was mean spirited, as close to 73 percent of the commercial airings were either attack or contrast ads.[1] The candidates clashed over health care and medical malpractice, and supporters of one questioned the character of the other. Volunteers for one of the candidates were even accused of rummaging through the opponent's trash. All of this was regularly covered in the print media. This was not a race for the U.S. Senate, as the amount of money spent, the tone of the campaign, the issues raised, and the media coverage might imply. It was an election for a seat on the Illinois Supreme Court.

The Illinois Supreme Court race between Karmeier and Maag is not an outlier. According to one study, in 2003–2004, supreme court candidates combined to raise over $46.8 million. Combined candidate spending in ten races broke the $1 million mark, and nine candidates spent more than $1 million by themselves. In the 2000, 2002, and 2004 election cycles, candidates raised $123 million compared with only $73.5 million in the preceding three cycles.[2] The spending didn't stop at the supreme court level; one candidate for a Georgia intermediate appellate court seat raised $3.3 million.[3] Nor was the spending confined only to candidates. While the controversial 527 organizations took a major role in the 2004 presidential election, they weren't silent in judicial elections, either. In West Virginia, one 527 group raised at least $3.6 million to successfully beat an incumbent.[4] The organization, known as "And for the Sake of the Kids," accused

Justice Warren McGraw of being lenient on child molesters and was funded primarily by the chief executive officer of Massey Energy.

Twenty years ago, judicial elections such as the ones in Illinois and West Virginia would have been relatively uncommon. Today, they are ordinary. Judicial elections have changed immensely, perhaps more so than elections for any other office. Once compared to playing a game of checkers by mail,[5] many of today's judicial races are as rough and tumble as any congressional election. As one observer famously remarked, judicial elections are getting "noisier, nastier, and costlier."[6] Candidate spending in judicial elections, both at the supreme court and intermediate appellate levels, has skyrocketed. Interest groups and political parties, recognizing the extreme importance of electing judges who support their views, are becoming more active.

The changes occurring in judicial elections involve more than the massive amounts of money that are flooding campaigns. Judicial elections are governed by rules different from those of other elections, and those rules are coming under attack (see chapter 2). Courts have declared some of the rules that guide judicial elections to be unconstitutional (most notably the announce clause, which prohibited judicial candidates from "announcing his or her view on disputed legal or political issues"),[7] and many more lawsuits challenging other rules remain or are likely on the horizon. The decisions have the potential to dramatically affect the way judicial elections are run by campaign consultants and covered by the media, the kinds of issues that are raised in the races, and the ability of citizens to cast informed votes. All of these occurrences have worried many judicial reformers because, in their eyes, races for judgeships are becoming more and more political. As a result, several states and municipalities are considering judicial election reform (see chapter 11).

Discussion of the judicial selection process isn't restricted to reformers. Because of the increasing contentiousness of the federal judicial selection process, questions about whether judges should be elected or appointed are common in newspapers, magazines, and even blogs. In short, interest in judicial elections among scholars, practitioners, and the media has grown substantially. Yet systematic studies of judicial elections are surprisingly somewhat rare. Certainly, there are an enormous number of law review articles on the judicial selection process, and there are an increasing number of interesting articles on the topic published in academic journals (many by several of the contributors to this book). But with what Deborah Goldberg and her colleagues at the Brennan Center for Justice call the

"New Politics of Judicial Elections"[8] emerging and recent court rulings regarding the rules of judicial elections (and several more pending), a systematic study of judicial elections is needed. The goal of *Running for Judge* is to fill in this void by providing some answers to important questions regarding judicial elections, ranging from the role of interest groups and political parties to the coverage of these elections by the media. The chapters will tie together the current state of the judicial elections literature and offer some new, empirical analyses on a wide spectrum of topics.

Much of the work that is published on judicial elections, especially in law reviews is normative in nature. Some recent titles, including "Judicial Elections versus Merit Selection: The Futile Quest for a System of Judicial 'Merit' Selection,"[9] "Had Enough in Ohio? Time to Reform Ohio's Judicial Selection Process,"[10] "The Case for Adopting Appointive Judicial Selection Systems for State Court Judges," and, most bluntly, "Why Judicial Elections Stink"[11] make the point. Certainly there is nothing wrong with people debating the pros and cons of certain judicial selection methods, but our purpose here is different. While the contributors will raise some normative questions, they will let the readers provide their own normative answers. The goal is to describe and explain the current state of judicial elections in a nonnormative way; we leave the pros and cons of our findings as they relate to judicial elections to be debated by others.

Why Study Judicial Elections?

Recently, I started a job at Northern Illinois University. During the new faculty orientation we were asked to introduce ourselves and briefly discuss our research areas of interest. When I said that I was currently studying the politics of judicial elections, many of my new colleagues gave me a quizzical look. My colleagues are not much different from others who ask what I study. "Why would you study judicial elections?" one friend once asked. "Aren't presidential elections more interesting and important?" Some people are not even aware that there are judicial elections to study.

While I certainly understand my friend's puzzlement, the study of judicial elections is enormously important (whether it is more important than studying presidential elections is irrelevant). While a member of Congress is just one of 535, a judge may be one of a few people—and, indeed, may often be the sole person—responsible for a decision. Even in cases where a jury is ultimately responsible for a verdict, the judge has great discretion in terms of ruling on the procedural aspects of the case, and, in many states it is the judge who is responsible for the sentencing. Also, post-trial motions are quite common. While they are usually denied, the judge still has the potential power to overrule a jury's verdict or to issue a new trial. And, as Paul Brace and Brent Boyea make clear in chapter 10, judges regularly have the power to reverse capital punishment decisions. Simply put, judges have more power and discretion than most office holders have.

Moreover, the issues that state judges must confront are often as important as those before federal judges. Judges have a great deal of power and are deeply involved in dividing up scare resources and deciding what kind of society we will live in. Clearly, state judges may be limited in their rulings by federal court precedent—a state court cannot overturn *Roe v. Wade,* for example—but the issues before state judges are likely to be quite relevant to many people who live in the state. While a state court cannot overturn *Roe,* it can make rulings that would limit or uphold abortion rights under certain circumstances. Perhaps the power of state courts is most apparent with the controversy over the Massachusetts Supreme Court's ruling that same-sex marriage was protected under the state's constitution. The Massachusetts Supreme Court is not elected, but that doesn't mean that a similar ruling couldn't be handed down in a state where judges are elected (or, maybe not because of the judges' fear of backlash, which raises a host of other interesting questions regarding judicial independence). In short, state court judges make important rulings and have significant influence; as a result, it is necessary that we understand the selection process that puts the vast majority of state judges in that position of power.

Studying the judicial selection process—in this case, specifically elections—can allow us to better understand the conditions under which state judges make their rulings and how, if at all, the selection process influences those rulings (a topic that is addressed in chapter 10). While the research in this book is nonnormative, it certainly has normative implications. Should judges be accountable to the public in a manner similar to that of other elected officials? Should they be concerned with public opinion? How important is judicial independence? Is it appropriate for political parties and interest groups to be active in judicial campaigns? Are these actors needed to help the public make sense of these low-information elections?

The study of judicial elections has relevance beyond how they affect what happens on the bench. As someone who studies political behavior, I initially became interested in judicial elections because they raise some intriguing questions about campaigns and citizens' vote choices. Much of the voting behavior literature is focused on national or high-profile state elections (e.g., the president, Congress, governor), and understandably so. But elections for these offices actually constitute an extremely small percentage of the total number of offices in which Americans are asked to vote. Many questions emerge regarding contests for so-called down-ballot offices. How are these down-ballot races covered in the media? Can citizens obtain enough information about the candidates to cast "rational" votes? If party identification is removed from the ballot—as it is in many judicial elections—and we know that party identification is a (if not *the*) central influence on voter choice,[12] then how informed are people when they vote in these races? What other cues might they be looking for? Do interest groups and political parties come to wield more influence in these low-information elections? How do candidates for these offices campaign? Judicial elections are one outlet to answer some of these questions about political behavior in low-information elections.

So why have scholars generally focused more on elections for higher-profile offices? Because the offices have higher profiles, there is more interest in these races (nobody flinches when I tell them I study presidential elections). Many citizens are engrossed in the competitive nature of presidential elections, and they may be more apt to see the relevance of elections for Congress or governor. People are more likely to understand the issues discussed in, and the importance of the outcomes of, these elections. They haven't always felt the same way about judicial elections. For example, most people don't get too worked up about tort reform, a subject that is regularly an issue in judicial elections.

There is also a more practical reason why scholars are less likely to examine judicial elections (or, for that matter, other down-ballot contests as well). Data collection makes presidential, congressional, and even gubernatorial elections much easier to study. Every two years the Inter-University Consortium for Political and Social Research (ICPSR), housed at the University of Michigan, conducts the American National Election Study (ANES), a comprehensive pre/post survey that asks respondents a plethora of questions about presidential and congressional elections. Exit polls— conducted as voters leave the voting booth—are usually available to provide scholars with information on how people voted and why they voted that way. A variety of polling and news organizations conduct preelection polls that give researchers even more data to analyze. Usually, none of these sources of data asks questions about judicial elections.

The complexity of the state court systems makes judicial election research more difficult, too. If you are studying trial court elections, for instance, there are thousands of seats to be filled (although many of these seats are uncontested) and information about these races is sporadically available; the data that are available are contained in several places. Furthermore, as Brian Schaffner and Jennifer Segal Diascro discuss in chapter 7, media coverage of judicial elections is not frequent, especially when compared with races for the Senate and governor and, especially, for the presidency. All of these things can make studying judicial elections difficult and frustrating.

Judicial Selection in the States

Before we get into the more substantive chapters of this volume, it is important to illustrate the judicial selection process in the states, as well as the reasons that judicial elections came about. These are the subjects of the next two sections.

Judicial selection of federal judges is straightforward. The Constitution clearly states that the president is to nominate all federal judicial candidates who then must be confirmed by the Senate. Although it is easy to explain the federal judicial selection process, judicial selection in the states is much more complex because of federalism. There are nearly as many different rules for selecting judges as there are states. Each state determines how their judges will be initially selected, the length of the judges' terms, and whether they will be reappointed or reelected, which leads to many different variations.

There are two broad types of judicial selection methods: appointment and election. Some states, such as New Jersey and Maine, follow the federal model of judicial selection. The governor independently chooses a judicial candidate, who is then subject to legislative confirmation. However, unlike the federal model in which judges serve for life, judges in New Jersey and Maine each serve seven-year terms and then must be reappointed in the same manner as they were first appointed. Virginia continues to use the plan adopted by many of the states after the ratification of the Constitution. Its judges are appointed (and reappointed) by the state legislature. Finally, in some states, such as Hawaii, New Hampshire, and Rhode Island, a nominating committee—often comprising state lawyers and judges—presents a list of potential nominees to the governor from which

to choose. South Carolina is slightly different. The state's Judicial Merit Selection Committee—comprised of six members of the General Assembly
and four people chosen by the state legislature from the general public—
provides a list of three candidates to the state legislature, not the governor.

In the vast majority of states, however, at least some of the judges face
some sort of election. Thirty-nine states use some form of election to select or retain some or all of their judges. Almost 90 percent of all state
judges must face voters to retain their seats on the bench.[13] There are three
types of judicial elections: partisan, nonpartisan, and retention elections.
Some states, including Alabama, Illinois, Pennsylvania, and Texas, elect
their judges in partisan elections. In theory, then, these elections are no
different from elections for president and for Congress. A political party
nominates candidates, who then run under the party's name. Because
judges are supposed to be above politics, partisan judicial elections are
quite controversial (see chapter 6). As a result, many states hold nonpartisan judicial elections, in which no political party is listed next to the candidates' names. These elections are similar to all of the elections for local
office, for instance, in California and Texas. In 2004, North Carolina became the most recent state to switch from partisan to nonpartisan elections. Michigan and Ohio use a strange combination of partisan and nonpartisan elections for seats on their state supreme courts. In both states
candidates are nominated by political parties (by a party convention in
Michigan and a party primary in Ohio), but the candidates' party affiliations are not listed on the general election ballot.

Partisan and nonpartisan elections are regularly used in elections for
other offices, but there is one election that is unique to the selection of
judges: retention elections. In retention elections, judges are appointed to
the bench (usually by the governor, in some cases with a merit commission, in some cases without) for a set term. After a judge's term is completed, the public then votes whether to retain the judge. The judge does
not run against an opponent; voters simply vote "Yes" to keep him or
her on the bench or "No" to remove the judge. As I discuss momentarily,
retention elections were a solution offered by the American Judicature
Society as an attempt to generate a compromise between judicial independence and judicial accountability. Retention elections are also getting
more expensive and nastier, which raises questions about how independent even judges selected under this method can be.

What makes judicial selection in the states even more complex is the
variations that are used *within* several states. For example, California holds

retention elections for its supreme court and courts of appeals justices after they serve twelve-year terms. Alternatively, candidates for superior court must run in nonpartisan elections and are elected to six-year terms. In Arizona, all judges are nominated by the governor through a nominating committee, unless the county's population is under 250,000. In that case, superior court judges are then chosen through nonpartisan elections. California's and Arizona's judicial selection processes are simplistic compared to Indiana's. In Indiana, supreme court and appellate court justices are appointed by the governor through a nominating commission and must be retained every ten years. At the circuit court level, judicial candidates generally run in partisan elections, unless the seat's jurisdiction is in Vanderburgh County, in which case the election is nonpartisan. Superior court seats are also generally decided in partisan elections, but Allen and Vanderburgh Counties hold nonpartisan elections and Lake and St. Joseph Counties appoint through a nominating commission.

History of Judicial Elections

The complex nature of the states' judicial selection processes raises the question, why do we have judicial elections in the first place? After all, Alexander Hamilton was quite clear that if a judge were forced to run for reelection, judicial independence—and hence the judiciary itself—would be threatened. As with many aspects of government at the time, Hamilton's and the founders' beliefs about the importance of judicial independence were developed largely because of their experiences with England and colonial government. Founders like Hamilton strongly favored judicial independence because of the conflict they saw in England between judges and the king. They also believed judicial independence was needed based on the colonial experience where governors often appointed friends to the bench no matter the person's qualifications.[14] As a result, the founders settled on a selection system in which federal judges would be appointed by the president with a senatorial check on the president's appointment power. To keep federal judges free from political influence, they would serve life-time terms (although the judges would have the possibility of being impeached under extraordinary circumstances).

The thirteen original states also adopted an appointment system for their judges. In 1780, seven states selected their judges by the legislature and five states had the governor appoint judges who would then be approved by a special council appointed by the legislatures to serve as a check on the governor. Delaware followed the model eventually adopted in the Constitution: the governor would appoint followed by legislative confirmation.[15] No state elected judges. All the states that entered into the Union after the original thirteen until 1830 followed the appointment method as well.[16]

However, the idea of an elected judiciary was not foreign at this time. Montesquieu, for example, supported the selection of judges by the people.[17] In the Declaration of Independence, Jefferson accused King George of having "made Judges dependent on his Will alone, for the Tenure of their Offices, and the Amount and Payment of their salaries." As a result, the idea of judicial accountability began to emerge as well. In the early 1800s, Vermont, Indiana, and Georgia became the first states to allow localities the option to elect trial court judges. It wasn't until 1832, however, when Mississippi became the first state to amend its constitution to require that all state judges be elected. New York followed suit in 1846, with apparently little debate over the subject.[18] Rapidly, states began to follow the leads of Mississippi and New York. According to Evan Haynes, "In the year 1850 alone, seven states changed to popular election of judges; and, thereafter, year by year until the Civil War, others followed."[19] By the time of the Civil War, twenty-four of thirty-four states had an elected judiciary.[20] In fact, every state that entered the Union between 1846 until Alaska's admission in 1959 allowed for the election of some—if not all—all its judges.[21]

Scholars have put forth several reasons behind the surge in state-elected judiciaries, including concern over an independent judiciary after the Supreme Court's controversial ruling in *Marbury v. Madison*,[22] resistance to English common law,[23] imitation by the states,[24] the fact that impeachment was difficult to enact,[25] the belief that judges at the local level should be responsive to their communities,[26] and the legal profession's belief that the judiciary needed more independence from the state legislatures.[27] Perhaps more than anything, the rise of Jacksonian democracy gave more power to the people and raised questions about the accountability of judges. Not electing state judges was considered to be undemocratic, and the Jacksonian era was dominated by beliefs in expanded suffrage and popular control of elected officials.

However, the creation of judicial elections introduced a whole new set of problems. The first judicial elections established were partisan and dominated by the machine politics of the time, which led to cronyism and

corruption. In fact, as Steven P. Croley notes, "By the early twentieth century, elective judiciaries were increasingly viewed as plagued by incompetence and corruption."[28] Roscoe Pound concurred, arguing in 1906 in an
often-cited speech before the American Bar Association that "putting
courts into politics, and compelling judges to become politicians, in many
jurisdictions has almost destroyed the traditional respect for the bench."[29]
These problems led to a new round of judicial selection reform pushed by
groups including the Progressives, the American Bar Association, and the
American Judicature Society. One particularly popular reform was nonpartisan elections in which the candidates' party affiliations would not be
listed on the ballot. This Progressive reform was designed to cripple the
powerful city machines' control over the nomination process and remove
divisive national partisan interests from state and local elections. In the
process, Progressives believed, government would become less corrupt.
Since judges are supposed to be "above politics," this reform was particularly popular regarding judicial selection. Nonpartisan judicial elections
were perceived as a way to clean up corruption and cronyism in the judicial selection process while still keeping judges accountable to the people. Judicial candidates first ran in nonpartisan elections in Cook County,
Illinois, in 1873. By 1927, twelve states employed this method of judicial selection.[30]

Yet, nonpartisan judicial elections did not quell the concerns of the
critics. Judges still had to campaign for office (both to be elected and reelected), meaning that politics would still likely play a part. Also, not
everyone was convinced that parties completely removed themselves from
involvement in judicial elections.[31] Furthermore, some began to question
the ability of citizens to cast informed ballots in nonpartisan judicial elections. Political science research has noted the difficulty that citizens have
in making educated evaluations when their cheapest voting cue is not
available.[32] If this is the case, then the quality of justices could suffer.
While twelve states elected judges in nonpartisan elections by 1927, three
states had already tried nonpartisan elections but switched back to partisan elections as a result of these reasons.[33]

Because of concerns over partisan and nonpartisan judicial elections,
the American Judicature Society pushed for another judicial selection reform that they believed captured the positive effects of all selection systems: retention elections. Again, the idea behind retention elections was to
combine judicial independence (judges would not have to run against an
opponent) with judicial accountability (they would still face the possibility

of being removed from office if they had ruled against the wishes of the people). While California first adopted a merit plan in 1934, in 1940 Missouri became the first state to adopt the more familiar option today; hence, retention elections are also called the "Missouri Plan."[34] Merit selection with retention elections is the most common judicial selection method today. Even it has encountered criticism, however, as the role of money becomes larger and the tone of these elections becomes nastier. In 2005, for example, citizen groups targeted Pennsylvania Supreme Court justices Russell Nigro and Sandra Schultz Newman after the state legislature voted to enact pay raises for the legislature and judges. Neither judge had anything to do with the vote, but since no one in the legislature was up for reelection in 2005, groups such as Clean Sweep and Democracy Rising turned their attention to ousting Nigro and Newman in their retention elections. While Newman was barely retained, Nigro was not as lucky. In 2006, a Nebraska man targeted two state supreme court justices, Kenneth Stephan and Michael McCormack, because of what he saw as the "tendency [of justices] to rely on personal philosophies in reaching legal decisions." Stephan and McCormack were not challenged because of any decisions they had personally made, but simply because they were the only justices up for retention in 2006.[35] If retention elections continue to follow in the footsteps of their partisan and nonpartisan counterparts, it is possible that they will lose favor as the preferred method of judicial selection as well.

Overview of the Book

Running for Judge examines many different facets of judicial elections from the rules that guide these elections to the campaigns conducted by judicial candidates and from the news coverage of these campaigns to the effects that running for election has on the judge once on the bench. In chapter 2, Richard Hasen provides an overview of the current canons by which judicial candidates must abide and an analysis of the Supreme Court decision in *Republican Party of Minnesota v. White,* a case that explicitly declared one canon—the announce clause—to be unconstitutional. Hasen argues that, given the Court's ruling in *White,* many of the remaining canons may no longer pass constitutional muster.

Chapters 3–7 examine judicial campaigns from a variety of perspectives. In chapter 3, Rachel Caufield assesses how the tone of judicial campaigns has differed since *White*. While only one electoral cycle has passed since *White* at the time of Caufield's writing, she finds that, to some extent, campaign tone has changed since *White*. For example, while negative advertising didn't necessarily increase in 2004, the number of contrast ads in states with "broad" interpretations of *White* did rise.

Chapters 4 and 5 examine the increasing role that money is having in judicial elections. In chapter 4, Chris Bonneau illustrates that judicial campaigns are becoming more expensive across the board, but especially when those elections are partisan and no incumbent is running. In chapter 5, Deborah Goldberg notes the increasing role of interest groups in judicial campaigns. This role hasn't been limited to campaign donations and running campaign commercials but has extended to grassroots activities as well.

In chapter 6, I turn to the question of partisan involvement in judicial campaigns. While many reformers want to limit the involvement of parties in judicial campaigns to keep judicial candidates "above politics," the evidence indicates that parties do have a role in judicial campaigns. While that role is much greater in partisan judicial elections, it is hardly absent from nonpartisan elections.

The focus of chapter 7 turns away from the candidates' campaigns to the news coverage of those campaigns. Brian Schaffner and Jennifer Segal Diascro find that news coverage of state supreme court races is lacking, both in terms of quality and quantity, when compared with coverage of Senate elections. However, coverage is not constant across elections. Partisan races, competitive races, and those races covered by independently owned newspapers all receive more news coverage than those races that are nonpartisan, uncompetitive, or covered by chain newspapers. Nevertheless, most judicial races fail to receive substantial coverage from the print media.

Chapter 8 analyzes judicial elections from a voter's perspective. Lawrence Baum and David Klein compare voting in high-visibility and low-visibility judicial elections. They find that, while voter participation was greater in the high-visibility election, the determinants of vote choice changed little between elections.

Chapters 9 and 10 move away from analyzing different aspects of judicial elections to examining the *effects* of those elections. In Chapter 9, Melinda Gann Hall addresses whether judicial elections have the capacity to fulfill their goal of holding state supreme court justices accountable. She finds that judicial elections are increasingly contested and competitive, and that incumbents are more susceptible to defeat. As a result, Hall argues, judicial elections can promote accountability and thus fulfill their essential function.

In chapter 10, Paul Brace and Brent Boyea look at whether judicial elections influence a judge's decision, specifically regarding the reversal of capital punishment cases. Brace and Boyea find that the prospect of an upcoming election, among other things, is a significant factor on a judge's vote.

Finally, in chapter 11, Brian Frederick and I discuss some of the recent judicial selection reform efforts and comment on the future of judicial elections and judicial elections research.

NOTES

1. Percentage calculated by author from the Brennan Center's report on television advertising for the 2004 judicial elections. Brennan Center for Justice, "Buying Time 2004."

2. Goldberg et al., *New Politics of Judicial Elections 2004.*

3. Rankin, "Bernes Wins Judicial Election."

4. Goldberg et al., *New Politics of Judicial Elections 2004.*

5. Bayne, "Lynchard's Candidacy."

6. Woodbury, "Is Texas Justice for Sale?"

7. Coyle, "It Won't Be Long."

8. Goldberg et al., *New Politics of Judicial Elections 2004.*

9. Dimino, "Judicial Elections versus Merit Selection."

10. Link, "Had Enough in Ohio?"

11. Dimino, "Judicial Elections versus Merit Selection"; Link, "Had Enough in Ohio?"; Behrens and Silverman, "Case for Adopting"; Geyh, "Why Judicial Elections Stink."

12. Campbell et al., *American Voter*; Brody and Page, "Assessment of Policy Voting"; Jackson, "Issues, Party Choices, and Presidential Votes"; Markus and Converse, "Dynamic Simultaneous Equation Model."

13. Schotland, "Should Judges Be More Like Politicians?" The percentages are slightly lower for initial selection as many justices are appointed and then, after their term is over, must face reelection or retention.

14. Sheldon and Maule, *Choosing Justice.*

15. Price, "Selection of State Court Justices."

16. Sheldon and Maule, *Choosing Justice.*

17. Johnson, "Judicial Campaign Speech."

18. Berkson, "Judicial Selection in the United States."

19. Haynes, *Selection and Tenure of Judges,* p. 100.

20. Berkson, "Judicial Selection in the United States."

21. Croley, "Majoritarian Difficulty"; Berkson, "Judicial Selection in the United States."

22. Croley, "Majoritarian Difficulty."

23. Ibid.

24. Sheldon and Maule, *Choosing Justice.*

25. Ibid.

26. Zaccari, "Judicial Elections."

27. Sheldon and Maule, *Choosing Justice.*

28. Croley, "Majoritarian Difficulty," p. 722.

29. Pound, "Causes of Popular Disaffection," p. 45.

30. Sheldon and Maule, *Choosing Justice*; Epstein et al., "Selecting Selection Systems."

31. Epstein et al., "Selecting Selection Systems."

32. Schaffner et al., "Teams without Uniforms"; Schaffner and Streb, "Partisan Heuristic"; Squire and Smith, "Effect of Partisan Information."

33. Cheek and Champagne, "Political Party Affiliation."

34. Epstein et al., "Selecting Selection Systems."

35. Mabin, "North Platte Man Seeks Judges' Ouster."

Chapter 2

First Amendment Limits on Regulating Judicial Campaigns

Richard L. Hasen

In 2002, the U.S. Supreme Court held that a provision of Minnesota's rules regulating the conduct of judicial elections violated the free speech guarantees contained in the First Amendment to the United States Constitution.[1] By a 5–4 vote, the Court in *Republican Party of Minnesota v. White*[2] held that Minnesota could not prevent judicial candidates from "announcing" their views on disputed legal or political issues. *White* left open many questions, but some lower federal courts have relied on it to strike down a host of other judicial campaign regulations, from those that prohibit judicial candidates from making campaign promises to those that bar such candidates from directly soliciting campaign contributions. State courts have read *White* more narrowly and upheld challenged judicial election rules, leading to a great deal of uncertainty over precisely which judicial campaign regulations pass constitutional muster. In addition, some state supreme courts, perhaps in anticipation of legislation, have changed the rules for conducting of judicial elections. The law is in a high state of uncertainty, which is likely to persist at least until the Supreme Court hears another case resolving these issues.

White emerged at a time—perhaps not coincidentally, as we shall see— when judicial campaigns were becoming "nastier, noisier, and costlier,"[3] and *White* has the potential to inject judicial candidates more directly into the tumult of these newly invigorated campaigns. Other chapters in this volume explore how changes in judicial regulations are beginning to affect judicial campaigns. This chapter considers only the legal question whether, in light of *White*, the most important judicial campaign regulations can survive a First Amendment challenge.[4] The question is important and urgent in the thirty-nine states that select or retain at least some of their judges through elections.

This chapter first lays out the major regulations of judicial conduct in various states. It then summarizes *White*'s holding and reasoning. The remainder of the chapter considers arguments that have been advanced since *White* for and against the constitutionality of the major judicial campaign regulations. The analysis concludes that most of the major regulations are of uncertain constitutionality under *White*. This constitutional analysis must be considered with caution, however. Two of the five Justices in the *White* majority (Chief Justice William Rehnquist and Justice Sandra Day O'Connor) have left the Supreme Court, and it is unclear whether the new Roberts Court will follow *White* faithfully or go forward in a moderately or radically different direction. Only time will tell if remaining longstanding special regulations for judicial elections will survive a legal challenge.

Judicial Campaign Regulation in the States

Judicial campaign regulations, which vary from state to state in those that conduct judicial elections, trace their roots to the "Canons of Judicial Ethics" promulgated by the American Bar Association (ABA) in 1924.[5] Among other things, the canons set forth limits on certain speech and political activities by judges, such as soliciting contributions for political parties. Though the ABA first intended the canons simply as ethical guidelines, the canons later became enforceable in many states through adoption of legal rules (promulgated by state supreme courts).

As states began creating their own disciplinary bodies to deal with complaints against judges, the ABA reworked the judicial canons. The ABA adopted the Model Code of Judicial Conduct in 1972, and all but three states adopted it for use.[6] Like the earlier 1924 canons, the 1972 canons regulated judicial speech. In 1990 the ABA substantially revised the code: "The new code revised the sections providing that a judge should not engage in various actions, replacing these with new provisions declaring what a judge shall not do. This approach was consistent with the perception of the ABA authors that judicial discipline needed to be tougher."[7] States varied in how much they adopted their rules to conform with the 1990 code, and the ABA itself has amended the code three times since

1990. The ABA is currently considering additional revisions to the code in part to respond to the Supreme Court's *White* decision.[8]

The *White* case itself involved the so-called Announce Clause, which had existed in various forms in the ABA canons since 1924.[9] Minnesota's version, at issue in *White*, was adopted from the 1972 ABA Judicial Code and provided that "a candidate for judicial office, including an incumbent judge" shall not "announce his or her views on disputed legal issues."[10] The Announce Clause was dropped from the 1990 code, and "by the time of *White*, due to constitutional challenges and canon revisions, only nine state canons continued to retain the Announce Clause, and several of these [versions of the Announce Clause] were narrower . . . than the Clause at issue in *White*."[11]

Other canons which have been questioned on constitutional grounds since *White* include the following important provisions:

- *The Pledges or Promises Clause.* The 1972 ABA Judicial Code and the 1990 revision bar judicial candidates from making "pledges or promises of conduct in office other than the faithful and impartial performance of the duties of the office."[12] Nearly every state holding judicial elections had adopted this canon.[13] In 2003 the ABA modified this language to preclude "pledges, promises or commitments,"[14] removing the separate "Commit or Appear to Commit" clause discussed below.[15]

- *The Commit or Appear to Commit Clause.* When the 1972 code dropped the Announce Clause, it replaced it with a new provision barring candidates for judicial office from making "statements that commit or appear to commit the candidate with respect to cases, controversies or issues that are likely to come before the court."[16] Twenty-seven states had adopted this canon by the time the Supreme Court decided *White*,[17] though some states no doubt will modify their codes to meet with the ABA's 2003 amendment, which collapses this provision with the pledges and promises canon.

- *Partisan Political Activity.* Since 1924, the ABA canons have limited the political activity of judicial candidates. The 1990 code, as amended, currently prohibits judges and judicial candidates from acting as a leader or holding an office in a political organization,[18] publicly endorsing or publicly opposing another candidate for public office, making speeches on behalf of political organizations, attending political gatherings, soliciting funds, paying an assessment, and making a contribution to a political organization or candidate.[19] Most states with judicial elections have adopted these provisions.[20]

- *Personal Solicitation of Campaign Funds.* The 1990 code prohibits judicial candidates from personally accepting or soliciting campaign contributions. To collect campaign funds, the candidate must establish a political committee of responsible persons to solicit and accept contributions on the candidate's behalf.[21] Most states with judicial elections ban the direct solicitation of contributions by judicial candidates.[22]
- *Misrepresentation Clause.* Building on the 1972 code, the 1990 code prohibits a judicial candidate from "knowingly misrepresent[ing] the identity, qualifications, present position or other fact concerning the candidate or an opponent."[23] Most states have adopted the 1972 or later versions of this misrepresentation clause.[24]

As we shall see, the constitutionality of at least part of each of these provisions has been challenged since the Supreme Court's *White* decision.

Understanding White

In brief,[25] *White* concerned a challenge initially brought by Gregory Wersal, a former and would-be judicial candidate, to a number of Minnesota rules for the conduct of judicial elections. He was later joined by other plaintiffs, including the Republican Party of Minnesota. The Eighth Circuit rejected plaintiffs' arguments that some Minnesota judicial campaign regulations, including the Announce Clause, violated plaintiffs' First Amendment rights of free speech and association.[26] The Supreme Court agreed to hear only the challenge to the Announce Clause, leaving the Eighth Circuit to reexamine the other challenged regulations on remand after the Court's decision.[27]

Justice Antonin Scalia, writing for a five-Justice majority, began by setting forth the Court's understanding of the scope of the Announce Clause. Rejecting a narrower interpretation of the Announce Clause accepted by the lower court, the Court construed it as prohibiting a judicial candidate "from stating his views on any specific nonfanciful legal question within the province of the court for which he is running, except in the context of discussing past decisions—and in the latter context as well, if he expresses the view that he is not bound by *stare decisis.*"[28] The Court then judged the constitutionality of the law based on this understanding of its meaning.

Having defined the meaning of the Announce Clause, the Court then considered the applicable level of scrutiny to apply in the constitutional challenge. This determination is crucially important, because the level of scrutiny usually determines the outcome of constitutional cases: plaintiffs usually (though not always) win First Amendment cases decided under "strict scrutiny," but the government usually (though not always) wins when the Court applies a lower level of scrutiny such as "rational basis" scrutiny. Under strict scrutiny, the state must demonstrate it has a *compelling interest* that justifies infringing on the rights of free speech and association guaranteed by the First Amendment and that the means the state has advanced are *narrowly tailored* to achieve the state's interest. In contrast, under rational basis review, the state need only demonstrate a *legitimate interest* and that the means it has adopted are *rationally related* toward achieving that interest.

Viewing the Announce Clause as a content-based restriction on speech in the midst of an election campaign (where political speech is entitled to great protection from government interference), the Court held that strict scrutiny must apply. It then considered and rejected the state's argument that the Announce Clause was a narrowly tailored means of achieving Minnesota's compelling interests.

The lower court had held that the Announce Clause was constitutional under strict scrutiny, serving as a narrowly tailored means of preserving the impartiality or the appearance of impartiality of the state judiciary. The Supreme Court rejected this analysis. It declared that "impartiality" could have three different meanings, and depending on the meaning attributed to it the Announce Clause was unconstitutional either because the interest was not compelling or because the Announce Clause was not a narrowly tailored means of achieving a compelling interest.

The Court first considered the meaning of impartiality as "lack of bias for or against any *party* to the proceeding."[29]

> We think it plain that the announce clause is not narrowly tailored to serve impartiality (or the appearance of impartiality) in this sense. Indeed, the clause is barely tailored to serve that interest *at all,* inasmuch as it does not restrict speech for or against particular *parties,* but rather speech for or

against particular *issues*. To be sure, when a case arises that turns on a legal issue on which the judge (as a candidate) has taken a particular stand, the party taking the opposite stand is likely to lose. But not because of any bias against that party or favoritism toward the other party. *Any* party taking that position is just as likely to lose. The judge is applying the law (as he sees it) evenhandedly. (Emphasis in original.)[30]

The Court then rejected the argument that the law could be justified based on impartiality as a "lack of preconception in favor of or against a particular *legal view*" (emphasis in original). Though the Announce Clause "may well" serve this interest, the Court rejected the argument that this version of impartiality could constitute a compelling interest: "For one thing it is virtually impossible to find a judge who does not have preconceptions about the law. . . . Indeed, even if it were possible to select judges who did not have preconceived views on legal issues, it would hardly be desirable to do so."[31]

Finally, the Court rejected the argument that impartiality as "openmindedness" could serve as a compelling interest to justify the Announce Clause against First Amendment attack: "This sort of impartiality seeks to guarantee each litigant, not an *equal* chance to win legal points in the case, but at least *some* chance of doing so" (emphasis in original).[32] The Court stated that the Minnesota Supreme Court did not enact the Announce Clause with this goal in mind, so it "need not pursue that inquiry." In the Court's view, however, even if openmindedness constituted a compelling state interest, the Announce Clause was "woefully inadequate" in pursuing this goal: Judicial candidates could have made the same statements before they were candidates or after they took on the bench, until litigation on the issue is pending. Seeing such "underinclusiveness" in the reach of the canon, the Court rejected the argument that the Announce Clause was narrowly tailored toward serving an interest in openmindedness. In other words, the Court reasoned that preventing judicial candidates from announcing their views only during the limited time period of the judicial campaign would neither keep judges openminded nor create the public perception of openmindedness.

Ultimately, the majority saw the true purpose of the Announce Clause as impermissibly "undermining judicial elections." Justice O'Connor in her separate concurrence seemed sympathetic to arguments against judicial elections as a whole, and Justice Anthony Kennedy in his separate concurrence would have imposed an even stricter First Amendment test than that set forth in Justice Scalia's opinion; Justice Kennedy would not have even *balanced* state interests against First Amendment rights having found that the state imposed a content-based restriction on protected speech. Nonetheless, these two Justices joined with Justices Scalia, Clarence Thomas, and Chief Justice Rehnquist to form a five-member majority endorsing the holding and reasoning of Justice Scalia's opinion. The majority concluded: "We have never allowed the government to prohibit candidates from communicating relevant information to voters during an election,"[33] and it certainly did not allow the government to do so in this case.

In addition to the Court's holding striking down the Announce Clause on First Amendment grounds, the Court offered some significant *dicta* (statements of a court not necessary to the holding) that courts and commentators have latched on to in considering the constitutionality of other judicial campaign regulations. First and foremost, responding to Justice Ruth Bader Ginsburg's dissent accusing the majority of a "unilocular 'an election is an election' approach,"[34] the majority wrote:

> We neither assert nor imply that the First Amendment requires campaigns for judicial office to sound the same as those for legislative office. What we do assert . . . is that, *even if* the First Amendment allows greater regulation of judicial election campaigns than legislative election campaigns, the announce clause still fails strict scrutiny because it is woefully underinclusive, prohibiting announcement by judges (and would-be judges) only at certain times and in certain forms. (Emphasis in original.)[35]

The Court quickly undermined its own point, however, noting that Justice Ginsburg "greatly exaggerates the difference between judicial and legislative elections."[36]

The Court also discussed two other judicial campaign regulations. It distinguished the Pledges and Promises Clause twice. First, the Court noted that the clause was "a prohibition not challenged here and about which we express no view."[37] Second, the Court conceded that the state's interest in openmindedness might "plausibly" be advanced by the Pledges and Promises Clause, on grounds (as Justice John Paul Stevens put forward in his dissent) "that statements made in an election campaign pose a special threat to openmindedness because the candidate, when elected judge, will have a *particular* reluctance to contradict them."[38] But it rejected the argument that limits on *nonpromissory* statements such as those covered by the Announce Clause could be justified by this interest in openmindedness.

The Court also dropped a confusing footnote responding to Minnesota's argument that the Announce Clause was no broader that the Commit or Appear to Commit Clause contained in the 1990 ABA canons. The Court failed to reach the question whether the two provisions were the same and noted that "no aspect of our constitutional analysis turns on this question."[39] It is unclear whether the Court meant to cast doubt on the constitutionality of the Commit or Appear to Commit Clause; if it had that intention, it expressed it quite obliquely.

Constitutionality of Judicial Campaign Regulations after White

The timing of the Supreme Court's *White* decision—coming alongside the well-documented increase in the politicization of judicial campaigns[40]—is perhaps not coincidental. For many years the canons stood unchallenged as the rules of the game for low-salience judicial elections. With voter interest low, there was little need for judicial candidates (especially incumbents) either to engage in much direct campaigning or to raise significant campaign funds.

As judicial elections gained a higher profile and attracted the attention of more interest groups, a Supreme Court majority endorsed the view that judicial candidates should be freed from constraints on their ability to campaign for office more aggressively. The majority in *White* took the view that as judicial elections started looking more and more like legislative elections, with interest group and party politics taking an increasingly important role (see chapters 5 and 6), it was somewhat anomalous that the person at the center of the campaign—the judicial candidate—should be the only person precluded from much campaign activity. For the dissenters, however, the First Amendment costs of special judicial campaign rules that no doubt limited some judicial campaign speech were justified by the special nature of the judicial office. Judicial candidates were not simply running for election; they were poised to serve as impartial arbiters of the law, and not as elected representatives who are accountable to the people for the campaign promises that they make.[41]

The rift in *White* looked like a typical conservative-liberal split in the last nine years of the Rehnquist Court, with perennial swing-voter Justice O'Connor this time siding with the conservatives but expressing sympathy with the position of the dissenters that judicial elections were inconsistent with the proper judicial role. Perhaps Justice O'Connor sided with the majority in the hopes that when judicial elections began to look more like other elections, states would move toward the appointment of judges. So far, however, that has not happened. No state has moved from election to appointment of judges since the *White* decision—indeed, the North Carolina Supreme Court surprisingly acted without any public input to change judicial campaign rules so as to allow for greater political activity by judicial candidates.[42]

White staked out new territory for the Supreme Court. To its credit, rather than issue broad pronouncements on the scope of judicial campaign rules, the Court began slowly crafting its constitutional rules for judicial campaigns, beginning only with the Announce Clause—recall that the Court refused to hear other challenges to Minnesota's campaign rules, leaving those issues to be resolved by the Eighth Circuit on remand. The post-*White* period gives the Court a chance to observe how lower courts apply the holding of *White* and to consider more carefully the precise contours of the Court's new jurisprudence in this area.[43]

And there is plenty for the Supreme Court to consider from lower court developments in the few years since the decision. Though the courts have split on the constitutionality of various campaign rules since *White*, the anti-regulation forces scored some major victories, including the recent decision of the Eighth Circuit on remand in the *White* case striking down the partisan activities and solicitation provisions of Minnesota law. The Supreme Court declined to hear the Eighth Circuit case, but other cases are working their way through the appellate system. The remainder of this section considers the constitutional arguments related to the major remaining judicial regulations.

The Pledges or Promises Clause

Any analysis of the constitutionality of the judicial canons should begin with the framework of *White*. Because a ban on pledges or promises by candidates is a direct content-based speech restriction, it is likely that courts will follow *White* in applying strict scrutiny to the analysis. Under strict scrutiny, courts must consider whether the state could assert a compelling interest in impartiality or some other compelling interest and that the Pledges or Promises Clause is narrowly tailored to promote that interest.

Considering the three meanings of "impartiality" in *White,* a ban on campaign pledges or promises to decide certain disputed legal or political issues in a certain way cannot be justified as a means of promoting impartiality of *parties.* As with the Announce Clause, a judge promising to decide an *issue* in a certain way will do so regardless of which *party* is before him raising the issue. Nor could the law be justified as a means of preventing a candidate from expressing a *legal view,* which the *White* Court held was more a sign of incompetence for a judge than a lack of bias.

The biggest question mark for applying the *White* analysis to pledges and promises comes from the analysis of impartiality as openmindedness. A court could hold that openmindedness is not a compelling state interest, an issue left open in *White.* That seems somewhat unlikely, because it is hard to quarrel with openmindedness (as defined by the Court) as a compelling interest in a state's justice system.

More likely, a court wishing to strike down the clause could hold that it is "woefully inadequate" to assure openmindedness or the appearance of openmindedness. Now that the *White* Court has held the Announce Clause as unconstitutional, a judge could still signal his views about a particular case through an "announcement" without making a promise or pledge (or commitment for that matter). A statement such as "I believe same-sex marriage is unconstitutional" (an example used by the majority in the *White* case) would not violate the Pledges or Promises Clause (while a statement promising to strike down such laws would), but it could still leave litigants and the public questioning the openmindedness of a judge. In this view, the Pledges and Promises Clause stands ready to catch sloppy judicial candidates who fail to speak carefully, but it does little to assure either that candidates remain openminded or that they appear openminded.

Proponents of the clause will argue against the lack of narrow tailoring, claiming that there is something special about promissory speech in the election context, as Justice Stevens argued in his *White* dissent: if it is indeed true that judges will have a special reluctance to contradict their campaign *promises* when on the bench, the clause could be found to serve this compelling interest in openmindedness. In addition, if the state has a compelling interest in assuring *public confidence* in the openmindedness of judicial decisionmakers, then the Pledges and Promises Clause could be narrowly tailored. Under this argument, it is worse when judges make explicit promises as judicial candidates than when they simply announce their positions on disputed issues: promises signal a prejudgment of issues in a way that announcements do not.[44]

It is not clear that the Court would accept that promissory speech is in fact special compared to nonpromissory announcements of disputed positions.[45] Nor is it clear that the *appearance* of a lack of openmindedness would count as a sufficiently compelling interest even if assuring *actual* openmindedness could do so. In addition, because judges can and should recuse themselves from hearing a case when their impartiality can be reasonably questioned, it might be that recusal rather than a ban on campaign speech is the *more narrowly tailored way* to assure openmindedness on those issues likely to come before the Court.

Finally, the Supreme Court in a 1982 case had already held that campaign promises in legislative elections enjoyed First Amendment protection, and for the Court to distinguish this case would require some notion that judicial elections are special—a point currently unresolved by *White*.[46]

The Commit or Appear to Commit Clause

To some extent, the constitutional analysis of this provision tracks the analysis of the Pledges and Promises Clause. The Commit or Appear to Commit Clause is a content-based restriction of the speech of judicial candidates, triggering strict scrutiny. As in the Pledges and Promises context, the same problem with applying the first two meanings of impartiality applies here as well. But the Commit or Appear to Commit Clause is on shakier legal ground than the Pledges and Promises Clause. First, as Richard Briffault has noted, the "Appear to Commit" portion of the canon raises issues of unconstitutional vagueness.[47] How would a candidate know when his statement would appear to commit him with respect to cases or controversies likely to come before his court? Consider Briffault's example of a candidate who labels himself "pro-life" or "tough on crime." Does this statement appear to commit a candidate to striking down abortion laws or to imposing criminal sentences that are harsh? It is hard to see the Appear to Commit Clause being upheld under strict scrutiny by the *White* Court.

Perhaps because of this vagueness concern, the ABA recently eliminated the "Appear to Commit" portion of the canon and combined "commitments" with "pledges or promises" under the most recent amendments to the canons—the result being a ban on "pledges, promises, or commitments" by judicial candidates.

Even as amended, it is uncertain whether the "commitments" provision alone is constitutional. If "commitments" are understood as simply pledges and promises made without the express words "I promise" or "I pledge," then the analysis of the constitutionality of this provision would track the Pledges and Promises Clause. If the government can lawfully tell judicial candidates that they cannot say "I promise to strike down a same-sex marriage law under the state constitution," the government should equally be able to tell judicial candidates that they cannot say "You have my word that I will strike down a same-sex marriage law under the state constitution." The latter is arguably a "commitment" that lacks the express words of promise, and the presence of "magic words" should not matter for the outcome.[48] However, if the Court reads commitments as covering statements somehow *broader* than the functional equivalent of a promise and closer to statements covered by the Announce Clause, the canon could be in serious constitutional jeopardy.

Partisan Political Activity

No question, the Partisan Political Activities canon interferes with the speech and associational activities of judicial candidates. In states running nonpartisan judicial elections, judicial candidates cannot seek the endorsement of political parties or give speeches to political groups, nor can the candidates associate with political parties in various ways such as by assuming leadership positions. Such restrictions "do not easily square with a system that uses a partisan ballot for judicial elections" and may be "particularly burdensome for challengers who need to demonstrate their partisan bona fides to win a party nomination."[49]

Turning to the constitutional analysis, it is hard to see how any of the three versions of impartiality could serve as a compelling interest to justify this canon. As to the first interest, affiliating with political parties in the ways proscribed by the canon could lead observers to believe that in the *small class of cases* (such as redistricting cases) where political parties are parties in a lawsuit, a judge might exhibit bias. A court following *White* could well conclude that *recusal* is a more narrowly tailored solution to the problem of this lack of impartiality,[50] a solution recently imposed in the case of former Republican House majority leader Tom DeLay, who was accused of criminal violations of campaign financing.

Nor does it appear that the state's interest in (at least the perception of) openmindedness could justify this provision. It might be argued that a judge closely aligned with a party that has a strong a pro-life or pro-choice position would not be openminded on such an issue. But now—with the Announce Clause eliminated—that a judge can declare himself pro-life or pro-choice, the force of this argument is quite attenuated.

Supporters of the Partisan Political Activities Clause have begun raising a different, potentially compelling interest to justify it: a separation of powers between the branches of government. Judges who are beholden to political parties for support or whose interests are too closely aligned with the interests of party bosses might be overly influenced by the wishes of the party leadership. If a state wants to commit to an independent judiciary—that is, a judiciary willing to assert its constitutional power separate and apart from the other branches of government under the control of party leaders—it could well seek to place barriers between normal partisan activities and the judiciary. As Minnesota put it in its petition for certiorari in the recent *White II* case: "Most courts should have a Chief Judge or Chief Justice. None has, nor should have, a majority whip."[51] The interest is especially strong in those states that have made a policy decision that judicial elections should be nonpartisan—that is, judicial candidates running without party labels. When the state has made a deliberate decision to insulate the judicial election process from usual party politics, arguably that decision should be subject to some deference.

It remains to be seen if this "separation of powers" argument would gain support from the Supreme Court. In the campaign finance context, a slim majority of the Court has recognized the special dangers that political parties can have in the political process because of their unique role in shaping political competition. But those cases concerned the role of parties as a corrupting influence in area of campaign financing, not in endorsing and supporting candidates for office. The Court has upheld the right of parties to endorse candidates, even in nonpartisan elections.[52]

In addition, at least some courts are dubious of rules that prohibit judicial candidates from associating too closely with political parties but still allow the candidates to associate closely with interest groups such as the National Rifle Association or the Sierra Club.[53] Once candidates are involved in heavy political activity, there may be less reason to disfavor association *solely* with political parties. Support for the clause depends on recognizing special dangers from party association.[54] Still, supporters of the clause make analogies between limits on the partisan activities of judicial candidates and laws (upheld against constitutional challenge by the Supreme Court[55]) that limit the partisan activities of public employees, but this is a somewhat inapt comparison, given that these statutes do not apply to policymaking employees like judges.

The Solicitation Clause

The anti-solicitation rules may stand a better chance of being upheld against constitutional challenge, at least in those courts that view the question more as one of campaign finance than of judicial speech. In the campaign finance context, the Supreme Court has repeatedly upheld regulation, from *disclosure* laws to limits on the *amount* that candidates can collect for campaigns to *source limitations,* prohibiting corporations and unions from spending general treasury funds on election-related activity.

The solicitation rules bar some forms of personal solicitation of funds by judges, allowing the judges to set up committees to accomplish the task for the judge. Because judges can still collect contributions, albeit indirectly, a court might apply a more deferential level of scrutiny to the restrictions and uphold them as simply another of many regulations aimed at preventing the corruption or appearance of corruption of elected officials (in this case, elected judges) through limits on how money is collected in the political process. This would be no more remarkable than the Supreme Court's decision in the recent *McConnell* case limiting federal candidates from soliciting money for certain kinds of races or entities.[56] In the campaign finance contribution context especially, the Supreme Court has shown a great deal of deference to legislative determinations about the need for such regulation. Nothing is a greater threat to openmindedness than the sale of a judicial vote for dollars, and the solicitation rules could be said to sensibly put some distance between judges and the money that gets them (and keeps them) in office—an especially large concern, given that many contributions to judicial candidates comes from lawyers who appear before these same judges (see chapter 5).

Alternatively, courts that view the solicitation rules as content-based limits on the free speech of candidates (that is, the judicial candidate cannot say, "Please give me your money for my campaign") will subject the solicitation provisions to strict scrutiny.[57] Again, defenders of the law can raise an anti-corruption argument in favor of the law, but it will be harder to justify the law as narrowly tailored to prevent corruption; even under the rules, judges often can learn the identity of campaign contributors (in Minnesota, for example, the information is freely available over the Internet through public disclosure required by Minnesota's campaign finance law), and the public already believes that campaign contributions have too much influence over elected judges even with the solicitation rules in place. According to a 2001 poll, 72 percent reported being concerned that the money raised by judicial candidates compromised the judges' impartiality.[58] So it might be that the rules are not targeted enough toward preventing corruption or its appearance.

Misrepresentation Rules

The misrepresentation rules perhaps present the most clear-cut case on the question of constitutionality, and the issue turns less on the special nature of *judicial* elections than on the ability of states to regulate false campaign speech more generally. Generally speaking, the Supreme Court has held that the First Amendment limits the ability of the state to punish false speech unless such speech is made with knowledge of its falsity or in reckless disregard of the truth. The courts have generally applied the same principles to false campaign speech: speech can be nasty and misleading, but it cannot be punished unless it is false and made with the appropriate intent.[59]

To the extent the 1972 code allowed for the punishing of negligently made false campaign speeches by judges, it is likely unconstitutional. The 1990 code stands a greater chance of being upheld against constitutional challenge. Even under strict scrutiny, the government likely has a compelling interest in assuring that voters receive accurate information, and a ban on knowingly false speech appears narrowly tailored toward achieving this goal.[60]

Having said that, it may be that some supporters of the ABA's misrepresentation rules hope they will achieve a certain level of civility (or at least a lack of mudslinging) in judicial campaigns. But for the clauses to be construed as constitutional, they cannot ban uncivil judicial campaign speech, including inflammatory statements of opinion.[61]

Conclusion

Though the Supreme Court in *White* was careful not to declare that judicial election campaigns must be treated the same as other elections in order to comply with the First Amendment, *White* is leading states in that direction. Most of the important judicial campaign canons are subject to at least serious question under *White*, and the post-*White* trend in the lower courts has been discouraging for those who seek to defend the ABA code.

As judicial campaigns begin to look more like campaigns for legislative and executive offices, states may begin to rethink whether judicial elections continue to make sense. We have not seen that rethinking yet, but another Supreme Court case striking down more judicial canons may leave little choice for states but to either accept judicial elections on the same terms as other elections or to make radical changes in longstanding judicial selection practices.

NOTES

1. Thanks to Roy Schotland for his patience and guidance, to Richard Briffault for useful comments, and to Regan Parker for excellent research assistance.

2. *Republican Party of Minnesota v. White*, 536 U.S. 765 (2002).

3. Schotland, "Comment," p. 150.

4. After the Supreme Court decided *White*, it remanded the case to the Eighth Circuit to consider issues not reached by the Supreme Court. On remand, the Eighth Circuit, in addition to striking down additional provisions of the Minnesota judicial code on First Amendment grounds, held that the Minnesota Supreme Court was without authority under Minnesota law to promulgate rules regulating judicial elections (*Republican Party v. White*, 416 F.3d 738 (8th Cir. 2005) (en banc) (*White II*)), p. 753 n.7. This *ultra vires* argument is beyond the scope of this chapter, but it is certainly an issue that observers of judicial elections will need to watch.

5. For a more detailed history, see Shepard, "Campaign Speech," pp. 1063–1067; see also Rapp, "Will of the People," pp. 110–116.

6. Shepard, Campaign Speech," p. 1066 n.33.

7. Ibid., p. 1066.

8. Information about the status of the proposed revisions is available on the American Bar Association website, at http://www.abanet.org/judicialethics/home .html (accessed July 7, 2006).

9. Rapp, "Will of the People," p. 112.

10. *Republican Party of Minnesota v. White*, 536 U.S., p. 768 (quoting Minn. Code of Judicial Conduct, Canon 5(A)(3)(d)(i) (2000)).

11. Briffault, "Judicial Campaign Codes," p. 203.

12. American Bar Association, *Model Code of Judicial Conduct*, Canon 7B(1)(c) (1972); *Model Code of Judicial Conduct*, Canon 5A(3)(d)(ii) (1990).

13. Briffault, "Judicial Campaign Codes," p. 209.

14. American Bar Association, *Model Code of Judicial Conduct*, Canon 5A(3)(d)(i) (2003).

15. American Bar Association, *Annotated Model Code of Judicial Conduct*, p. 466 (noting 2003 amendment collapsing commit clause and pledges and promises clause "to provide a clearer enumeration of what judicial speech was prohibited and to state more clearly the interest protected by that prohibition").

16. American Bar Association, *Model Code of Judicial Conduct*, Canon 5A(3)(d)(ii) (1990).

17. Briffault, "Judicial Campaign Codes," p. 214.

18. "'Political organization' denotes a political party or other group, the principal purpose of which is to further the election or appointment of candidates to political office" (American Bar Association, *Annotated Model Code of Judicial Conduct*, p. 8).

19. American Bar Association, *Model Code of Judicial Conduct*, Canon 5A(1) (2003). A judge or judicial candidate may not "publicly endorse or publicly oppose other candidates for the same judicial office in a public election in which the judge or judicial candidate is running" (Canon 5C(1)(iv) (2003)). In addition, a judge or judicial candidate at any time may not purchase tickets and attend political gatherings, identify himself as a member of a political party, or contribute to a political organization (Canon 5C(1)(a) (2003)).

20. Briffault, "Judicial Campaign Codes," p. 228.

21. American Bar Association, *Model Code of Judicial Conduct*, Canon 5C(2) (1990).

22. Schotland, "Myth, Reality, Past and Present," p. 666.

23. American Bar Association, *Model Code of Judicial Conduct*, Canon 5A(3)(d)(ii) (1990).

24. Moerke, "Must More Speech Be the Solution?" p. 310.

25. Readers may find a more detailed summary of the case in Briffault, "Judicial Campaign Codes."

26. *Republican Party v. Kelly*, 247 F.3d 854 (8th Cir. 2001).

27. On remand, the Eighth Circuit, sitting en banc, struck down the solicitation and partisan activities provisions of the Minnesota judicial code. *Republican Party v. White*, 416 F.3d 738 (8th Cir. 2005) (en banc) (*White II*).

28. *White*, 536 U.S., p. 788. "*Stare decisis*" is respect for court precedent. The dissent read the clause more narrowly, as proscribing only "statements that essentially commit the candidate to a position on a specific issue" (ibid., p. 810) (Ginsburg, J., dissenting).

29. *White*, 536 U.S., p. 775.

30. Ibid., pp. 776–777.

31. Ibid., pp. 777–778.

32. Ibid., p. 778.

33. Ibid., p. 782. The Court also rejected the argument that limits on judicial campaign speech were part of a universal and longstanding tradition, entitled to a strong presumption of constitutionality (ibid, p. 784).

34. Ibid., p. 805 (Ginsburg, J., dissenting).

35. *White*, 536 U.S., p. 783 (footnote omitted). In the past, the Court had held on at least one occasion that judicial elections could be treated differently from other elections in that there was no need to comply with the generally applicable "one person, one vote" requirements for judicial elections (*Wells v. Edwards*, 409 U.S. 1095 (1973)).

36. *White*, 536 U.S., p. 784.

37. Ibid., p. 770.

38. Ibid., p. 780.

39. Ibid., p. 773 n.5.

40. Schotland, "Financing Judicial Elections."

41. Johnson, "Judicial Campaign Speech," pp. 400–401 ("The difficulty with [*White*] is not that it equates judicial elections for popular representatives. Rather it confuses judicial accountability with a politician's accountability. . . . Politicians break faith with the people when they abandon their advocacy. Judges break faith with the people when they abandon their neutrality.").

42. The North Carolina Supreme Court made it easier for judges to ask for campaign contributions and to make certain promises on the campaign trail.

43. For an argument in favor of this slow approach in election law cases under the Equal Protection Clause, see Hasen, *Supreme Court and Election Law*, ch. 2.

44. For example, *In re Watson*, 100 N.Y.2d 290 (2003), pp. 302–303.

45. *North Dakota Family Alliance, Inc., v. Bader*, 361 F. Supp. 2d 1021 (D.N.D. 2005), p. 1041. The court struck down North Dakota's Pledges and Promises Clause, noting:

> This Court is of the opinion that there is little, if any, distinction between the "announce clause" which was struck down by the United States Supreme Court in *White*, and the "commitment clause" and "pledges and promises clause" contained in Canon 5A(3)(d)(i) and (ii) of the North Dakota Code of Judicial Conduct. All of the clauses sweep constitutionally-protected speech within its scope. All of the clauses forbid the same type of speech the Supreme Court held was constitutionally-protected in *White*, namely, speech announcing a judicial candidate's views on disputed legal, political, or social issues. There is no real distinction between announcing one's views on legal or political issues and making statements that commit, or "appear to commit," a judicial candidate with respect to cases, controversies, and issues that are likely to come before the court.

46. On this argument, see Briffault, "Judicial Campaign Codes," p. 210 (citing *Brown v. Hartlage*, 456 U.S. 45 (1982)).

47. Briffault, "Judicial Campaign Codes," pp. 217–218.

48. Ibid., p. 216.

49. Ibid., p. 230.

50. *Republican Party v. White*, 416 F.3d, 738 (8th Cir. 2005) (en banc) (*White II*), p. 755.

51. *Dimick v. Republican Party of Minnesota*, No. 05-566, Petition for Writ of Certiorari, pp. 19–20; available at http://www2.mnbar.org/committees/judicial-elections/WhiteIIPetition.pdf (accessed July 7, 2006).

52. *Eu v. San Francisco County Democratic Central Committee*, 489 U.S. 214 (1989).

53. *White II*, 416 F.3d.,,p. 760 n.13.

54. Ibid., p. 778 (Gibson, J., dissenting).

55. See *In re Raab*, 793 N.E.2d 1287 (NY 2003), p. 1291; *U.S. Civil Serv. Commission v. Nat'l Ass'n of Letter Carriers*, 413 U.S. 548 (1973). See also *White II*, 416 F.3d (Gibson, J., dissenting), p. 769 .

56. *McConnell v. FEC*, 540 U.S. 93 (2003).

57. *Weaver v. Bonner*, 309 F.3d 1312 (11th Cir. 2002), p. 1322; *White II*, 416 F.3d, p. 763.

58. Justice at Stake Campaign, *Poll of American Voters.*

59. See generally Lowenstein and Hasen, *Election Law*, pp. 582–594.

60. Briffault, "Judicial Campaign Codes," p. 222.

61. *Weaver v. Bonner*, 309 F.3d, p. 1321.

Chapter 3

The Changing Tone of Judicial Election Campaigns as a Result of *White*

Rachel P. Caufield

As Matt Streb notes in chapter 1, the vast majority of state judges in the United States face election. In total, thirty-nine states use some form of election to select or retain some or all of their judges. For state trial courts of general jurisdiction, 76 percent of judges are elected to their initial term, and 88 percent face the voters for subsequent terms on the bench. For state appellate level courts, 53 percent of judges are elected to their initial term, and 89 percent face the voters for subsequent terms on the bench.[1] As a result, the change in judicial elections affects the vast majority of state judges across the country.

While judges may be elected in partisan, nonpartisan, or retention elections, similar patterns emerge in each case. Historically, studies have emphasized two basic patterns that characterize judicial elections. First, research confirms a strong incumbency advantage in judicial elections. Lawrence Baum's research confirms that between 1962 and 1980, judges on the Ohio Court of Common Pleas had remarkable job security. He found that 95.1 percent of incumbents who had been previously elected were not even opposed in their party primary, and 73.1 percent ran unopposed in the general election. In addition, only 2 percent of incumbent judges were defeated in a party primary and only 4.5 percent were defeated in the general election.[2] Larry Aspin and William K. Hall reported that of the 4,588 judges that faced the public in retention elections between 1964 and 1998, only fifty-two were defeated.[3] Clearly, incumbents do well.

Why do so many incumbent judges keep their job? One explanation, and the second significant historical finding, is that voters do not understand or know enough to effectively evaluate judicial candidates. Baum, in his study of judges on the Ohio Court of Common Pleas, writes that "the advantage of incumbent judges is strengthened by the low visibility of judicial elections. Judgeship campaigns usually receive little publicity and their issue content is severely limited by the Code of Judicial Conduct. As a result, most voters attain a low level of knowledge about judicial candidates."[4] Similarly, Philip DuBois concluded that "voters have preciously little information upon which to base their voting decisions [in judicial elections]. Indeed, judicial campaigns are so uninteresting that voters scarcely take advantage of those sources of information that *are* available" (italics in original).[5]

Why do voters lack information? One of the most prominent reasons is that, traditionally, judicial candidates have been restricted in what they can say on the campaign trail. As Rick Hasen discussed in chapter 2, most states have adopted language from the American Bar Association's *Model Code of Judicial Conduct,* including several provisions that limit judicial campaign speech. Provisions such as the pledges or promises clause or the announce clause were designed specifically to limit campaign speech in an effort to preserve the unique character of the judicial branch and to promote the impartiality of state court judges. But they also have limited what voters can learn about the candidates for judgeships.

The fact that voters lack information about judicial candidates' positions on specific issues is, in the eyes of some, quite significant in explaining voter decisionmaking in judicial elections. Marie Hojnacki and Baum examined the elections of 1986 and 1988 in Ohio, two races that attracted considerable attention because of high campaign expenditures and heavy advertising.[6] In assessing the information that voters had in these races, they distinguished between the quantity of information and the quality of that information. According to their theory, lack of voter interest was not due to a lack of information but to a lack of quality information that would help the voter determine the differences between the candidates. They identified high-information cues (like the judicial candidates' issue positions or ideology, or both), moderate-information cues (including a candidate's qualifications for the job or "character"), and low-information cues (such as a general impression of the candidate and the demographic characteristics of the candidate—usually such things can be gleaned from the name printed on the ballot alone). Despite the advertising in the race, voters generally explained their votes by referring to low- and moderate-information cues. Hojnacki and Baum argued that even increased information in a judicial campaign (through advertising in these cases) would not necessarily result in high-quality information that would allow voters to easily distinguish between candidates. They tied this directly to the limits imposed by the Ohio Code of Judicial Conduct by saying that "rules regarding judicial campaign speech have impeded past attempts to inject high-information cues, such as policy issues and a candidate's position, into campaigns."[7]

The traditional patterns of judicial elections are changing. In this chapter, I analyze one aspect of judicial campaigns—what I call the "tone and tenor" of judicial campaigns. Judicial elections, once unremarkable, quiet, dignified affairs, are increasingly becoming political. Judicial candidates are frequently attacked in ways that were previously reserved for those competing for legislative or executive positions. These attacks frequently come from interest groups (see chapter 5) but may also come from party organizations or the candidates themselves. One thing is clear, however: recent judicial elections across the country have seen more overtly political messages, more negative advertising, and more coordinated attacks on candidates. In many states, the extent of change is directly related to the 2002 U.S. Supreme Court decision in *Republican Party of Minnesota v. White*. Here, I examine how states have reacted to the *White* decision and the extent to which state interpretations of *White* have influenced the tone and tenor of judicial elections.

Recent Changes and the Rise of Issue-Based Judicial Campaigns

Most scholars writing before 2000 easily concluded that, with a few notable exceptions, judicial elections were unlikely to generate much controversy or excitement and the voting public was consistently uninformed about judicial elections. Increasingly, however, current research has demonstrated that judicial campaigns are more political than they have been in the past.

Two trends deserve attention, although the discussion will be limited, as other authors in this volume have covered them well. First, as Chris Bonneau makes clear in chapter 4, there has been an influx of money into judicial campaigns. Today, it is not uncommon to see judicial races attract several millions of dollars. In 2003, the Pennsylvania Supreme Court race cost an estimated $3.34 million.[8] In the 2003–2004 election cycle, state supreme court candidates raised almost $47 million for their campaigns.[9] The previous high-water mark was 2000, when candidates in state supreme court races spent a combined $45 million.[10] Between 2000 and 2002, average candidate spending in state supreme court races increased 167 percent. From 2002 to 2004, spending increased an additional 168 percent on average.[11]

Second, as Deborah Goldberg argues in chapter 5, interest groups have become increasingly active in judicial elections. In 2000, the U.S. Chamber of Commerce spent over $10 million in judicial elections in eight states, spending a combined $6 million in Alabama, Michigan, Mississippi, and Ohio.[12] Since 2000, the chamber and its affiliated organizations have poured tens of millions of dollars into judicial races around the country. What is particularly noteworthy about the growth of interest group participation is their emphasis on campaign advertising. In 2000, television advertising was used in only four states' judicial contests. By 2004, fifteen states saw television ads aimed at influencing the outcome of the judicial elections.[13]

Today's judicial elections are unlikely to be low-profile, quiet, or dignified affairs. Although spending on judicial races and the presence of interest groups began to receive extensive scholarly attention in 2000, some scholars saw the writing on the wall in the 1980s and 1990s. As early as 1985, Roy Schotland noted that judicial elections were becoming "nosier, nastier, and costlier."[14] John T. Wold and John H. Culver, with remarkable foresight, commented that "it is not unreasonable to forecast less expensive but nevertheless well-organized challenges against individual justices in the future."[15]

In addition, some states experienced "the new politics of judicial elections"[16] long before scholars were paying much attention. In 1986, three California Supreme Court justices were removed from office in a retention election. Never before had multiple judges been defeated in a single election cycle. But the California retention elections of 1986 were notable, not only for their effect on the court itself (the California Supreme Court had a total of seven justices, six of whom were up for retention in 1986). What was perhaps most notable was the fact that the campaign to unseat Chief Justice Rose Bird and Justices Cruz Reynoso and Joseph Grodin came from a well-coordinated coalition of public figures and interest groups within the state. That coalition was made up of Governor George Deukmejian and other Republicans in state government, a group called Crime Victims for Court Reform, and state and local prosecutors. Furthermore, both sides crafted campaign messages based on political issues, although Chief Justice Bird herself relied exclusively on a platform of judicial independence.

Those who campaigned to defeat Chief Justice Bird referred to prominent Democrats in the state, like Jerry Brown and Jane Fonda, in their campaign literature that painted her as being soft on crime and against the death penalty. The pro-retention campaign literature charged that "if . . . fanatics are successful in defeating Rose Bird and other targeted Supreme Court Justices in November, it will send an unmistakable message to every judge in every county in California who has ever drawn the line between Church and State or tried to protect and enhance our civil rights: either do what the radical right says, or we'll be coming after you."[17] In total, the pro- and anti-Bird campaigns spent $7.5 million dollars.[18] A poll of voters in the 1986 California retention elections indicated that the more important factor in a voter's decision to vote against Bird, Reynoso, and Grodin was a perception that they were opposed to the death penalty.[19]

In 1996, Justice David Lanphier of Nebraska and Justice Penny White of Tennessee were both defeated in their retention elections. In his excellent analysis of these defeats, Traciel Reid writes that both justices "lost their seats when a cluster of special interest groups and other political actors challenged their retentions. Neither was accused of judicial malfeasance or judicial incompetence. Rather, the campaigns that led to their removal stemmed from frustration over selected decisions rendered by their courts."[20] Also in 1996, Alabama voters were targeted with a campaign advertisement that has become notorious. The ad featured a picture of a skunk, and the image slowly morphed into a picture of Harold See, the Republican candidate for a seat on the Alabama Supreme Court. Clearly, the writing was on the wall even before 2000—judicial election campaigns were becoming more political, more interest groups were participating in judicial elections, the costs associated with judicial campaigns were rising, and attacks on judicial candidates were more frequent.[21]

Even the rising cost of judicial campaigns and the increased presence of interest groups, however, may not significantly alter the nature of judicial campaigns, particularly if the quality of information does not allow voters to easily distinguish between candidates. As Hojnacki and Baum argued, state codes of judicial conduct have severely limited the type of information that voters have in judicial elections. But, if we consider these recent developments in combination with the U.S. Supreme Court's decision in *Republican Party of Minnesota v. White* (2002) (see chapter 2 for a discussion of *White*), the significance of state codes of judicial conduct becomes very clear.

The White *Decision*

When the Supreme Court handed down the *White* decision, it significantly altered the landscape of judicial elections. Eight states had language that was identical to Minnesota's announce clause. In addition, however, the reasoning provided by the Court in *White* could easily be used to strike down other campaign speech restrictions, including the pledges or promises clause or the commit clause, forcing virtually all states to abandon their existing codes of judicial conduct. In fact, the 8th Circuit has relied on the Supreme Court's reasoning to declare portions of Minnesota's code that forbade candidates from personally soliciting campaign contributions and actively participating in party activities unconstitutional in *Republican Party v. White,* on remand from the U.S. Supreme Court, in August of 2005.[22] Similarly, the 11th Circuit has declared two provisions of the Georgia Code of Judicial Conduct unconstitutional. One of those provisions prohibited candidates from making false and misleading statements. The other forbade candidates from personally soliciting campaign funds.[23] A federal judge in New York ruled that a clause in the New York code that restricted candidates' participation in inappropriate political activities was unconstitutional.[24] In 2004, a U.S. district court in Kentucky ruled that the state's commit clause was unconstitutional, a decision that was upheld by the circuit court of appeals.[25]

To summarize the implications of the Supreme Court's ruling, returning to Hojnacki and Baum's argument, the *White* decision has allowed candidates to openly provide high-information cues to voters—including ideological positions, party affiliation (even in states that have nonpartisan elections, like Minnesota), and stances on controversial issues. Combined with the influx of money and the growing interest group presence, the *White* decision is thought to open the door to fully politicized judicial elections. Robert Hirshon, president of the American Bar Association when the *White* decision was announced, opined that "now we are going to have judicial candidates running for office by announcing their positions on particular issues. They will know that the voters will evaluate their performance in office on how closely their rulings comport with those positions. This is not impartial justice."[26] Georgetown law professor Schotland concluded that "the decision will make a change in judicial election campaigns that will downgrade the pool of candidates for the bench, reduce the willingness of good judges to seek reelection, add to the cynical view that judges are merely 'another group of politicians,' and thus directly hurt state courts and indirectly hurt all our courts."[27]

What are the practical effects of *White*? How has *White* changed judicial elections? Are judicial candidates more likely to speak about their issue positions? Are campaigns for judgeships becoming more similar to campaigns for legislative and executive positions? In order to answer these questions, we must first examine how states are interpreting *White* as they reevaluate and revise their codes of judicial conduct. As each state strives to balance the need for judicial impartiality while still accommodating the Supreme Court's ruling protecting the First Amendment rights of judicial candidates, they must determine how to change their own codes of judicial conduct. Here I evaluate the fallout from the *White* decision by examining how states have interpreted *White* in their efforts to revise or reevaluate their codes of judicial conduct.

How States Are Interpreting White

Nearly every state has devoted some attention to a reevaluation of their code of judicial conduct in the wake of *White*, but state interpretations have demonstrated remarkable variation.[28] In Missouri, one of the eight remaining states with the announce clause, the state supreme court repealed the provision in July 2002, just after it announced that it would not enforce the provision for the remainder of the 2002 judicial elections.[29] In November 2002, Pennsylvania amended its code of judicial conduct to remove the announce clause.[30] Texas changed its code after the *White* decision to repeal a provision that prohibited statements that disclosed candidates' opinions "on any issue that may be subject to judicial interpretation." Instead, Texas adopted the following language:

> A judge or judicial candidate shall not make pledges or promises of conduct in office regarding pending or impending cases, specific classes of cases, specific classes of litigants, or specific propositions of law that would suggest to a reasonable person that the judge is predisposed to a probable decision in cases within the scope of the pledge.[31]

In August 2002, the California Commission on Judicial Performance "dismissed a proceeding against a former judge charged with campaign speech violations."[32] Similarly, the Alabama Judicial Inquiry Commission withdrew an advisory opinion that suggested that judicial candidates should not respond to a questionnaire from the Christian Coalition.[33] In Ohio, the Supreme Court Board of Commissioners on Grievances and Discipline offered an advisory opinion, including eleven guidelines for judicial candidates.[34]

Among the most drastic alterations of a state code, North Carolina changed its code to repeal the pledges or promises clause and to allow candidates greater freedom to endorse other candidates and personally solicit campaign contributions.[35] The justices justified these changes as a reasonable response to the decisions in *White* and its progeny. A number of other states, most notably North Dakota, Georgia, Ohio, Indiana, Kentucky, and Florida, issued a series of advisory opinions clarifying the implications of *White* for their judicial codes.[36] Many of these advisory opinions simply stated that the state code would not be altered as a result of *White,* but given ongoing legal battles in the courts, it is unclear whether existing provisions like the pledges or promises clause and the commit clause will withstand judicial scrutiny. In light of *White* and cases spawned by *White,* states will be in a continuing state of uncertainty regarding the constitutionality of their speech restrictions. Nonetheless, many states have already engaged in substantial efforts to revise or reevaluate their codes of judicial conduct to determine necessary changes after the *White* decision.[37]

But what effect have these revision efforts had? For the purposes of this chapter, I restrict my analysis to those states that held supreme court elections in 2004.[38] For each state, I have engaged in an analysis of their post-*White* revision efforts to determine the breadth of their interpretation. Based on this classification, we can then assess whether state interpretations of *White* have had a discernable influence on the tone of judicial elections in the states. It is reasonable to expect that states that rely on a broad interpretation of *White* in their reevaluation and revision efforts will have looser speech restrictions than states that use a narrow interpretation of *White.* We should, then, see increasing negativity and more attacks in states that use broad interpretations.

My classification is necessarily subjective and rather rudimentary. Among the many difficulties in categorizing state response, states had different provisions in their codes of judicial conduct prior to the *White* ruling; therefore, the status quo is not uniform across all states. In addition, several states have undergone multiple revisions based on different interpretations. As a general rule, these states adopted one "advisory" set of rules in the immediate aftermath of the *White* decision and were later forced to alter those rules in the wake of new judicial rulings within the state or judicial circuit. Therefore, revision and reevaluation efforts are frequently ongoing, and interpretations of *White* may have changed in the two and a half years between the *White* ruling and the 2004 elections. Nonetheless, based on published statements by state supreme courts and commissions that have been established to assess the canons in light of *White*, it is possible to begin categorization of each state's interpretation of the *White* decision.

Each state is placed in one of two possible categories: one indicating a narrow interpretation and one indicating a broad interpretation of *White*. This categorization is based on whether the state voluntarily removed speech codes other than the announce clause (specifically, the pledges or promises clause or the commit clause) from their code of judicial conduct after the U.S. Supreme Court handed down the ruling in *White*. If a state supreme court or a state commission evaluating the implications of *White* issued an advisory opinion stating a belief that other speech codes would also be unconstitutional, or otherwise amended the state code to eliminate speech restrictions based on the *White* decision, I classify it as a "broad" interpreter. If, alternatively, a state authority issued any advisory opinion or ruling arguing that existing speech restrictions were permissible under *White* (usually based on the fact that the Supreme Court did not consider the commit clause or the pledges or promises clause in its *White* decision), I classify it as a "narrow" interpreter.

Classification of States as Broad or Narrow Interpreters of White

Before examining whether the tone of judicial campaigns was different depending on how the state interpreted the *White* decision, I must first provide a brief description of each state's revision and reevaluation efforts and justify my classification of each state.

ALABAMA—Before the *White* decision, Alabama did not have an announce clause. After the decision by the Alabama Judicial Inquiry Commission to withdraw an opinion that advised judicial candidates not to respond to a questionnaire from the Christian Coalition,[39] the Alabama Supreme Court amended the state's code of judicial conduct in September of 2004. Although the revisions did borrow from the ABA recommendations, adding "political" to the types of relationships that a judge should not allow to influence judicial conduct of judgment, the court retained a clause prohibiting candidates from making "any promise of conduct in office other than the faithful and impartial performance of the duties of the office" and retained a clause that prohibits candidates from "announcing in advance the candidate's conclusions of law on pending litigation." In addition, however, the court altered language to add the word "knowingly" to the prohibition against "misrepresenting his or her identity, qualification, present position, or other fact" and deleted a provision that disallowed candidates' distribution of "true information about a judicial candidate or an opponent that would be deceiving or misleading to a reasonable person." While these revisions are substantial, the decision to retain existing clauses that comply with the ABA recommendations indicates that this is a narrow interpretation of *White.*

ARKANSAS—Under today's canon 5 of the Arkansas Code of Judicial Conduct, judicial candidates and judges are governed by the pledges or promises clause and the commit clause. After the *White* decision, no substantive changes were made to the state's code of judicial conduct before the 2004 supreme court elections. Therefore, Arkansas is classified as a narrow interpreter.

GEORGIA—As previously discussed, Georgia's revision efforts were substantially influenced by the 11th Circuit decision in *Weaver v. Bonner,* which struck down two speech provisions in the Georgia code. In January of 2004, the Georgia Supreme Court issued a revised version of the canons of judicial conduct. The court removed the pledges or promises clause and a provision that requires candidates to maintain the dignity appropriate to judicial office. The commentary clarifies:

> This Canon does not prohibit a judge or candidate from publicly stating his or her personal views on disputed issues, see *Republican Party of Minnesota v. White* (2002). To ensure that voters understand a judge's duty to uphold the constitution and laws of Georgia where the law differs from his or her personal belief, however, judges and candidates are encouraged to emphasize in any public statement their duty to uphold the law regardless of their personal views.[40]

Given the removal of the pledges or promises clause and the commentary that boils down to a recommendation about candidates' behavior rather than any real restriction, I classify Georgia's as a broad interpretation.

IDAHO—Idaho is the only state in the Union that has no judicial candidate speech restrictions at all.[41] For the purposes of the following analysis, therefore, Idaho is considered separately.

ILLINOIS—The Illinois Code of Judicial Conduct has not been substantially altered in the wake of *White,* and the state continues to use the commit clause to regulate candidate speech. Nonetheless, reform activists and policy makers have begun to address concerns that elections in Illinois (where nearly $10 million was spent in a single race for the supreme court in 2004) have gotten out of hand. This would indicate revision efforts within the next few years. For present purposes, however, Illinois is categorized as a narrow interpretation.

KENTUCKY—Following the *White* decision, the Kentucky Judicial Conduct Commission issued a memorandum noting that the state supreme court had ruled the announce clause unconstitutional in 1991. The memo went on to say that the Kentucky Code of Judicial Conduct contains only the pledges or promises clause and the commit clause, both of which should be permissible since the U.S. Supreme Court did not expressly consider or overturn these provisions. The memo concludes by stating that "Canon 5(B)(1)(c) of the Kentucky Code of Judicial Conduct is not affected by the ruling on the Minnesota Canon, and remains effective as promulgated by the Supreme Court of Kentucky."[42] Although the pledges or promises clause was challenged by the Family Trust Foundation in the fall of 2004, the U.S. District Court for the Eastern District of Kentucky denied the motion and wrote that "to the extent that the promises and commit clauses attempt to prevent judicial candidates from promising to rule a certain way on cases, controversies or issues likely to come before the court, the state has a compelling interest in such a restriction."[43] This is clearly a narrow interpretation of *White,* although future appeals may alter this interpretation.

LOUISIANA—After the *White* decision was handed down, the Louisiana Supreme Court revised the state judicial ethics code to provide that a judicial candidate "shall not, while a proceeding is pending or impending in any court, make any public comment that might reasonably be expected to affect its outcome or impair its fairness" (this language is adopted from the 2003 ABA recommendations). The commentary that accompanies the court order adds that the amendments are "not intended to apply to in-court comments by lawyer candidates, or comments regarding a case or proceeding that the lawyer candidate is participating in."[44] By adopting the language from the amended 2003 ABA

Model Code, which strives to maintain the most restrictive rules possible under current law, Louisiana is classified as a narrow interpreter.

MICHIGAN—The Ethics Committee of the State Bar of Michigan stated that, although the pledges or promises clause in the Michigan code "is presumed constitutionally valid and enforceable," it must be "narrowly construed and cautiously applied to campaign speech."[45] The committee advised that judicial candidates may use campaign slogans that represent some expression of philosophy, like "A strict sentencing philosophy! A hard working man!" Similarly, the committee gave judicial candidates permission to respond to questionnaires eliciting the candidates' opinions on matters pending or impending in any court and to criticize the majority opinion of a divided court of last resort and the legal philosophy that underlies it. Thus, even though they have retained the pledges or promises clause, they have not adopted the ABA's revised commit clause. Furthermore, the advisory opinion undermines the meaning of the clause, and the committee has endorsed very broad latitude for campaign speech. Michigan is clearly using a broad interpretation of *White*.

MINNESOTA—Minnesota is, of course, the most telling of all states, given that its canon was the impetus for the *White* decision. Once the decision was handed down by the U.S. Supreme Court, the case was remanded to the 8th Circuit. In September of 2004, the Minnesota Supreme Court altered the state's canons. The revised canons adopted language from the ABA recommendations that prohibit candidates from "with respect to cases, controversies, or issues that are likely to come before the court, mak[ing] pledges or promises that are inconsistent with the impartial performance of the adjudicative duties of the office." But Minnesota did not go as far as the ABA; the ABA also included "commitments," as well as "pledges and promises." However, the court refused to adopt language recommended by the Advisory Committee to Review the Minnesota Code of Judicial Conduct that would have loosened restrictions on candidates' partisan political activities (the refusal was based on the desire to retain nonpartisan elections even after *White*). The recommendations to loosen restrictions on partisan political activity were based on a perception that *White* required that candidates be allowed to identify and participate in political party activities if they wished to do so. The Minnesota Supreme Court, however, noted that it was "not convinced the recommended changes are either necessary or desirable on their merits."[46] This is a particularly difficult state to classify since the interpretation of the state supreme court and that of the advisory committee are contradictory. In addition, however, it is telling that the supreme court's language did not go as far as the ABA recommendations. For that reason, and because the issue of partisan political activity is unique to nonpartisan elections and therefore not comparable across all states, I classify Minnesota as a broad interpreter.

MISSISSIPPI—Mississippi is a unique case. Before 2002, Mississippi's code included the announce clause, but its revisions started prior to *White*. The Supreme Court of Mississippi removed the announce clause in April of 2002, just before the *White* decision was handed down, based on questions about its constitutionality. Nonetheless, the Mississippi code also included the pledges or promises clause and the commit clause. On July 10, 2002, Mississippi Chief Justice Edwin Pittman stated that the decision in *White* would not influence the Mississippi code. He said: "We are untouched. . . . I'm very proud of the Mississippi Supreme Court in that we carefully drafted a Code of Judicial Conduct that was undisturbed by the Minnesota case."[47] Mississippi is therefore listed as a narrow interpreter.

MONTANA—On June 24, 2003, the Montana Supreme Court established the Commission on the Code of Judicial Conduct. Unlike any other state, Montana had retained a version of the announce clause from the 1924 model code, which provides that a judicial candidate should not "announce in advance his conclusions of law on disputed issues to secure class support" and "should do nothing while a candidate to create the impression that if chosen, he will administer his office with bias, partiality or improper discrimination." Other portions of the code provide that a candidate for judicial office "should not make [promises] of conduct in office which appeal to the cupidity or prejudices of the appointing or electing power" and prohibit candidates from making "statements that commit or appear to commit the candidate with respect to cases, controversies or issues that are likely to come before the court."[48] As yet, no revisions have been made, although revisions may be necessary in the near future. Therefore, Montana is classified a narrow interpreter.

NEVADA—In September of 2004, the Nevada Supreme Court promulgated new rules for judicial conduct in the state. The new code adopts the changes made by the ABA in 2003. Because the ABA recommendations try to retain as many restrictions as possible under the reasoning in *White*, I classify this as a narrow interpretation.

NEW MEXICO—The New Mexico code included the announce clause prior to the *White* ruling. In August of 2004, the supreme court amended the state's judicial conduct rules to adopt the 2003 recommendations of the ABA. I classify New Mexico, like Nevada, as a narrow interpretation.

OHIO—Like Minnesota, Ohio holds nonpartisan elections. The Ohio Supreme Court Board of Commissioners on Grievances and Discipline issued an advisory opinion after *White*. The opinion noted that Ohio's code did not include the announce clause and the U.S. Supreme Court did not consider the constitutionality of the provisions that were included in the Ohio code, namely the pledges or promises clause and the commit clause. In addition, the board issued eleven speech guidelines for judicial candidates. Because Ohio uses nonpartisan elections, prior to *White*, the state code provided that "after the day of the primary election, a judicial candidate shall not identify himself or herself in advertising as a member of or affiliated with a political party," that campaign materials may not use the term judge when a judge is running for judicial office, and that judges and judicial candidates must "maintain the dignity appropriate to judicial office."[49] These restrictions were challenged when a state representative filed a complaint against William O'Neill, a judicial candidate who declared he was a Democrat on his campaign literature and on his website. After the Ohio Supreme Court suspended the provisions, the U.S. District Court for the Northern District of Ohio issued a preliminary injunction that prohibited the Ohio Disciplinary Counsel from investigating or threatening to investigate these provisions. Ohio is clearly using a narrow interpretation in assessing its code of judicial conduct.

OREGON—Oregon's code of judicial conduct was last amended in August of 2002, shortly after the *White* decision was handed down. Currently, Section 4 of the code prohibits candidates from knowingly "mak[ing] pledges or promises of conduct in office that could inhibit or compromise the faithful, impartial and diligent performance of the duties of the office." This re-wording of the pledges or promises clause is similar to those recommended by the ABA in 2003, but Oregon has not added any further commit clause. Oregon's speech restrictions were not very severe prior to *White*, but the revisions weaken the earlier code. Therefore, Oregon is classified as a broad interpreter.

TEXAS—In August of 2002, immediately after the Supreme Court's decision in *White* was announced, the Texas Supreme Court announced changes to the Texas Code of Judicial Conduct in an advisory opinion:

> The first change the Texas Supreme Court made was to Canon 3(B)(10). The court extended to judicial candidates the prohibition on public comment on certain types of litigation. The amended provision effectively prohibits both judges and judicial candidates from announcing their views on the outcome of potential litigation within their court. The court also modified Canon 5, which was modeled after the rules that Minnesota had in place before *White*. The court eliminated the "announcement clause" for judicial candidates in Canon 5(1). . . . The court also modified Canon 5(2) from the original. . . . In updating Canon 5, the Court replaced sections 1 and 2 with an amended version of Section 2 which prohibits judicial candidates from "making pledges or promises of conduct in office regarding pending or impending cases, specific classes of cases, specific classes of litigants, or specific propositions of law that would suggest to a reasonable person that the judge is predisposed to a probable decision in cases within the scope of the pledge. . . ." Furthermore, the court added a comment prohibiting candidates from making statements that "may cause a judge's impartiality to be reasonably questioned in the context of a particular case and may result in recusal."[50]

Given the recognition that these changes may not withstand further analysis, it is fair to classify Texas as a narrow interpreter.

WASHINGTON—Washington's Canon 7 was last revised in 1995. Today, the canon includes the pledges or promises clause and the commit clause. Before the *White* decision, Washington had removed a version of the announce clause. Noting that the U.S. Supreme Court declined to rule on the pledges or promises clause and the commit clause, legal observers in Washington have not pushed for any revision of the Washington canons.[51] Therefore, Washington is clearly a narrow interpreter.

Recognizing that my classification scheme is fairly simplistic, it still allows a first glimpse of whether state interpretations influenced the tone of judicial elections in these states.

So what do the 2004 supreme court elections across the country tell us about the influence of state interpretations? Is it true that those states that used a broad interpretation and weakened their codes of judicial conduct had more contentious judicial campaigns in 2004?

The Data

As a result of *White*, and subsequent state interpretations of *White*, many have predicted a dramatic change in the tone and tenor of judicial elections. As candidates are freer to speak their minds about controversial questions of law and policy, there is a greater chance that judicial campaigns will see more discussion of political issues, more efforts to attract interest group support on those issues, and more overt efforts to curry favor with voters. Specifically, the rise of TV advertising in judicial campaigns may have significant effects. To examine the effects of *White* in the states, I use data collected by the Justice at Stake Campaign, which tracked all supreme court advertising in 2002 and 2004 and has published brief summaries of the advertising that took place in many of the states examined here. Specifically, they have recorded the number of ads that were produced and the number of airings that occurred in each judicial race. In addition, they have done content analyses to examine the tone of each ad and the themes that were used. Ads were then classified based on their tone and put into one of three categories: "promotion of one candidate," "attack on the opponent," or "contrasting two or more candidates based on issues." Further classification was done to determine the themes that were used in the ad—whether the ad discussed specific issues or used campaign themes, or both. To determine whether *White* has produced more contentious judicial campaigns, it is worthwhile to examine the tone and content of advertising in each state.

To assess whether state interpretations matter, Table 3.1 examines how broad interpreters and narrow interpreters differed in terms of the amount of money spent in 2004 compared with that spent in 2002 judicial races. On average, those states that used broad interpretations of *White* saw a 72.6 percent average increase in campaign expenditures from 2002 to 2004. In contrast, states that used a narrow interpretation saw a 233.8 percent increase. When outliers Arkansas and Illinois are excluded from that average, narrow interpreters averaged a 72.2 percent increase between 2002 and 2004. Excluding the extreme outliers, we see virtually no difference between the two.

While *White* may prompt candidates and interest groups to spend more money, in the short term (and given that at the time of this writing we have only had one full election cycle since the *White* decision, the short term is most fitting here), the most immediate effects should be seen in the type of campaign information that candidates are using in their

TABLE 3.1

Average Percentage Increase in Candidate Spending by Interpretation

Interpretation	States	Average percentage change in candidate spending, 2002–2004
Broad	Georgia, Michigan, Minnesota, Oregon	72.6
Narrow	Alabama, Arkansas, Illinois, Kentucky, Louisiana, Mississippi, Montana, Nevada, New Mexico, Ohio, Texas, Washington	233.8 (72.2 excluding Arkansas and Illinois)
None	Idaho	–82.9

Source: Goldberg et al., *The New Politics of Judicial Elections 2004*, and Goldberg and Sanchez, *The New Politics of Judicial Elections 2002*.

campaigns. In those states that have used a broad interpretation, speech codes are significantly looser today than in those states that have opted for a narrow interpretation. Therefore, we should see changes in the tone and content of campaign messages. In Tables 3.2 and 3.3, I have included summary data about the tone of television ads in each state for 2002 and 2004. The data are compiled by dividing the total number of airings that featured any one category of content by the total number of airings in the state. Table 3.4 examines the difference in the tone of advertising in 2004 state supreme court elections between states that used a narrow interpretation and those that used a broad interpretation.

Patterns in the tone of campaign ads become clear. In those states that used a narrow interpretation, an average of 86 percent of all campaign ads focused on promoting one candidate—in short, they were positive ads. In contrast, narrow interpreters witnessed only 8.2 percent attack ads and 16.5 percent contrast ads (Table 3.4). The overwhelming majority of advertising in these states focused on positive messages promoting one candidate. But, in states that used a broad interpretation of *White* during their revision or reevaluation process the number of positive ads promoting one candidate falls to just 45.4 percent. While the number of attack ads remains low (8.6 percent), the number of ads that draw contrasts between candidates is significantly higher than states that use narrow interpretations—a whopping three and one-half times higher—at 46 percent. Contrast ads are not necessarily negative ads (while attack ads are, by definition, negative), but the fact that judicial races in those states that opted for broad interpretations drew such intense competition is clearly indicative that these races are different from those in states that used a narrow interpretation.

If it is true, however, that state interpretations of *White* have a significant role in determining the nature of judicial elections, it should also

TABLE 3.2
Tone of Judicial Ads, by State, 2002

State	Interpretation	Total number of ads	Total number of airings	Percentage of airings promoting a candidate	Percentage of airings attacking the opposing candidate	Percentage of airings contrasting candidates
Alabama	Narrow	8	3,594	69.9	8.5	21.6
Illinois	Narrow	10	1,473	76.3	0.0	23.7
Michigan	Broad	5	1,030	100.0	0.0	0.0
Mississippi	Narrow	18	1,479	64.8	30.9	4.3
Nevada	Narrow	5	233	89.3	0.0	10.7
Ohio	Narrow	29	13,105	64.6	6.2	29.2
Washington	Narrow	1	37	0.0	100.0	0.0
Average		10.9	2,993	66.4	20.8	12.8

Source: Goldberg and Sanchez, *The New Politics of Judicial Elections 2002*.

TABLE 3.3
Tone of Judicial Ads, by State, 2004

State	Interpretation	Total number of ads	Total number of airings	Percentage of airings promoting a candidate	Percentage of airings attacking the opposing candidate	Percentage of airings contrasting candidates
Alabama	Narrow	24	9,377	88.7	4.3	7.0
Arkansas	Narrow	6	242	100.0	0.0	0.0
Georgia	Broad	2	453	27.8	0.0	72.2
Illinois	Narrow	21	7,500	26.0	49.2	24.7
Kentucky	Narrow	12	205	64.4	27.3	8.3
Louisiana	Narrow	9	315	89.1	2.6	8.3
Michigan	Broad	4	1,512	74.2	25.8	0.0
Mississippi	Narrow	18	1,479	100.0	0.0	0.0
Nevada	Narrow	9	867	100.0	0.0	0.0
New Mexico	Narrow	4	326	100.0	0.0	0.0
Ohio	Narrow	28	14,139	77.4	7.2	15.4
Oregon	Broad	2	181	34.3	0.0	65.7
Washington	Narrow	2	273	100.0	0.0	0.0
Average		10.8	2,836	77.3	8.3	14.4

Source: Goldberg et al., *The New Politics of Judicial Elections 2004*.

TABLE 3.4
Tone of Judicial Ads, by Interpretation, 2004

Interpretation	States	Average percentage of ads promoting a candidate	Average percentage of ads attacking the opposing candidate	Average percentage of ads contrasting candidates
Broad	Georgia, Michigan, Oregon	45.4	8.6	46.0
Narrow	Alabama, Arkansas, Illinois, Kentucky, Louisiana, Mississippi, Nevada, New Mexico, North Carolina, Ohio, Washington	86.0	8.2	16.5

Source: Goldberg et al., *The New Politics of Judicial Elections 2004*.

have a significant effect on the types of issues that are discussed during the campaign. Candidates have always been free to discuss some things, like their qualifications, with voters. But are candidates taking advantage of the new opportunities to discuss political issues during their campaigns? Tables 3.5 and 3.6 examine the content of ads in 2002 and 2004 to determine whether there are any patterns that we can discern about the candidates' discussion of issues. There are several notable features here. First, traditional campaign messages, about qualifications, experience, and personal characteristics, were slightly less likely to appear in 2004 election campaigns than they were in 2002. Similarly, messages emphasizing criminal justice issues were slightly less likely in 2004, family values images were slightly more likely, and attack ads were slightly less likely. Civil justice themes, however, were more than twice as likely to appear during the 2004 campaign cycle. Messages emphasizing a candidate's ties to special interests were significantly less likely in 2004, and the number of campaign ads that criticized court decisions was up about 50 percent (although they still comprise only 9 percent of campaign messages on average).

When we compare advertising content between states that used a broad interpretation and those that used a narrow interpretation (Table 3.7), we see a few trends that may be important. First, contrary to predictions, campaign ads in states that used a broad interpretation were much more likely to feature traditional judicial messages, like qualifications, background, experience, and personal characteristics. Second, states that used a broad interpretation were much more likely to see campaign ads that featured messages about civil justice issues. Similarly, broad interpreters were more likely to produce campaign ads featuring charges of special interest influence. Family values messages were about equal regardless of state interpretations, as were criticisms of court decisions. Last, in states that used broad interpretations, campaign ads were less likely to feature messages about criminal justice concerns. Here, although some patterns emerge, it is difficult to draw many conclusions about the influence of *White*.

The picture becomes a little clearer when we analyze both the tone and content of judicial campaign ads (Table 3.8). Attack ads tended to favor themes related to criminal justice, claims of special interest connections, and direct criticism of court decisions across all states in 2004. Nonetheless, the emphasis on all three themes is much higher in states that use a broad interpretation, which bolsters the claim that *White* will make campaigns even nastier. Attack ads are more pointed and are particularly focused on direct claims that judicial candidates are influenced by special

TABLE 3.5
Percentage of Ad Airings Using Issues or Themes, 2002

	Traditional	Civil justice	Criminal justice	Special interests	Criticism of decisions	Family values	Other	Attack ad (no theme)
Alabama	42.5	0.0	0.0	30.1	0.0	27.4	0.0	0.0
Illinois	41.8	15.3	42.9	0.0	15.3	26.5	0.0	0.0
Michigan	13.3	0.0	86.7	50.7	0.0	29.5	0.0	0.0
Mississippi	17.6	3.1	50.9	21.8	22.6	39.8	0.0	8.2
Nevada	83.6	0.0	0.0	0.0	0.0	16.3	0.0	0.0
Ohio	19.2	43.7	30.5	16.1	6.2	16.8	1.1	4.0
Texas	71.4	0.0	14.8	0.0	0.0	0.0	13.9	0.0
Average	41.3	8.9	32.3	17.0	6.3	22.3	2.1	1.7

Source: Goldberg and Sanchez, *The New Politics of Judicial Elections 2002*.

TABLE 3.6
Percentage of Ad Airings Using Issues or Themes, 2004

	Traditional	Civil justice	Criminal justice	Special interests	Criticism of decisions	Family values	Other	Attack ad (no theme)
Alabama	6.1	11.3	16.3	0.6	15.3	90.2	0.0	0.0
Arkansas	85.5	0.0	14.5	0.0	0.0	14.5	0.0	0.0
Georgia	72.2	27.8	27.8	0.0	0.0	27.8	0.0	0.0
Illinois	0.0	70.8	50.1	44.1	45.1	12.1	0.0	0.0
Kentucky	27.3	41.0	28.3	0.0	31.2	0.0	0.0	6.8
Louisiana	0.0	36.8	61.9	8.2	0.0	50.8	0.0	2.5
Michigan	0.0	53.3	46.4	25.5	25.8	53.6	0.0	0.0
Mississippi	31.7	6.6	29.8	1.1	0.0	50.3	7.3	0.0
Nevada	68.1	0.0	31.9	0.0	0.0	9.8	0.0	0.0
New Mexico	0.0	19.6	83.7	0.0	0.0	19.6	16.3	0.0
Ohio	73.3	10.8	19.3	0.0	0.0	3.4	0.2	4.9
Oregon	100.0	0.0	0.0	0.0	0.0	0.0	0.0	0.0
Washington	0.0	0.0	0.0	0.0	0.0	0.0	100.0	0.0
Average	35.7	21.4	31.5	6.1	9.0	25.5	9.5	1.1

Source: Goldberg et al., *The New Politics of Judicial Elections 2004*.

TABLE 3.7
Percentage of Ad Airings Using Issues or Themes by Interpretation, 2004

	States	Traditional	Civil justice	Criminal justice	Special interests	Criticism of decisions	Family values	Attack ad (no theme)
Broad	Georgia, Michigan, Oregon	57.4	54.1	24.7	8.5	8.6	27.1	0.0
Narrow	Alabama, Arkansas, Illinois, Kentucky, Louisiana, Mississippi, Nevada, New Mexico, North Carolina, Ohio Washington	29.2	19.7	33.6	5.4	9.2	25.1	1.4

Source: Goldberg et al., *The New Politics of Judicial Elections 2004*.

TABLE 3.8

Percentage of Ad Airings Using Issues or Themes by Tone and Interpretation, 2004

	Tone	Traditional	Civil justice	Criminal justice	Special interests	Criticism of decisions	Family values	Attack ad (no theme)
Broad	Promote	8.7	9.2	91.3	0.0	0.0	68.2	0.0
	Attack	0.0	0.0	99.0	99.0	100.0	1.0	0.0
	Contrast	100.0	0.0	0.0	0.0	0.0	0.0	0.0
Narrow	Promote	40.3	11.4	23.2	0.1	2.8	39.1	0.0
	Attack	0.0	65.7	57.0	38.1	63.9	6.9	0.1
	Contrast	49.2	42.8	12.6	30.2	20.3	15.9	0.2

Source: Goldberg et al., *The New Politics of Judicial Elections 2004*.

interests and that state courts are making bad decisions. In addition, in those states that used narrow interpretations, attack ads were far more likely to focus on civil justice. This might make sense, given that criminal justice issues in judicial campaigns, particularly campaign claims related to specific criminal cases—cases that may receive significant attention in the media—are likely to be more salient with the public. In those states that use broad interpretations, candidates can speak more freely about crime and issues like the death penalty, and it makes sense that they would do so, as these will likely resonate more with voters. Therefore, it comes as no surprise that, in those states that allow candidates to speak freely about these issues, they choose to emphasize these themes instead of civil justice issues.

Contrast ads, in both broad and narrow interpreter states, emphasize traditional themes. Issue-based themes, however, are more prevalent in those states that use narrow interpretations. This raises an interesting question, as we would expect that judicial campaigns in states using broad interpretations should feature more issue-based speech. Nonetheless, one could argue that candidates in broadly interpreting states are allowed to speak more freely about issues and therefore issue-based contrast ads become less important to their campaigns. Is this, in fact, the case?

It is. The most significant pattern that emerges (as shown in Table 3.8) is that, in those states with broad interpretations of *White*, television ads that promote a candidate are most likely to feature content that focuses on themes of criminal justice. Among broad interpreters, family values themes are also popular in promotion ads. In contrast, states that have narrow interpretations saw ads promoting a candidate that were more likely to feature traditional judicial campaign themes—the candidates' qualifications, background, and experience. As in states using broad interpretations, family values themes were popular, but much less so. While 68.2 percent of all ad airings in states with broad interpretations used some message related to family values, only 39.1 percent of ad airings in states using narrow interpretations included family values themes. Traditional themes were included in 40.3 percent of ads aired in narrow interpreting states, but were only included in 8.7 percent of airings in broadly interpreting states. Therefore, it is clear that candidates in those states that broadly interpreted *White* are leaving traditional themes behind, even in ads promoting themselves. They are now more likely to rely on criminal justice themes. Given the historic importance of the death penalty in judicial elections, we should not be surprised that candidates who are able to talk about political and social issues choose to focus on criminal justice debates when appealing to voters.

Conclusions

Is it true that judicial races are becoming more costly? Definitely. Has *White* driven the increase in costs? The answer is far from clear. Is it true that interpretation alters the tone of campaigns? To some extent, the data indicate that it is. Recognizing that these are merely preliminary patterns, it seems that some states saw very different campaign advertising than others. The emphasis on "contrast" ads in states that used broad interpretations of the Supreme Court's ruling might suggest that this is the case, but a closer look reveals that contrast ads in those states in 2004 always used traditional judicial campaign themes. Thus, this trend alone does not indicate that *White* is creating more contentious campaigns. But state interpretations of the *White* decision are changing the nature of judicial campaigns across the country. Those states that have read the decision broadly are seeing a change in how judicial candidates promote themselves and how they attack their opponents. In both cases, there is a significantly greater likelihood that candidates will use criminal justice concerns —concerns that will be particularly salient with voters—to campaign.

Because broad interpretations will lead to looser canons of judicial conduct, it is entirely possible that judicial candidates in these states will increasingly rely on the ability to distinguish themselves from their opponents based on controversial issue positions. Has *White* had a significant influence on the kinds of messages that voters are receiving during a judicial campaign? It seems clear that it has—or at least it did in 2004.

It is important to remember that 2004 was the first election cycle after *White.* Therefore, any effort to establish lasting patterns is necessarily preliminary. Only time will tell us what the effect of *White* will be on the politicization of judicial elections. Exacerbating this problem, many states continue to revise and reevaluate their codes, and state and federal courts continue to hear challenges to state speech codes. Therefore, candidates and special interests that are interested in shaping the state judiciaries have had a very unclear picture of which states allow what activities. Moreover, the analysis here is necessarily limited to a few states—some of which had extremely contentious elections, some of which did not. Given that 2004 is the only full election cycle since *White* that allows analysis, it is difficult to say that the patterns are the rule, when they may be driven by the exceptions. In addition, even within those states that have seen significant interest group activity, money, and political speech (like Arkansas and Illinois), the pressure is sometimes targeted at specific races, but not at entire states. Over time, we will be better equipped to see a more complete picture and make more extensive claims as all candidates become more familiar with new speech codes and more states have more elections.

What does this tell us about the state of the state judiciaries in the wake of *White?* Once upon a time, judges were thought to serve a unique function, one that necessitated a pure adherence to legal doctrine and the absence of political predispositions. Whether or not one believes that this is possible, this ideal shaped how people thought about the courts. Today, in the aftermath of *White,* that ideal may be more difficult to achieve. How states choose to deal with the decision and how policymakers read the decision in *White* may have a substantial role in determining how much information voters get and how accountable judges will be to the voters. There is no doubt that we are witnessing significant changes in how judges are elected and how voters think about the courts. What is unclear, however, is exactly how today's changes will affect future judicial campaigns.

NOTES

1. Schotland, "Should Judges Be More Like Politicians?"
2. Baum, "Electoral Fates of Incumbent Judges."
3. Aspin and Hall, "Retention Elections and Judicial Behavior."
4. Baum, "Electoral Fates of Incumbent Judges," p. 422.
5. DuBois, *From Ballot to the Bench,* p. 67.

6. Hojnacki and Baum, "Choosing Judicial Candidates."

7. Ibid., p. 352.

8. Pennsylvanians for Modern Courts, *As Pennsylvania Goes.*

9. Goldberg et al., *New Politics of Judicial Elections 2004.*

10. Goldberg et al., *New Politics of Judicial Elections . . . 2000.*

11. Caufield, "In the Wake of *White.*"

12. Rizzo, "Chamber Ads Failed in Ohio."

13. Goldberg et al., *New Politics of Judicial Elections 2004.*

14. Schotland, "Elective Judges' Campaign Financing," p. 78.

15. Wold and Culver, "Defeat of the California Justices," p. 351.

16. The phrase "the new politics of judicial elections" comes directly from the series of reports that have been published by the Brennan Center for Justice at NYU School of Law, the Institute for Money in State Politics, and the Justice at Stake Campaign, all of which have been titled "The New Politics of Judicial Elections."

17. Wold and Culver, "Defeat of the California Justices," pp. 349–350.

18. Ibid., p. 350.

19. Ibid., p. 353.

20. Reid, "Politicization of Judicial Retention Elections," p. 46.

21. Noe, "Alabama Judicial Selection Reform," p. 215.

22. *Republican Party v. White,* 416 F.3d 738 (8th Cir. 2005) (en banc) (*White II*). It is important to note that Minnesota uses nonpartisan elections. Therefore, the limits imposed on judicial candidates' participation in party activities were instrumental in defining the electoral system in this case.

23. *Weaver v. Bonner,* 309 F.3d 1312 (11th Cir. 2002). See also Gallagher, "Judicial Ethics and the First Amendment."

24. *Spargo v. NY Commission on Judicial Conduct,* 351 F.3d 65 (2d Cir. 2003).

25. *Family Trust Foundation v. Kentucky Judicial Conduct Commission,* 388 F.3d 224 (6th Cir. 2004), p. 226.

26. Margolies, "Ruling Throws a Wrench into the Missouri Plan." See also Lieb, "Missouri Ruling Lets Candidates for Judge Speak Out."

27. Schotland, "Should Judges Be More Like Politicians?"

28. After the *White* decision, the ABA set up its own committee to review and revise the model code. Amendments to the speech codes were offered in 2003 and adopted by Arizona, Maryland, Minnesota, Nevada, New Mexico, and Wisconsin.

29. Margolies, "Ruling Throws a Wrench into the Missouri Plan." See also Lieb, "Missouri Ruling Lets Candidates for Judge Speak Out."

30. Gray, "States' Response," p. 163.

31. Ibid.

32. Kenworthy, *Judicial Campaign Speech.*

33. Gray, "States' Response," p. 164 (citing Alabama Advisory opinion 00-763).

34. Ibid.

35. Ibid. North Carolina is a unique case, as the state adopted nonpartisan elections and public financing before the 2004 elections.

36. Ibid.

37. Since the 2004 elections, there have been several additional court decisions regarding the status of state codes of judicial conduct. Because the data used here come from the 2004 election cycle, I have limited my analysis to those legal decisions and advisory opinions that came before the 2004 election cycle.

38. These states include Alabama, Arkansas, Georgia, Idaho, Illinois, Kentucky, Louisiana, Michigan, Minnesota, Mississippi, Montana, New Mexico, Ohio, Oregon, Texas, and Washington. While North Carolina, North Dakota, and West Virginia held supreme court elections in 2004, they are removed from the campaign spending analysis because data about the costs of judicial campaigns are unavailable. In the case of North Carolina, this is a result of the public financing system that was put into place in 2003, which eliminates any data for the 2004 costs. In the case of North Dakota, no data have been reported by the Institute for Money in State Politics, and therefore I cannot investigate the effects of the state's interpretation. Similarly, there is no available data for West Virginia in 2002, so it is impossible to know whether the state's interpretation has influenced the costs of campaigning in the state.

39. Alabama Advisory Opinion 00-763. The survey contained thirty questions that solicited candidates' views on issues. The opinion stated that the questions "[solicited] or appear to solicit the judicial candidate's predisposition toward specific legal views on matters pending or impending before any number of trial and appellate courts. Some of the questions call for the candidate to comment on issues that are likely to come before the candidate if elected judge."

40. Quoted by Gray, *Developments following* Republican Party of Minnesota v. White.

41. Brennan Center for Justice, "*Republican Party of Minnesota v. White.*"

42. Quoted by Gray, *Developments following* Republican Party of Minnesota v. White.

43. Ibid.

44. Ibid.

45. Ibid.

46. Ibid.

47. Administrative Office of Courts, "Candidate Free Speech Ruling."

48. Morris, "Free Speech in Judicial Elections."

49. Quoted by Gray, *Developments following* Republican Party of Minnesota v. White.

50. Williams, "*Republican Party of Minnesota v. White,*" pp. 216–218.

51. Thornton, *Judicial Campaign Ethics.*

Chapter 4

The Dynamics of Campaign Spending in State Supreme Court Elections

Chris W. Bonneau

The 2004 election between incumbent Justice Warren McGraw and attorney Brent Benjamin for a seat on the West Virginia State Supreme Court was considered "one of the nastiest in the nation."[1] In this race (which led to McGraw's defeat), an alliance of mining executives, businesses, and physicians combined to spend millions of dollars in opposition to McGraw. Unlike ugly races in other states like Alabama and Mississippi, opposition was not focused on business issues like tort liability or caps on damages. Instead, these business interests (broadly defined) attacked McGraw for being "soft on crime." An interest group named "And for the Sake of the Kids," which was described as "West Virginia's version of Swift-boat Veterans for Truth,"[2] ran several advertisements criticizing McGraw for supporting the 3–2 majority extending probation for a convicted child molester.[3] One of the chief fundraisers for And for the Sake of the Kids was Don Blankenship, CEO of Massey Energy Company, a coal company that is one of the largest employers in the state. Blankenship donated $1.7 million (of the roughly $2.5 million it raised) to the group. Not surprisingly, Massey "is expected to have several cases on appeal before the state Supreme Court."[4] After his defeat, McGraw sued And for the Sake of the Kids and Blankenship (among others) for libel, a case that was subsequently dismissed.[5] Clearly, state supreme court races in West Virginia are no longer the obscure, low-salience elections they used to be.

Perhaps this is not surprising, since West Virginia elects their judges on a partisan ballot. In this way, these elections do not differ from elections to other offices, such as the legislature. But not all states elect their judges in this way (see chapter 1). Georgia, for example, elects their judges in nonpartisan elections. While there are competitive elections between multiple candidates in Georgia, voters do not know the political parties of the candidates. In 2004, incumbent Justice Leah Sears was challenged by Grant Brantley. This is noteworthy because, in Georgia, very rarely are incumbent justices challenged. Moreover, on the rare occasions when there is a contested race, it tends to be relatively low-key in terms of campaigning and spending. However, this was not the case for the Sears-Brantley race, where Sears spent almost $500,000 and Brantley spent over $340,000. Unlike the West Virginia race, the major issues in this race were same-sex marriage and "judicial activism," as opposed to crime.[6] Despite the fact that the race was nonpartisan, the Republican governor of Georgia, Sonny Perdue, supported Brantley via automated phone calls to voters. Sears countered by having the Democratic mayor of Atlanta, Shirley Franklin, campaign on her behalf (for more on the involvement of parties in nonpartisan judicial elections, see chapter 6).[7] Also, for the first time ever, the Atlanta Press Club invited candidates for the state supreme court to participate in a live debate, a sign that the race was unusual in its high profile.[8] Thus, despite the official "nonpartisan" nature of the race, many officials and interest groups participated in the election in a way that revealed the candidates' ideologies and political party affiliations. In fact, after this race, a constitutional amendment was introduced in the state legislature to change the method of selection in Georgia from nonpartisan to partisan, and the governor said that while he did not support this change "at this time," he "could see himself supporting a constitutional amendment" in the future.[9] As in West Virginia, judicial races in Georgia have also been quite different recently than they were in preceding years. While Sears still won her election, the campaign to do so was more vigorous than in previous races.

However, both of these elections pale in comparison with the 2004 race in the Fifth District for the Illinois Supreme Court discussed in chapter 1. Unlike in West Virginia and Georgia, in Illinois, candidates for the state high court run in judicial districts, not statewide. Cook County (Chicago) elects three judges, and four other districts each elect one member of the seven-member court. The Fifth District encompasses thirty-seven southern (mostly rural) Illinois counties.[10] Two lower court judges—Republican Lloyd Karmeier (who won the election) and Democrat Gordon Maag —raised and spent in excess of $8 million on the campaign, an average of about $16 per vote.[11] The race was so nasty that both candidates were reprimanded by the Illinois State Bar Association for negative and misleading advertisements.[12] The major issue in this race was tort reform, with the Chamber of Commerce supporting Karmeier and the AFL-CIO backing Maag.[13] Part of the reason this race was seen as so important is that the judges on the Illinois Supreme Court serve ten-year terms, and the court had recently struck down tort reform legislation. Given the five to two advantage enjoyed by Democrats on the court, and the fact that another election was not expected until 2010, this contest was the last chance that tort reform advocates had to elect a judge sympathetic to their views. Even though the election was held in a district, the same trend observed in other states toward large amounts of campaign spending and vigorous campaigning prevailed.

These cases illustrate that contemporary state supreme court elections possess many of the same characteristics as elections for executive or legislative offices. In the rest of this chapter, I examine changes in these elections from 1990 to 2004. Specifically, I look at changes in campaign spending by state, across time, and by selection system. While I do not take a position as to whether judges *should* be elected, the data suggest that there are certain institutional arrangements that can promote (or inhibit) campaign spending. I conclude the chapter with a discussion of the public financing of judicial elections, a reform gaining popularity among those who seek reform of judicial elections but that seems to have little public support.

Campaign Spending: The Good, the Bad, and the Ugly

Most of the research that has been done on campaign spending in judicial elections has taken an "advocacy" tone: campaign spending leads to the erosion of the perception of fairness in the judiciary.[14] This is true even though, to date, there is *no evidence* that judges are affected by campaign spending, once one controls for other factors.[15] Critics respond that, to a certain extent, it does not matter whether judges are influenced by campaign contributions; rather, all that is important in terms of perceptions of fairness is that people *think* judges are influenced. And, on this front, the empirical evidence is clear: people do think judges are influenced by campaign funds.[16] Interestingly, 26 percent of state judges also agree that campaign contributions influence judicial decisionmaking, though, presumably, none would admit that *they* are influenced.[17]

Yet, it is far from clear that campaign spending in judicial elections has purely negative consequences. For example, when candidates spend money on their campaigns, they provide information to allow voters to make a more informed decision. Moreover, the more money that is spent in these elections, the higher the levels of voter participation.[18] A vigorous campaign serves as a way to stimulate voter interest in the election. Campaign spending also helps make the election more competitive. Melinda Gann Hall and Chris W. Bonneau find that the larger the spending difference between the candidates, the larger the incumbent's percentage of the vote.[19] Conversely, if the candidates spend roughly equivalent amounts of money, the election will be closer. This again suggests that voters are responsive to competitive elections, and thus campaign spending allows candidates to provide voters with information they need to make decisions.

Of course, the positives associated with campaign spending do not go to the question of whether judges *should* be elected. And there is a very good reason for that: whether judges should be elected is a normative question that cannot be answered by empirical data. There is no amount of evidence that will convince an opponent of judicial elections that judges should be elected. However, there *is* empirical evidence that can refute some of the reasons that are given for why judicial elections are bad. For example, one of the reasons given for opposition to judicial elections is that voters do not have enough information to make informed choices. However, Hall and Bonneau have demonstrated this claim to be false.[20] On the campaign spending front, Bonneau showed that not all races are similarly costly.[21] Moreover, the amount of campaign spending can be understood systematically, and the institutional rules of the game are important determinants of the amount of spending. Thus, if policymakers are concerned with the amount of spending, they can change certain institutional structures to limit spending while preserving elections.

Normative questions aside, looking at the elections since 1990 will allow us to understand the changes that have been occurring, as well as suggest some possible reasons for these changes.

Data

I collected data on campaign spending by all candidates in state supreme court races from 1990 to 2004. These data were gathered from official state reports, obtained through the secretary of state's office in each state (in some states, these reports are kept with an elections board). Here, I look only at states that elect their judges in partisan and nonpartisan elections. Given the significant differences between these elections and retention elections, and the fact that many candidates who stand for retention do not raise and spend money (since they face no opposition), I omit retention elections from this analysis.[22]

State Supreme Court Elections over Time and by Selection System

Figure 4.1 shows the amount of total spending over time by method of judicial selection. As can be seen clearly, campaign spending in state supreme court elections has increased steadily over the period 1990–2004. The average contested race in 1990 (all elections) involved $364,348 in spending, while a similar race in 2004 cost $892,755. While there have been some fluctuations, the general trend is toward more expensive races.

Figure 4.1 also shows the differences between partisan and nonpartisan elections. In every election from 1990 to 2004, partisan elections were more expensive, on average, than nonpartisan elections. Indeed, in most years, partisan elections are *much* more expensive than their nonpartisan

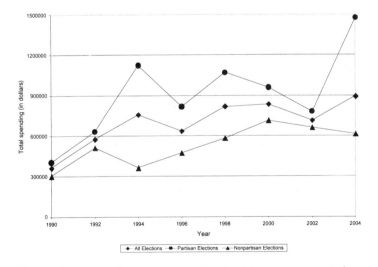

Fig. 4.1. Average total campaign spending in state supreme court elections, 1990–2004

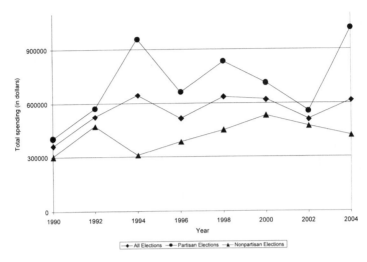

Fig. 4.2. Average total campaign spending in state supreme court elections, 1990–2004 (1990 dollars)

counterparts. Over the fifteen-year period examined here, contested partisan elections average spending of $885,177, while nonpartisan elections average $549,160.

While Figure 4.1 documents that state supreme court elections are getting more expensive, this result could be because of inflation. That is, what costs $1 in 1990 is going to be more expensive in 2004. Thus, in Figure 4.2, I graph the same data, but this time converting the spending figures to 1990 dollars. As Figure 4.2 indicates, while the average amount of campaign spending has changed, the overall trend has not. Thus, we can be confident that the increases in campaign spending that we have observed over this time period are not due to inflation and rising costs. Rather, there are other explanations for this increase.

The major explanation for this increased cost has to due with the importance of state supreme courts. State courts "have become more visible and controversial by 'actively protecting constitutional rights' and taking up 'lightning rod issues.' During the 1970s the judicial branches in many states began to use state constitutions to extend rights beyond those guaranteed under the federal constitution."[23] State supreme courts are the courts of last resort in their states, and they address a variety of important issues to both individuals and businesses. Given the small number of cases heard by the U.S. Supreme Court (and this number has become even smaller in recent years), state supreme courts are effectively the end of the road for the vast majority of litigation.[24] Thus, decisions about tort liability and damages, the death penalty, and the funding of education, for example, are all definitively made by state supreme courts. The power of state supreme court justices makes them attractive positions to both seek and control.

Moreover, state supreme courts range in size from five to nine members, with terms from six to twelve years. Consequently, from a business perspective, it is much more efficient to try to elect judges who are sympathetic with your interests than it is to try to control the legislature. This is especially true since state supreme courts have the last say on the constitutionality of enacted state legislation. Thus, if you believe in tort reform and capping damages, your best strategy is to have a sympathetic supreme court (and, as Deborah Goldberg illustrates in chapter 5, organizations in favor of tort reform have had major roles in recent state supreme court elections). Without that, any legislation passed may be struck down. As control of the court has become more important, campaign fundraising and spending has risen.

Campaign Spending by Type of Election

In addition to the differences between partisan and nonpartisan elections, another important distinction is between open seat races and incumbent-challenger races. In open seat races, there is no incumbent justice present. In general, these races have been found to be more competitive and more expensive.[25]

In Table 4.1, I show the campaign spending by type of election. While, on average, open seat races are more expensive than incumbent-challenger races, there are some important qualifications to this general observation. For example, partisan incumbent-challenger races are more expensive

TABLE 4.1
Average Campaign Spending (in dollars) by Type of Election, 1990–2004
(number of elections in parentheses)

	Open seat	Incumbent-challenger
Partisan	1,142,597 (53)	712,477 (79)
Nonpartisan	619,803 (40)	521,990 (104)
All elections	917,739 (93)	604,222 (183)

than nonpartisan open seat races. Thus, it appears that even though the presence of an incumbent is important, it is not as important as the type of election—partisan versus nonpartisan.

The reason open seats are more expensive than incumbent-challenger races is straightforward. Just like legislative incumbents, judicial incumbents possess resources and name recognition that most challengers do not. Moreover, the vast majority of incumbents are likely to be reelected, though not at as high a rate as many suggest.[26] Thus, the best chance a potential candidate has to ascend to the bench is to run for an open seat, as scholars of legislative elections have argued.[27] Likewise, open seat races are also the best opportunity for interest groups to elect a candidate who shares their positions on key issues. Consequently, they will pour more money into these races in an attempt to secure a victory. For these reasons, open seat races tend to be more expensive than races where an incumbent is involved.

Campaign Spending by State

In addition to the differences in state supreme court spending over time and by type of election, other differences between states are interesting. For example, since some states are larger than others (both geographically and in terms of population), we would expect greater levels of spending in states like Texas than in those like West Virginia.

In Table 4.2, I show the average amount of total spending by each state in the analysis. Not surprisingly, given what we saw earlier, the most expensive states are those that have partisan elections (Pennsylvania, Alabama, Illinois, Texas, and Louisiana). Moreover, the top two most expensive nonpartisan states (Ohio and Michigan) are states that nominate their candidates in partisan primaries or conventions, even though the general election is nonpartisan. At the bottom of the list in terms of cost are nonpartisan states like Oregon, Idaho, and Minnesota.

There also some interesting variations within selection system. For example, consider the neighboring states of Wisconsin and Minnesota. Despite both being nonpartisan, elections in Wisconsin are, on average, five times more expensive than those in Minnesota. Even though many similarities exist between the two states, state supreme court elections have become more politicized in Wisconsin than in Minnesota. Indeed, in Chief

TABLE 4.2
Average Campaign Spending, by State, 1990–2004
(number of elections in parentheses)

State	Average spending (dollars)
Pennsylvania	2,250,773 (6)
Alabama	1,450,673 (21)
Illinois	1,371,590 (11)
Ohio	1,193,205 (20)
Texas Supreme Court	1,155,125 (27)
Louisiana	1,080,113 (9)
Michigan	927,019 (18)
West Virginia	887,218 (7)
Mississippi	599,251 (16)
Nevada	593,816 (11)
Wisconsin	559,505 (9)
Kentucky	422,063 (10)
North Carolina	366,742 (16)
Montana	359,974 (6)
Georgia	289,865 (8)
New Mexico	273,398 (2)
Arkansas	264,320 (9)
Washington	205,601 (22)
Oregon	183,107 (7)
Idaho	124,579 (5)
Texas Court of Criminal Appeals	116,841 (26)
Minnesota	108,185 (10)

Justice Shirley Abrahamson's reelection race in 1999, four of her colleagues endorsed her challenger and total spending was around $1.5 million.[28] In Minnesota, the most costly race barely exceeded $300,000. Also, Texas is an interesting example since there are two courts of last resort in the state. The Texas Supreme Court is the court of last resort for all civil cases, and the Texas Court of Criminal Appeals is the final arbiter of criminal cases. Despite both courts being of the same size, with the same salary, term of office, and resources, Texas Supreme Court elections average over $1.1 million in spending, while those for the Texas Court of Criminal Appeals average just under $117,000. As discussed earlier, the importance of issues like tort liability have made elections to the Texas Supreme Court significantly more expensive than elections to the Texas Court of Criminal Appeals. Given that everything else between these courts is identical, the only variation is the jurisdiction of the court, and this shows the importance of the docket on the costs of state supreme court elections.

To control for the size of the state, I divide the total cost of the race by

TABLE 4.3
Average Campaign Spending per Capita,
by State, 1990–2004

State	Average spending (dollars)
Illinois	8,789.31
Louisiana	2,140.27
Kentucky	1,014.57
Mississippi	874.33
West Virginia	633.36
Montana	565.05
Nevada	475.32
Alabama	446.96
Pennsylvania	246.30
New Mexico	212.15
Wisconsin	145.33
Arkansas	143.96
Ohio	143.45
Idaho	141.34
Michigan	128.10
Texas Supreme Court	87.13
Oregon	72.84
North Carolina	64.57
Georgia	52.26
Washington	49.90
Minnesota	31.42
Texas Court of Criminal Appeals	8.77

the size of the voting population in the state (in 1,000s). For those states that do not elect judges statewide, the size of the voting population in the district in which the election is held is used. These results are presented in Table 4.3. What jumps out immediately is that the four most expensive states per capita all hold elections in districts, as opposed to statewide. There is more spending per voter, on average, in Illinois, Louisiana, Kentucky, and Mississippi than there is in any other state. Thus, holding elections in districts does not decrease the amount of money spent per capita in the election. If anything, the opposite is true.

Also, high-spending states like Alabama, Pennsylvania, Ohio, and Texas (Supreme Court) are not at the top of the list once the size of the voting age population is taken into account. Ohio, which was ranked fourth in average spending, is only thirteenth in spending per capita; the Texas Supreme Court moves from fifth to sixteenth. While the total amount of campaign spending is interesting, Table 4.3 shows that failing to take into account the size of the voting age population can lead to misleading conclusions.

Reforming Judicial Elections: Public Financing

For years, people interested in reforming the selection of state court judges have focused their attention on the eradication of judicial elections. However, the electorate has repeatedly refused to relinquish their right to elect judges.[29] Failing the eradication of elections, which many reformers still prefer, the focus has shifted to trying to make judicial elections as apolitical as possible. Specifically, many reformers now advocate the full public financing of judicial elections.

Proponents of public financing cite one major advantage of such a system: it is a way to minimize private campaign contributions and protect the judiciary from the perception of impropriety that arises when judges receive money from parties that will appear before them.[30] Given both that a perception of impropriety exists and the public still supports electing judges, the public financing of judicial elections may be the most practical solution. Indeed, the American Bar Association is now recommending that "states that elect judges in contested elections finance judicial elections with public funds," though Charles Gardner Geyh and others argue that nothing short of the elimination of elections is sufficient to preserve judicial independence and eliminate the perception of impropriety.[31]

Of course, public financing of campaigns also has significant drawbacks. First, while public financing does eliminate the need for candidates to raise money, it "does little to rein in groups making independent expenditures or conducting issue advocacy campaigns. . . . Restricting candidate fundraising activities makes these other forms of campaign support more important and increases the influence of the groups that provide them."[32] Thus, it is unclear whether public financing will affect the amount of money spent in judicial elections; rather, it may simply shift the spending of money from candidates to interest groups.

Second, there is some evidence that the current system of financing judicial elections discourages some candidates from running.[33] On the surface, one would think this is an advantage: public financing can remove one of the barriers to candidate entry, thus promoting competition and allowing the electorate to better hold judges accountable. Reformers, though, do not see increased competition as necessarily desirable.[34] Indeed, "increased competition may undermine ongoing efforts to cool judicial campaign rhetoric and dissuade candidates and the electorate from compromising judicial independence by turning elections into referenda on the popularity of incumbent judges' isolated decisions."[35]

Finally, there is the issue of how to publicly fund judicial campaigns. To date, only two states—Wisconsin and North Carolina—have attempted to publicly finance judicial elections (North Carolina has only done it for one election cycle, 2004). In both cases, these systems are funded via "check-offs" on state tax returns (Wisconsin has a $1 check-off; North Carolina has a $3 check-off). It is important to note that check-off plans simply appropriate a sum of already paid taxes from each taxpayer to the fund; it is not an additional tax. The response by the public in terms of support has been underwhelming. For example, only 7 percent of North Carolina taxpayers chose to allocate $3 of their taxes for the public financing of campaigns, and in Wisconsin the number has hovered between 8 percent and 9 percent in recent years.[36] This lack of public support has led to elections being underfunded, and in Wisconsin, only 14 percent of judicial candidates opted to participate in the public funding program in 2000.[37] Thus, there does not seem to be much support for the public financing of judicial elections.

Conclusion

This chapter has shown that campaign spending in state supreme court elections has increased from 1990 to 2004. Further, partisan elections are more expensive than nonpartisan elections, and open seat races are generally more expensive than incumbent-challenger contests. That being said, there are also important variations in spending by state, with some states having more expensive elections than others.

What does all this mean? The data presented here indicate that state supreme court seats have become more "valuable" in recent years, both to those who seek to hold them and to those who seek to elect like-minded candidates. This is most clearly shown in the differences between the Texas Supreme Court and the Texas Court of Criminal Appeals. Moreover, we can expect this trend to continue, especially in the wake of *Republican Party of Minnesota v. White* (2002) (see chapter 2). The ability to provide meaningful information about their positions on a variety of legal and political issues makes campaigning more meaningful to candidates, and thus money assumes greater importance to candidates to ensure they can buy television and radio airtime and actively campaign.

Because of the importance of state supreme courts and the *White* decision, we can expect campaign spending to continue to increase over the next several years. While some would argue that this is a negative development since it gives rise to the appearance of impropriety, it is important to remember that there has been no evidence that judges are being "bought" or "influenced" by campaign money.[38] Furthermore, campaign spending can help provide information to voters, so as to better allow them to make an informed decision. In response to the increase in campaign spending and the threat to the impartiality of the judiciary, some judicial reformers have advocated moving to a system of publicly financing elections. While there has not been much experience with this reform, evidence from the two states that have enacted public financing schemes indicates that there is not much support for this from the public.

NOTES

1. Morello, "W.Va. Supreme Court Justice Defeated."
2. McElhinny, "McGraw Campaign Cries Foul."
3. Morello, "W.Va. Supreme Court Justice Defeated."
4. Ibid.
5. Bundy, "Judge Dismisses Former Justice's Libel Lawsuit."
6. Seely, "'Activist' Judges Targeted."
7. Rankin, "Divisive Supreme Court Fight Ends in Victory for Sears."
8. Badertscher, "Justice Candidates Trade Barbs on TV."
9. Basinger, "Perdue Looks at Partisan Judicial Races."
10. Dreiling, "Supreme Fight."
11. Hampel, "Big-Money Race Sets Record."
12. Gustin, "Candidates Are Asked to Pull Ads."
13. Howard, "Chamber Backs Judicial Candidate."
14. For example, Hansen, "High Cost of Judging," and Schotland, "Financing Judicial Elections, 2000."
15. Cann, "Campaign Contributions and Judicial Behavior."
16. National Center for State Courts, *How the Public Views State Courts*; Jackson and Riddlesperger, "Money and Politics in Judicial Elections."
17. Goldberg, *Public Funding of Judicial Elections.*
18. Bonneau and Hall, "Mobilizing Interest."
19. Hall and Bonneau, "Does Quality Matter?"
20. Ibid. Although see Baum and Klein, chapter 8 in this volume.
21. Bonneau, "What Price Justice(s)?"
22. Abbe and Herrnson, "Public Financing for Judicial Elections?"; Bonneau, "Patterns of Campaign Spending and Electoral Competition."
23. Abbe and Herrnson, "Public Financing for Judicial Elections?" p. 539.

24. Carp and Stidham, *Judicial Process in America*.

25. Bonneau, "Patterns of Campaign Spending and Electoral Competition"; Bonneau, "What Price Justice(s)?"

26. Bonneau, "Electoral Verdicts."

27. Banks and Kiewiet, "Explaining Patterns of Candidate Competition"; Bond et al., "Partisan Differences in Candidate Quality"; Jacobson, *Politics of Congressional Elections*.

28. Bonneau and Hall, "Wisconsin Judiciary."

29. Goldberg, *Public Funding of Judicial Elections*; Geyh, "Why Judicial Elections Stink."

30. Geyh, "Publicly Funded Judicial Elections"; Goldberg, *Public Funding of Judicial Elections*.

31. American Bar Association Standing Committee on Judicial Independence, *Report of the Commission on Public Financing of Judicial Elections*; Geyh, "Why Judicial Elections Stink."

32. Abbe and Herrnson, "Public Financing for Judicial Elections?" p. 547.

33. Ibid.

34. Goldberg, *Public Funding of Judicial Elections*.

35. Geyh, "Publicly Funded Judicial Elections," p. 1480.

36. Ibid.; Democracy North Carolina, *Judicial Campaign Reform Successes*.

37. Participation is higher in North Carolina (Democracy North Carolina, *Judicial Campaign Reform Successes*). However, it is interesting to note that participation in the Wisconsin program used to be much higher as well—55 percent in 1986. Thus, we should be careful about concluding too much on the basis of one election cycle.

38. Cann, "Campaign Contributions and Judicial Behavior."

Chapter 5

Interest Group Participation in Judicial Elections

Deborah Goldberg

"Justice for Sale." For almost twenty years, variants of this phrase have headlined exposés about the role of interest group money in judicial elections.[1] The presumption behind all of the reports is that interest group contributions to candidates for the bench and expenditures on independent advertising campaigns pose profound risks to a crucial institution and the fundamental values it serves.[2] What is it about the judiciary and judicial elections that raises special anxiety about interest group influence? What have interest groups been doing to generate alarm? Is the threat real, or are interest groups providing an important service to the electorate? If our courts are in danger, what options are available to protect them? These questions are the focus of this chapter.

Judicial Elections and the Role of Courts

In the constitutional democracy of the United States, courts have a special role. Members of the executive and legislative branches are expected to make policy commitments and to represent the interests of their constituents. But the third branch is a check on the popular will—a bulwark against "tyranny of the majority"—an institution charged with safeguarding the fundamental rights of even the least powerful and most unpopular minorities. These values are embedded in constitutional principles of due process and the separation of powers.

With those ideals in mind, judicial elections may seem a contradiction in terms. How can judges who secure their positions through popular election be expected to maintain the integrity, independence, and impartiality necessary to do their jobs? To the skeptics asking that question, it may come as a surprise that judicial elections actually began as a means of *increasing* the independence of judges, who were widely regarded as incompetent political cronies of the elected officials who appointed them.[3] Progressive thinkers reasoned that elections would open the judiciary to more qualified candidates and that the public would be better served by judges accountable to the electorate, rather than a single powerful politician.

Judicial elections thus began on the model of most other elections, as a contest between candidates whose partisan affiliation appeared on the ballot. Over time, as political parties increased their hold on candidates for the bench, presenting a new sort of threat to judicial independence, a majority of states holding contested elections switched to a nonpartisan system. Today's proponents of nonpartisan elections contend that judges owe their allegiance to the law, not to a particular political party or its favored policies, so elections should be structured to reduce the influence of partisan affiliation. But disillusion even with nonpartisan elections led some states to abandon contested elections altogether, replacing them with a system often called "merit selection," in which initial appointments are followed by retention elections.[4]

Other strategies have been adopted, even in states with partisan elections, to mitigate political influence on judges.[5] Judges typically serve for longer terms than other elected officials, so they face the pressures of re-election less frequently. For many years, the judiciary also has been subject to special canons of ethics, usually adaptations of the American Bar Association's *Model Code of Judicial Conduct,* which helped to keep judges and judicial candidates largely removed from the ordinary political fray. As Rick Hasen explains in chapter 2, however, the canons have been subject to increasing—and increasingly successful—attack by candidates and political parties as they seek to make campaigns for the bench more like other elections.

Even with the canons in place, but more so as they are invalidated or diluted, judicial elections present numerous opportunities for interest group involvement. In fact, judicial elections may be especially susceptible to interest group influence, because voters typically do not have much information about judicial candidates.[6] Deprived of that information, voters often decline to vote for any of the candidates on the ballot.[7] A relatively high level of voter "rolloff" means that a small, but well-informed, sector of the electorate can disproportionately affect electoral outcomes. In this environment, even grassroots interest groups operating on a limited budget can wield substantial power by targeting their message to a select group of receptive voters. Wealthy interest groups can fill the information gap with mass advertising. An affirmative strategy mobilizes supporters for a favored candidate. Negative ads are known to increase cynicism and depress turnout, leaving the remaining voters with enhanced power.[8]

Retention elections are particularly vulnerable to such strategies. Unlike elected judges, appointed judges do not have a preexisting donor base from which they can raise funds to respond to an attack. Judges facing retention elections thus are sitting ducks for coordinated interest group campaigns to unseat them because of unpopular decisions. Even judges who have been able to secure political contributions and the support of the organized bar have found it difficult, and in some cases impossible, to repel coordinated interest group attacks, which are often orchestrated shortly before elections to maximize the difficulty of a meaningful response.

A retention election in Tennessee is a notorious example of this phenomenon. Tennessee adopted merit selection in 1994 as means of avoiding the growing politicization of its judicial elections. In June 1996, the Supreme Court of Tennessee decided a controversial capital case, unanimously upholding the defendant's conviction but invalidating his death sentence. The court split only with respect to the reason that the defendant deserved a new sentencing, with Justice Penny White joining (but not writing for) a narrow majority who held that the lower court had misinterpreted the state's aggravating circumstances statute. In reaction to the decision, the Tennessee Conservative Union, "along with victims' rights groups, religious conservatives, and law enforcement organizations," mobilized a campaign against Justice White, who had the misfortune of being up for retention in August of that year.[9] She was branded as "pro-criminal" and lost her seat.

This example illustrates why concern is rising about the involvement of interest groups in judicial elections. Sitting judges facing an imminent election, whether a contested election or a retention election, know that every decision is potentially fodder for the opposition. When well-heeled or well-organized interest groups can seize on isolated opinions—even well-reasoned decisions that have been joined by a majority of other judges on the court—as the basis for attack ads in the next campaign, it takes extraordinary integrity and real courage for a judge facing reelection to support a ruling that plainly will be unpopular.

Ignoring the electoral threat is not an easy matter, as some well respected judges have candidly admitted:

> The late Honorable Otto Kaus, who served on the California Supreme Court from 1980 through 1985, used a marvelous metaphor to describe the dilemma of deciding controversial cases while facing reelection. He said it was like finding a crocodile in your bathtub when you go in to shave in the morning. You know it's there, and you try not to think about it, but it's hard to think about much else while you're shaving.[10]

Research suggests that the prospect of electoral defeat does in fact influence judicial decisions. For example, one study indicated that elected judges are more likely to support local parties to litigation against out-of-state parties who cannot vote.[11] Another demonstrated that "criminal defendants [convicted of murder] were approximately 15% more likely to be sentenced to death when the sentence was issued during the judge's election year."[12] And, in chapter 10 of this book, Paul Brace and Brent Boyea clearly show that an appellate judge's impending election influences whether she will vote to reverse a capital punishment case.

Interest group involvement in judicial elections raises a second type of concern. The highly visible participation of interest groups in campaigns for the bench, whether through contributions of large sums directly to candidates or through expensive advertising campaigns, gives rise to the perception (in addition to the reality) that money influences judicial decisionmaking. The perception that our courts are tilted toward wealthy interests—that there are two systems of justice in this country, one for the rich and one for everyone else—undermines respect for the judicial system and erodes the trust in government necessary to motivate compliance with the law. To the extent that interest group involvement in judicial elections is rising, it may reinforce that perception and jeopardize the legitimacy of the courts.

Interest Group Involvement in Judicial Elections

Interest group participation in judicial elections is not a new phenomenon. In 1986, law enforcement organizations were prominently involved in the successful attacks on California Supreme Court Justice Rose Bird and two of her colleagues, whose bids for retention were defeated. Also, the

1988 supreme court elections in Texas drew national attention to the role of business and professional groups in partisan elections, as the battle over "tort reform" began to heat up. But, until recently, these multimillion-dollar races and organized campaigns against judges seeking retention were anomalies in what were otherwise relatively tame and nearly invisible elections.[13]

The year 2000 marked a watershed for interest group involvement in judicial elections.[14] In that year, major television advertising campaigns radically changed the tenor and profile of supreme court races in several states.[15] Studies of the two election cycles since then have documented both increased numbers of interest groups making expenditures and more geographically diverse interest group spending on television airtime in those elections.[16] Moreover, although the different types of elections—partisan, nonpartisan, and retention—present different incentives and opportunities for interest group participation, we have seen high-profile involvement spread fairly rapidly into all of them. Lower-profile, grassroots activity is more difficult to track but also appears to be growing.

Monied Interests in Judicial Campaigns

In 2000, thirty-eight states conducted some form of election for their supreme courts. Total candidate fundraising in that year reached $45.6 million—a 61 percent increase in just one election cycle and double the amount raised in 1994.[17] Average candidate fundraising in three states—Illinois, Michigan, and Ohio—exceeded $500,000, and in Alabama, candidates raised more than $1 million, on average.[18]

The multimillion-dollar campaigns of 2000 took place only in contested elections and, in most cases, in partisan elections. Only one state with nonpartisan elections—Mississippi—passed the $2 million mark, with eleven candidates raising a total of nearly $3.3 million.[19] On average, candidates in partisan elections attracted more than three times the money of candidates in nonpartisan elections during the decade leading up to 2000.[20] By contrast, the 2000 retention elections remained quiet: only four of twenty-five candidates seeking retention raised any money at all, and those four averaged less than $20,000.[21]

High levels of fundraising by candidates tend to correlate with high levels of interest group participation in campaigns. Over the decade leading up to 2000, approximately half of the funds collected by supreme court candidates came from two major categories of donors: business interests and lawyers.[22] But interest group involvement in judicial elections attracted unusual attention in 2000, when controversial television advertisements first hit the airwaves.

In 2000, interest groups spent an estimated $2.8 million on airtime in Alabama, Michigan, Mississippi, and Ohio.[23] More than half of the spots aired in one state—Ohio—where interest group expenditures accounted for more than half of the TV spending.[24] Ohio also took the prize for the nastiest ad, an attack sponsored by Citizens for a Strong Ohio that catapulted interest group involvement in state supreme court elections into the national news.[25]

The ad that raised eyebrows around the nation was directed at an incumbent member of the Ohio Supreme Court, Alice Resnick. The ad depicted her as Lady Justice, lifting her blindfold to watch "$750,000 from personal injury lawyers" tilt the scales she held aloft. The voiceover concluded: "Alice Resnick. Is Justice for Sale?" The ad was so extreme, and was perceived to be such an unfair slur on the candidate and the courts, that it appears to have backfired. Notwithstanding the ad, and another financed by the U.S. Chamber of Commerce drumming the same theme, Justice Resnick won reelection in 2000.

Although the anti-Resnick campaign failed to unseat her, it succeeded in triggering substantial new interest group involvement in Ohio's supreme court elections. Trial attorneys and labor responded to the attack on Justice Resnick and other candidates, including through ads sponsored by a newly formed group, Citizens for an Independent Court. But in the three other states seeing television ads in supreme court elections, only the Chamber of Commerce and other business allies ran advertising campaigns (although state Democratic parties responded with their own ads in Alabama and Michigan).

The first year of supreme court air wars suggested that the chamber's investment in television advertising paid off. Justice Resnick kept her seat, as did two of the four candidates in Mississippi, where the chamber's advertising—the only noncandidate advertising in the elections—was evidently perceived to some extent as outsider meddling in the state's affairs. But supreme court candidates endorsed by the Chamber of Commerce won one seat in Ohio, two in Mississippi, three in Michigan, and five in Alabama. The lesson was not lost on interest groups hoping to influence supreme court elections in 2002.

In 2002, interest group involvement in supreme court elections was significant by a number of measures. First, interest groups ran TV ads in six states—Idaho, Illinois, Michigan, Mississippi, Ohio, and Washington—a 50 percent increase over 2000, with three new states seeing television advertising.[26] Second, ten separate groups ran television advertisements in 2002, as compared with only five in 2000.[27] In two states, interest groups were the only sponsors of advertising; in two others, they spent more on television than all of the state's supreme court candidates combined.

Although business financed almost 50 percent of the ads,[28] the chamber's name appeared on none of them. Its conspicuous absence in Mississippi, after its prominence on the air but only mixed success in 2000, provoked speculation that it was funneling money through the Law Enforcement Alliance of America (LEAA). The LEAA ran about 650 spots in Mississippi's major media markets, focusing on the death penalty and criminal justice themes, in support of a candidate whose financial support came almost entirely from business interests.[29]

The tone of interest group ads was more moderate in the 2002 campaigns than in those of 2000. In 2000, approximately 80 percent of ads run by interest groups attacked a disfavored candidate.[30] Perhaps chastened by the chamber's Ohio experience in 2000, interest group advertisers in 2002 ran twice as many spots promoting a candidate as they ran attacking a candidate.[31]

Interest group advertising on television appeared to carry some influence in 2002, but it was not decisive for electoral outcomes. Of the six states seeing interest group ads, four saw ads from only one side; in three of those states, the candidate with interest group support on the air was the winning candidate. In Mississippi, the LEAA outspent its interest group opposition $174,799 to $25,153, a rate of almost 7 to 1. Business interests in Ohio were slightly outspent by trial lawyers and labor, $767,560 to $880,137.

Like expenditures on television airtime, interest group contributions directly to candidates also remained high in 2002. In the 2001–2002 cycle, business interests accounted for almost 30 percent of donations to supreme court candidates.[32] In Alabama, business associations contributed $680,000 of almost $1.6 million to the winning candidate.[33] The top interest group contributor was the Progress PAC, a political action committee affiliated with the Business Council of Alabama, which gave $284,000 to a single candidate.[34] The two winners in Ohio were the top two fundraisers nationwide; their respective warchests of almost $1.9 million and $1.8 million each included more than $500,000 from the health and insurance industries.[35] The losing candidates in Ohio received even larger sums—more than $800,000 each—from lawyers and lobbyists,[36] although trial lawyer associations spread only $75,400 across six states.[37] Labor contributed less than a tenth of the sum contributed by business—about $650,000 to $8.4 million.[38]

The supreme court campaigns of 2004 suggested that the rising tide of interest group contributions to supreme court candidates and independent expenditures on television advertising was likely to be a persistent feature of campaigns for the bench. Business contributions to candidates rose from approximately $8.4 million to nearly $15.8 million.[39] Labor contributions, while still comparatively low, rose 36 percent to just over $884,000.[40] Collectively, contributions from business, labor, and lawyers, including both the plaintiffs' and the defense bar, accounted for more than 60 percent of all funds donated to supreme court candidates.[41]

Television advertising appeared in fifteen states, almost quadrupling the number of states seeing ads in 2000. Interest groups bought airtime in six of the states, spending more than $1 million in Illinois, Michigan, Ohio, and West Virginia. The nearly $7.4 million spent in 2004 represented about 2.6 times the amount spent only four years earlier.[42]

Battle over Tort Liability

What is driving the intensifying interest group involvement in judicial elections over the past three cycles? The principal motivating force is the battle over what is sometimes known as "tort reform." "Tort" is a legal term meaning a civil (rather than a criminal) wrong, other than a breach of contract, for which the law provides a remedy, usually money damages. Medical malpractice is a type of tort, as is an injury caused by a defective product. Large tort awards against doctors, businesses, and insurance companies prompted them to press for limits on judgments and for other legal changes calculated to reduce their financial exposure. Because the plaintiffs in tort cases are usually individuals of limited means, plaintiffs' attorneys (who get a cut of the large verdicts when their clients win cases) appear as the principal opposition to "tort reform." The battle spread from state legislatures to state courts, as defense interests began campaigns to replace judges perceived to be too sympathetic to plaintiffs in tort cases. With plaintiffs' counsel and unions, which have their own concerns about business-friendly judges, arrayed on the other side, the stage is set for nasty and costly judicial elections.

The judicial elections in Texas, earlier identified as the first to see major interest group involvement, were driven by this dynamic. One scholar describes the situation as follows:

> In 1988, unhappy with the pro-plaintiff tinge of the Texas Supreme Court, business interests and professional groups decided to take a major role in Texas Supreme Court races. The 1988 Supreme Court elections saw two-thirds of the Court up for grabs and a chance in one election to set the tone of tort law at least until 1990 and possibly for years to come. As one might expect, a plaintiff-defense conflict emerged in the Supreme Court races. The 1988 elections were the most expensive in Texas history.[43]

The battles continued over several election cycles through the mid-1990s, when "the victory over the plaintiffs was complete."[44] The new judges completely changed tort law in Texas, so that it became far more favorable to defendants.

Businesses and professionals operating in other states borrowed a page from the Texas playbook. The states that attracted interest group spending on television advertising in subsequent years were invariably states with heavy legislative and judicial activity on tort issues. In the 2000 elections for the Ohio Supreme Court, interest groups spent more on television advertising than did the candidates and the political parties combined. The U.S. Chamber of Commerce and Citizens for a Strong Ohio spent nearly $1.8 million in an effort to capture two seats on the high court, one of them held by Justice Alice Resnick, who wrote a 1999 Ohio Supreme Court majority decision striking down caps on punitive damages as a violation of the right to trial by jury.[45] After she survived their attack in 2000, business interests focused on other seats in 2002 and 2004, until they could claim a majority of the court. Simultaneously, they moved through the legislature a series of bills directly at odds with prior 4–3 decisions of the Ohio Supreme Court and specifically asked the court to reconsider its earlier decisions protecting business from liability under the state constitution.[46] As one observer commented: "The fate of Ohio tort law and of the underlying stare decisis hangs in the balance."[47]

In Ohio, as in other states, the tort wars have pitted the plaintiffs' bar and labor organizations, aligned with Democratic candidates, against the defense bar and business, aligned with Republicans, although other factors sometimes intruded into the campaigns. In Alabama's 2004 elections, for example, the controversy over Chief Justice Roy Moore's refusal to remove a statue of the Ten Commandments from the courthouse complicated the elections. In the Republican primary, a candidate loyal to Justice Moore challenged and beat a business-backed sitting justice who had voted to remove the monument. Because the winner had accepted contributions from plaintiffs' attorneys in the primary, business groups refused to endorse him in the general election. (He won anyway.) Religious ideology thus added color to the elections, but it didn't change the fundamental dynamic. In 2004, *all* of the group spending on television advertising in Alabama came from pro-business groups intent on protecting sitting Republican justices perceived to be business-friendly. Nationwide, *all* of the interest group spending on television advertising in 2004 came from either plaintiffs' interests in favor of Democrats or defense interests in favor of Republican candidates. The latter outspent the former $5.7 million to $1.7 million, or more than three to one.[48]

In some cases, what is at stake in the air wars is clear from the content of the advertising. Citizens for a Strong Ohio recommends a candidate who believes in "protecting our jobs from frivolous lawsuits,"[49] while the West Virginia Consumers for Justice argues that "powerful, out-of-state, corporate interests" want a justice who "will rule for them against the working people of West Virginia."[50] Interest groups on both sides also take aim directly at each other. The Alabama Civil Justice Reform League complains of "trial lawyer money" going to candidates it opposes.[51] The (Illinois) Justice for All PAC attacks a candidate who allegedly received "piles of money . . . from big corporations" including "big tobacco" and "the asbestos industry."[52]

Although the tort wars drive the money in judicial elections, the battle over tort reform is not necessarily the issue that resonates most with the public. As a result, what the public sees in television advertising and what is really motivating the advertising sponsors are often two very different things. The example from Alabama is just one case in point: the business group defending the sitting justice advertised that she was a Sunday school teacher with "conservative values" but made no mention of her judicial decisions on business issues.

Interest groups also use judicial candidates' rulings in criminal cases as a focus of advertising, to mobilize voters who may not know or care much about tort liability but appear to want judges who are tough on crime. In

Illinois—a major front in the 2004 tort wars—groups on both sides used criminal justice themes to attack the opposition. In one ad, JUSTPAC, which received $1.4 million from business interests, accused Democrat Gordon Maag of voting "to overturn the jury conviction of a man who sexually assaulted a six-year-old girl." In return, the Justice for All PAC, which received nearly $1.3 directly and indirectly from plaintiffs' lawyers,[53] advertised that the Republican Lloyd Karmeier "gave probation to kidnappers who tortured a grandmother." In West Virginia, a group named And for the Sake of the Kids ran an ad asserting that the Democratic candidate voted to release a child rapist from prison and then let him work as a school janitor. And for the Sake of the Kids received $2.7 million from mining interests and more than $700,000 from an organization called Doctors for Justice.[54]

Ground Wars

The battle over tort liability is largely responsible for the surge of money seen in judicial elections. But interest group involvement is not limited to big business and trial lawyers with large sums to invest in judicial campaigns. Grassroots groups are also active on the ground, often promoting ideological agendas rather than economic interests. These groups also see the judiciary as an agency for advancing particular policy goals.

Grassroots involvement can be especially effective in retention elections, which so far have not figured as a high priority in the tort wars and thus have not attracted expensive television advertising campaigns. As Matthew Streb notes in chapter 1, the Pennsylvania state legislators' decision to grant themselves and state judges a pay raise in 2005 spawned a wave of grassroots activism aimed at unseating all incumbents. The judges became the object of backlash principally because the legislators were not up for reelection that year.[55] One of the justices retained her seat; the other became the first appellate judge in Pennsylvania's history to lose a retention election. The upset underscores the vulnerability of retention candidates to coordinated attacks even by groups with very modest budgets—the activists in Pennsylvania evidently relied on nothing more than the Internet, free media, and rallies.

In 2004, Missouri saw "an under-the-radar campaign to oust Judge Richard B. Teitelman from the Missouri Supreme Court."[56] Groups behind the effort, including the Missouri Family Network, Missourians against

Liberal Judges, and the Missouri branch of the National Rifle Association, portrayed the judge—the first Jewish and the first legally blind judge appointed to the high court—as out of touch with mainstream Missouri. The organizations used recorded telephone messages from Phyllis Schlafly, web postings, direct mail, and voter guides to mobilize the "no" vote. But the Missouri Bar Association and lawyers from both political parties stepped in to defend what they perceived as an attack on the state's non-partisan court plan. Without endorsing either the retention or the removal of Judge Teitleman, the bar used radio advertisements, free media, and mailings to educate the public about the selection system, the role of the judiciary, and the importance of judicial independence. After leading papers in the state echoed the message, and endorsed the judge, he retained his seat.

The voter guides developed by ideological interest groups in Missouri have appeared in both retention elections and contested elections. Often they are preceded by a group's questionnaire, which is distributed to all candidates for the bench in an effort to ascertain the candidate's views on hot-button issues. Questionnaires have been distributed by groups as diverse as the Christian Coalition of Alabama, Austin Lesbian/Gay Political Caucus, and Peaceable Texans on issues such as abortion, gay rights, and gun control. After the Supreme Court's 2002 decision in *Republican Party of Minnesota v. White*,[57] permitting judicial candidates to announce their views on issues that may come before them if elected to the bench, interest groups may find candidates more willing to provide answers to these questionnaires.

The Internet is also a new frontier for low-budget interest group participation in judicial elections. Websites can be created at little cost, while reaching large numbers of potential voters. They can be very effective in building power in otherwise low-salience elections. The Internet was a major weapon in the efforts to oust judges in Missouri and Pennsylvania.

Interest Groups as Educators?

Unquestionably, websites, questionnaires, voter guides, telephone recordings, and other messages from interest groups—including high-profile television ads—provide information to the public about the candidates among whom they must choose for their highest court. Some commentators have argued that interest groups have an especially important role in judicial elections, because the candidates have been constrained, until recently, not to announce their positions on issues that may come before them after they are elected to the bench. Even now that they can make such announcements, some candidates still decline to do so, believing that such behavior is inappropriate for people who are trusted to serve as impartial arbiters of controversial disputes. But if the candidates will not tell you where they stand on the burning legal issues of the day, who else can do it if not interest groups?

Assuming that most interest group ads and other communications are not seriously misleading, voters can learn from them about the predilections of the individuals seeking judicial office—at least as the interest groups understand them. Even when candidates do speak out on the issues, interest groups may speak to different concerns or reach different audiences. Television viewers and recipients of other campaign messages can also learn something about the candidates by observing which interest groups are investing in their election. Major expenditures by the Chamber of Commerce speak volumes about how the chamber expects the candidate to rule if elected to the bench. The same is true about spending by trial lawyers. Because judges, especially judges on state high courts, have considerable power to make law for the state, voters welcome information that helps them decide among the candidates.

Unfortunately, special interests eager to affect the outcome of campaigns for the bench are not always as eager to make their role transparent to the public. In many cases, front groups with inspirational but completely opaque names—Citizens for Independent Courts, Citizens for Truth in Government, And for the Sake of the Kids—are formed to purchase advertising in judicial elections. In other cases, the general perspective of an advertising sponsor can be gleaned from the sponsor's name—it is reasonably apparent that the West Virginia Chamber of Commerce and the West Virginia Consumers for Justice reflect opposing points of view—but the sponsor's name still obscures specifically who is funneling money through these groups.

After the 2000 elections, lawsuits filed in Mississippi and Ohio addressed the question whether major interest group advertisers could be compelled to disclose which of their members had financed their judicial campaign advertising. In both states, campaign finance laws required disclosure of contributors to groups that ran electioneering ads. In neither state did the advertisers file the required reports.

In defense of its failure to file the Mississippi reports, the U.S. Chamber of Commerce claimed that it was not engaged in electioneering. Its ads were carefully crafted not to advocate expressly for the election or defeat of any candidate; they avoided "magic words" such as "vote for Smith" or "defeat Jones," which triggered regulation under federal law. Instead, they warmly praised candidates that the chamber favored and sharply criticized candidates that the chamber opposed. According to the chamber, such ads run in the period shortly before an election counted as a form of public education that could not be regulated under campaign finance law.

The Chamber of Commerce won the case in Mississippi. Although sympathetic to the state's argument that the ads were plainly designed to affect judicial elections, the federal court of appeals deciding the case interpreted the First Amendment to preclude compelled disclosure.[58] The court relied on a U.S. Supreme Court decision (*Buckley v. Valeo*[59]) that had been repeatedly interpreted to require the use of "magic words" before an ad could be considered to express advocacy subject to regulation. According to the federal court in Mississippi, the Constitution trumped the state's disclosure laws and protected the U.S. chamber's right to conceal its donors.

But the Ohio Chamber of Commerce, which backed Citizens for a Strong Ohio (the sponsor of the notorious Lady Justice ad), fared differently. The Ohio Election Commission determined that, under Ohio law, "magic words" were not necessary to trigger state campaign finance provisions. The commission subpoenaed the Ohio chamber's financial records, and for every day that the chamber failed to comply with the subpoenas, it faced a fine of $25,000. On January 28, 2005, the Ohio Chamber of Commerce disclosed a list of 383 donors who gave $4.2 million to Citizens for a Strong Ohio.

The different outcomes in these two cases were in part the result of a change in governing First Amendment law. The Mississippi case was decided in 2002, whereas the Ohio case was decided in 2005. In December 2003, the U.S. Supreme Court ruled in *McConnell v. FEC*[60] that "magic words" were not in fact necessary before electioneering could be subject to campaign finance regulation. *McConnell* opened the door to state regulation of judicial campaign finance and, in particular, to disclosure of donors to interest groups that sponsor advertising.

Even after *McConnell*, however, efforts to obtain full disclosure of interest group finances have not come easily. In the 2004 elections in Illinois, monied interests on both sides of the most expensive supreme court race in history concealed the identities of donors by funneling their contributions through two layers of groups. As a result, the Justice for All PAC disclosed that it received contributions from the Justice for All Foundation, and the Illinois Coalition for Jobs, Growth and Prosperity PAC disclosed that it received contributions from its affiliated coalition, but donors to the foundation and the coalition remained obscured from public view. After complaints were filed with the Illinois State Board of Elections, the foundation agreed to disclose its donors, but as of early 2006 the coalition is still fighting to keeps its donors secret.

Responses to Interest Group Involvement

Not everyone is worried about the increasing involvement of interest groups in judicial campaigns or the resulting politicization of the judiciary. When asked about the influence of her telephone recordings on Missouri's nonpartisan election system, Phyllis Schlafly responded: "There's nothing the matter with it [the judicial system] being political."[61] But those who believe that something is the matter have proposed a number of measures to reduce the influence of money and partisan politics or at least to make sure that it is transparent to the public.

Campaign Finance Rules

The least intrusive campaign finance rules applicable to interest groups are disclosure rules ensuring that funds contributed to candidates and spent independently on advertising in judicial elections are fully reported and that the reports are easily reviewable by the public. In 2003, the U.S. Supreme Court upheld a law that requires such reporting when a broadcast or cable ad referring to a clearly identified federal candidate is aired close to election day in the jurisdiction where the candidate is running for office. Similar statutes have been enacted in several states, including some that also regulate such "electioneering communications" in media other than television and radio. The reports do not reduce the sums contributed or spent, but they provide information to the public that may help them evaluate the advertising and the extent to which it should affect their electoral decisions.

Under federal law, corporations and unions may not use their treasury funds to air electioneering communications. Instead, the ads must be financed by separate entities (the effective equivalent of political action committees, or PACs) that raise funds from corporate or union officers, employees, or members. Contributions to the PACs are limited in amount, so that large sums are not funneled from wealthy individuals through PACs to candidates. Such regulations could also be enacted by state legislatures to limit the influence of corporate and union interests on judicial campaigns.

Limits may also be placed on the amounts that interest groups are permitted to give to any one candidate for the bench. With lower amounts going directly into judicial campaign coffers, the potential for corruption is reduced. Caps on contributions may also address the perception that judges serve special interests instead of the public interest. Most states already have contribution limits; some states regularly marked by high levels of fundraising—including Alabama and Illinois—have no ceiling on contributions to judicial candidates. Texas has special rules limiting what lawyers and law firms can give to candidates. Unless such rules are matched by a limit on corporate giving, they will tilt campaigns toward candidates favored by business interests, because plaintiffs can rarely make contributions, but corporate defendants can.

Even if low contribution limits constrain how much may be given to candidates, interest groups will be free to make unlimited independent expenditures in judicial campaigns. The U.S. Supreme Court has consistently ruled that any limit on what may be spent in a campaign, independently of a candidate, is unconstitutional. Under current law, there is no way to regulate interest group spending in judicial elections.

Even without limiting interest group spending, there are ways to address interest group influence in judicial elections. Under certain public financing systems, candidates who participate in the program and face large independent expenditures attacking them or supporting their opponents receive matching funds that enable them to respond. The matching funds do not reduce the role of money—indeed, they enhance it—but they ensure that interest groups cannot monopolize the political marketplace or, in the words of one commentator, "swamp" the electorate with its own message.[62] Public matching funds ensure that candidates for the bench are not grossly outspent by interest groups, while protecting candidates from the potentially corrupting influence of money contributed by litigants and lawyers.

Official and Unofficial Voter Guides

Another way to mitigate the power of economic or ideological interest groups is to provide alternative sources of information to the public. Free voter guides providing information about the background and qualifications of judicial candidates can educate voters about the individuals running for office. North Carolina produced voter guides for its 2004 elections, when it first switched to nonpartisan judicial elections. When such guides were made available at polling sites, rolloff dropped, and voters expressed higher levels of satisfaction with the information available to them about the candidates.[63]

Some commentators have expressed doubt about whether voters actually use the guides. To make them more compelling, the guides may be produced on multimedia compact discs. Such a format gives the voters an opportunity to hear directly from the candidates, either individually or in the form of a debate. In one experiment during the 2000 presidential election, more than half of the recipients of a compact disc used it, and those who did were significantly more likely to vote.[64]

Printed voter guides and compact discs are expensive to disseminate to the entire voting public, but less-expensive versions may be made available on the Internet. In 2004, fifteen states published online voter guides with information about judicial candidates. Where official guides are unavailable, nonpartisan organizations, including bar associations, may produce unofficial guides. The guides may include additional educational information about the courts, how judicial decisions are made, and the role of judges in a system of divided government, which may help voters evaluate mass advertising or campaign materials they receive from interest groups.

Other Forms of Public Education

Concerns about misleading advertising, whether sponsored by interest groups or by the candidates, have prompted some communities to create committees to serve as watchdogs during elections. These committees monitor advertising and other campaign communications to ensure that the information provided in them is accurate and fair.[65] When an ad contains false or misleading information and when it impugns the integrity of the court or a candidate, the committees alert the news media and undertake other efforts to set the record straight. Knowing that advertising will be scrutinized and subject to public criticism may help keep advertisers honest and encourage them to temper the negative tone of their ads.

Obviously, the committees will be effective only if they are perceived to be independent and balanced. There should be representation of a spectrum of partisan affiliations, participation by lawyers and non-lawyers, and involvement by respected nonpartisan civic groups. The committees must scrupulously avoid endorsements of any candidate and apply consistent standards to all of the ads.

The most effective committees will actively educate the media about the monitoring project even before advertisements begin to run. In Ohio, for example, the committee meets with editorial writers of major newspapers and representatives of the electronic media once or twice during the year. The media then becomes a partner in the effort to ensure that judicial campaign advertisements do not misinform the public about a candidate or the court.[66]

Eliminating Judicial Elections

One measure that is often proposed as an answer to unwanted interest group involvement in judicial elections is the replacement of elective judiciaries with appointed judges. Eliminating elections will certainly end certain forms of interest group influence. Without judicial candidates, there will be no campaign contributions to candidates. Judges will also be freed of the threat that a "wrong" decision will galvanize interest group opposition at the next election.

But appointive systems are not free from interest group influence. Interest groups were actively involved, for example, in the recent confirmation process for nominees to the U.S. Supreme Court. One conservative interest group, Progress for America, spent $85,000 on ads even before the first nomination—indeed, even before Justice Sandra Day O'Connor announced her retirement—anticipating attacks by "liberals."[67]

All three nominees attracted substantial interest group investment. Approximately $3.7 million was spent to influence the confirmation of Judges John Roberts and Samuel Alito. Conservatives spent approximately $400,000 more than progressives on the Roberts nomination (about $850,000 to $450,000), and progressives spent approximately $330,000 more than conservatives on the Alito nomination (about $1.37 million to $1.04 million).[68]

But the aborted nomination of Harriet Miers is the more telling story of interest group participation in the U.S. Supreme Court appointment process. Her nomination produced a storm of conservative protest. Only conservative groups ran television advertising (about $325,000 of airtime[69]), which was initially supportive of the president's choice but became increasingly critical. A new web clearinghouse for her opposition appeared, WithdrawMiers.org, founded by the Center for a Just Society ("Where Faith, Law and Policy Meet"), Concerned Women for America, ConservativeHQ, Fidelis ("Defending Life, Faith and Family"), and Phyllis Schlafly.[70] The pressure was severe enough to force President George Bush to accept her withdrawal. Clearly, eliminating elections does not guarantee an end to interest group involvement in the selection of judges.

Conclusion

Elective judiciaries have been with us for a long time and are likely to be with us for a long time to come. Often elections are enshrined in state constitutions, and voters have proven reluctant to relinquish their right to select the judges that make law in their state. Even critics of judicial elections must confront this unassailable fact.

As long as judges must stand for election, whether in contested elections or retention elections, interest groups will be involved in the process. In the past, they have operated largely below the radar, and their influence has been tempered by canons of judicial ethics. Now, with increasingly professional and expensive campaigns, and decreasingly effective codes of conduct, interest group participation is more visible and very likely more influential. The growing role of interest groups is evident in both expensive mass media campaigns and grassroots organizing efforts. Over the last three election cycles, more groups began to air television advertising, earlier during the election cycle, and in more and more states; expenditures more than doubled in only four years. In addition, the Internet is making it possible even for organizations with very modest budgets to have a major impact. A highly energized minority of voters can make all the difference in otherwise low-salience elections, especially retention elections. The electoral successes and defeats for which these groups claim credit will only increase their momentum.

Both benefits and costs come with interest group involvement in judicial elections. Interest groups provide resources to candidates who otherwise might find it difficult to communicate with voters. The groups provide information about candidates that the public cannot otherwise easily find. Interest groups help mobilize voters and improve turnout in elections for the bench. Alternatively, the increasing power of interest groups brings the increasing risk that judges will tailor their decisions to the sources of their financial and electoral support. To the extent that interest group involvement carries threats to the integrity, impartiality, and independence of the judiciary, a variety of responses are available. Legislatures may enact new campaign finance laws that will make participation transparent and ensure that candidates' messages are not swamped by those of interest groups. In addition, both the government and ordinary citizens may initiate public education efforts to provide alternative sources of information and balanced critiques of interest group communications. Ultimately, voters will have to weigh the advantages and disadvantages of elective judiciaries and decide whether to temper the power that interest groups wield in judicial elections.

NOTES

1. In 1988, the CBS newsmagazine *60 Minutes* entitled a segment on judicial politics in Texas, "Is Justice for Sale?" *Frontline*'s 1999 version of "Justice for Sale" was an hour-long "investigation into how campaign cash is corrupting America's courts," featuring commentary by two sitting U.S. Supreme Court Justices. Frontline, *Justice for Sale,* available at http://www.pbs.org/wgbh/pages/frontline/shows/justice/ (accessed July 10, 2006). The Illinois Lawsuit Abuse Watch and the Illinois Civil Justice League used the same title for two recent studies of trial lawyer contributions in Illinois: *Justice for Sale: The Judges of Madison County* (2002) and *Justice for Sale II: Half-Million from Five Trial Lawyers Flood Campaign Coffers* (2004). Adding a question mark, *Justice for Sale?* was the title of an American RadioWorks program in January 2005. Law review articles also ask the question—for example, Baker, "Is Justice for Sale in Ohio?" This list is not close to exhaustive.

2. As used in this chapter, an "interest group" refers to any association or organization that is neither a candidate committee nor a political party—including a political action committee, labor union, law firm, trade association, or business entity.

3. The history of judicial elections is discussed in detail in chapter 1 in this volume. Recently, a federal district court overturned New York's unique judicial selection system, whereby judges are nominated in conventions controlled by political party leaders. *Lopez-Torres v. New York State Bd. of Elections,* F. Supp. 2d, 2006 WL 213955 (E.D.N.Y. Jan. 27), *appeal filed* (2d Cir. Feb. 8, 2006). The record in that case, documenting exchanges of judgeships for promises of patronage (p. 17), set the stage for a preliminary injunction establishing primary elections. (In the interest of full disclosure, I am employed by the Brennan Center for Justice, lead counsel in *Lopez-Torres.*)

4. Today, all three sorts of elections may be found in states across the country —sometimes all three in a single state, where the different systems are used for

different levels of courts; in different parts of a state; or at different times during the course of a judge's tenure on the bench.

5. Schotland, "To the Endangered Species List."

6. Iyengar, "Effects of Media-Based Campaigns."

7. Ibid., p. 692 n.9.

8. Ibid., p. 694.

9. Reid, "Politicization of Judicial Retention Elections," p. 70.

10. Uelmen, "Crocodiles in the Bathtub," p. 1133.

11. Tabarrok and Helland, "Court Politics."

12. Brooks and Raphael, "Life Terms or Death Sentences," p. 609.

13. Champagne, "Access to Justice."

14. Goldberg et al., *New Politics of Judicial Elections . . . 2000.*

15. For simplicity, in this chapter I refer to state high courts as "supreme courts." Most states do call their high courts "supreme courts," but some use other designations. In Maryland and New York, for example, the high court is called the "court of appeals." Studies of fundraising and spending in supreme court elections in 2000, 2002, and 2004 include the following: Goldberg et al., *New Politics of Judicial Elections . . . 2000*; Goldberg and Sanchez, *New Politics of Judicial Elections 2002*; Goldberg et al., *New Politics of Judicial Elections 2004*; Weiss, "Fringe Tactics."

16. Goldberg et al., *New Politics of Judicial Elections 2004*; Goldberg and Sanchez, *New Politics of Judicial Elections 2002.*

17. Goldberg et al., *New Politics of Judicial Elections . . . 2000*, pp. 4, 7.

18. Ibid., p. 8.

19. Ibid., p. 11. Michigan and Ohio have nominally nonpartisan elections— party affiliations do not appear on the general election ballot—but judicial candidates are identified by party during the electoral process, and they are nominated by parties in Michigan. For this reason, the "New Politics" studies treat elections in Michigan and Ohio as partisan elections.

20. Ibid., p. 12.

21. Goldberg and Sanchez, *New Politics of Judicial Elections 2002*, p. 21 n.23.

22. Goldberg et al., *New Politics of Judicial Elections . . . 2000*, pp. 4, 9. Some of the lawyers also represent business interests.

23. Ibid., p. 14. Estimated costs of advertising were provided by the Campaign Media Analysis Group (CMAG), now known as TNS Media Intelligence/CMAG. In 2000, CMAG tracked advertising in the 75 largest media markets. Its data reflected only the estimated costs of airtime, based on rate sheets provided by television stations. Cost estimates were not adjusted for proximity to the election and did not include costs for design or production of the ads. In 2002 and 2004, CMAG expanded its tracking to the top 100 media markets and refined its methods of estimating airtime costs. Still, the total cost estimates provided by CMAG understate, sometimes substantially, the actual costs of advertising. Short of visit-

ing every television station after the election to review files documenting media buys, however, there is no more systematic or accurate source for airtime costs.

24. Ibid., pp. 13, 15.

25. Glaberson, "Spirited Campaign."

26. Goldberg and Sanchez, *New Politics of Judicial Elections 2002*, p. 8.

27. Ibid., p. 10.

28. Ibid.

29. Institute on Money in State Politics, "Mississippi 2002." Corporate contributions to the candidate supported by the LEAA figured prominently in one of his opponent's ads, which described the LEAA's favorite as "U.S. Chamber of Commerce and corporate America approved" and called on the voters of Mississippi to "send them all packing back to Washington, DC." (A real player file and a storyboard of the advertisement are on file with the author.) The voters were not persuaded, and the business-backed candidate won.

30. Goldberg and Sanchez, *New Politics of Judicial Elections 2002*, p. 17.

31. Ibid., p. 12.

32. Ibid., p. 18.

33. Institute on Money in State Politics, "Alabama 2002."

34. Goldberg and Sanchez, *New Politics of Judicial Elections 2002*, p. 17.

35. Institute on Money in State Politics, "Ohio 2002."

36. Ibid.

37. Goldberg and Sanchez, *New Politics of Judicial Elections 2002*, p. 17. Lawyers accounted for nearly 37 percent of contributions, but donations from plaintiffs' attorneys and defense counsel are aggregated in this figure.

38. Ibid.

39. Goldberg et al., *New Politics of Judicial Elections 2004*, p. 20.

40. Ibid.

41. Ibid.

42. Compare ibid., p. 6, with Goldberg et al., *New Politics of Judicial Elections . . . 2000*, pp. 14–15.

43. Champagne, "Access to Justice," p. 1483.

44. Ibid.

45. *State ex rel. Ohio Academy of Trial Lawyers v. Sheward*, 715 N.E.2d 1062 (Ohio 1999), p, 1091. For a description, see "Recent Cases."

46. James T. O'Reilly has written an interesting pair of articles documenting the connections between Ohio's tort jurisprudence and the composition of its supreme court: "Writing Checks or Righting Wrongs" and "Tort Reform and Term Limits."

47. O'Reilly, "Tort Reform and Term Limits," p. 549.

48. Goldberg et al., *New Politics of Judicial Elections 2004*, p. 8.

49. Citizens for a Strong Ohio, Brennan Center for Justice downloads.

50. West Virginia Consumers for Justice, Brennan Center for Justice downloads.

51. Alabama Civil Justice Reform League, Brennan Center for Justice downloads.

52. Justice for All PAC, Brennan Center for Justice downloads.

53. Weiss, "Fringe Tactics," p. 11.

54. Ibid., p. 18.

55. Dao, "In a Rare Battle."

56. Lhotka, "High Court Judge Faces Ouster."

57. *Republican Party of Minnesota v. White*, 536 U.S. 765 (2002).

58. *Chamber of Commerce v. Moore*, 288 F.3d 187 (5th Cir. 2002).

59. *Buckley v. Valeo*, 424 U.S. 1 (1976).

60. *McConnell v. FEC*, 540 U.S. 93 (2003).

61. Hoover, "Conservative Groups Take Aim."

62. Goldberger, "Power of Special Interest Groups."

63. Crosson, *Impact of the 2004 North Carolina Judicial Voter Guide.*

64. Iyengar, "Effects of Media-Based Campaigns," p. 698.

65. Judicial campaign monitoring committees may assume a much broader array of responsibilities. In some states, the committees conduct trainings for judicial candidates and help them comply with the ethical canons that govern their conduct. For general information about such committees, see Reed and Schotland, "Judicial Campaign Conduct Committees." Guidelines for creating such committees may be found in National Ad Hoc Advisory Committee on Judicial Campaign Conduct, *Effective Judicial Campaign Conduct Committees.* As applied to interest groups, the subject of this chapter, the committee's oversight of mass advertising is probably its most important function.

66. Symposium, "Judicial Professionalism in a New Era of Judicial Selection."

67. The television advertising data reported here are from Brennan Center for Justice, *Advice, Consent and Advertising.*

68. Ibid.

69. Ibid.

70. Ibid.

Chapter 6

Partisan Involvement in Partisan and Nonpartisan Trial Court Elections

Matthew J. Streb

The American public strongly supports having an electoral component to judicial selection, but they are also clear that parties should play no part in the process.[1] According to one survey, respondents were close to three times more likely to support nonpartisan judicial elections than partisan contests.[2] Moreover, even adamant defenders of political parties often hold a different view when it comes to judicial elections. A colleague of mine, who is a fervent opponent of nonpartisan elections for legislative and executive offices, once told me, "Well, of course *judicial elections* should be nonpartisan." And clearly the founding fathers were skeptical of political parties in general, much less any involvement in the election of judges (of which many were also skeptical).

Parties are not supposed to have a role in judicial elections because judges are expected to be above politics. When a judge puts on her robe and walks into a courtroom, she is not a Democrat or Republican; she is an impartial interpreter of the law. As a result, most judicial elections in this country are nonpartisan, meaning that a candidate's party affiliation is not listed on the ballot. In some cases, parties may be legally prohibited from performing duties such as donating money to judicial candidates or coordinating the candidate's campaign.

In theory, nonpartisan judicial elections are meant to be nonpartisan in spirit. But, scholars have asserted that parties are taking an increasing role in judicial elections, even nonpartisan ones.[3] In other words, nonpartisan judicial elections may be nonpartisan in name only. Most of the discussion regarding political party activity in judicial elections is based on mere assertions or anecdotes; scholars have conducted few systematic studies. In this chapter, using a survey of county party chairs from twenty-five states, I analyze the role that party organizations have taken in partisan and nonpartisan trial court elections. The findings indicate that while parties are more active participants in partisan elections than in nonpartisan elections, they still are quite active in nonpartisan contests. Those reformers who argue that nonpartisan judicial elections are needed to limit political party involvement are correct, but perhaps not as correct as they might think.

Party Activity in Judicial Elections

While much has been written about the differences between nonpartisan and partisan judicial elections, most of this work examines citizen voting and not the role of party organizations. In one of the seminal works on judicial elections, Philip Dubois uncovers evidence that people have a much more difficult time voting in nonpartisan judicial elections than in partisan ones.[4] In his study of Ohio's 1984 supreme court elections, Lawrence Baum finds that party identification is a strong correlate of vote choice.[5] In their experiment on retention elections, Peverill Squire and Eric Smith determine that, when given an indirect partisan cue, people use that information when evaluating whether a justice should be retained.[6] In her study on the myths of judicial reform, Melinda Gann Hall examines the results of 643 elections to state supreme courts from 1980 through 1995 and provides compelling evidence that nonpartisan elections and retention races are not insulated from partisan politics. According to Hall, "the simple fact of having a partisan challenger reduces the vote share of incumbents by about 22%, even though partisan labels do not appear on the ballot. Clearly, partisan considerations have not been eliminated from these races."[7] These are just a sampling of the studies that address this subject.

However, scholars have performed few systematic studies of the role of party organizations in judicial elections. At the end of his influential 1961 *American Political Science Review* article on the effect of political parties on a judge's decisions, Stuart Nagel writes that "even non-partisan elections preceded by non-partisan primaries may have partisan interests behind the formalities of the election and nomination procedure."[8] But Nagel merely speculates that this is the case; he provides no evidence that party organizations are active in judicial elections (in fairness to Nagel, this is not the crux of his paper).

More recently, Anthony Champagne has written some interesting law review articles on the topic (and a book on Texas judicial politics with Kyle Cheek that tangentially touches on the subject).[9] According to Champagne:

> Partisanship in judicial elections is nothing new. Political parties jockeying for power in the selection of state court judges is an ancient political rite. After all, the main goal of parties is to gain and hold offices and that includes judicial offices. However, there is a new level of partisanship in many judicial elections. It is not limited to partisan election systems, but can be found in nonpartisan systems and in retention elections as well.[10]

He later writes, "There *appears* to be a new level of partisanship in many judicial races" (my emphasis).[11] Champagne is rightly cautious in the second quote because, while he provides anecdotal evidence of party involvement, he does not give any systematic proof of partisan involvement (nor does he show that partisan involvement has increased). It is unclear exactly *how* involved parties are and under what conditions parties are active. One of the few examinations of party involvement actually indicates that parties are of secondary importance in judicial races. Examining the financing of Pennsylvania's Supreme Court candidates from 1979 to 1997, James Eisenstein notes that parties contributed only 3.1 percent of the contributions over $50 to candidates, far less money than attorneys and law firms.[12] This result may be somewhat surprising because Pennsylvania's Supreme Court elections are partisan.

No study, to my knowledge, has attempted to actually determine how involved party organizations are in judicial races by examining a wide range of roles that parties have in national and other statewide and local elections. Eisenstein's results are interesting, but they apply only to one state and one type of campaign activity. It is my goal in this chapter to get a clearer understanding of how committed county party organizations are in both partisan and nonpartisan elections. It is my expectation that parties should be more apparent in partisan races than in nonpartisan contests, but, like Champagne argues, given the "new politics of judicial elections" it is likely that parties will be quite involved in nonpartisan judicial elections as well.[13] Before I lay out the study, a brief discussion of the involvement of party organizations in other local elections is needed.

Revitalization of Local Party Organizations

Like their national and state counterparts, the strength of local party organizations have ebbed and flowed. As John H. Aldrich notes in his influential book on political parties, Martin Van Buren and Andrew Jackson built a national Democratic Party from a coalition of strong, autonomous local party organizations.[14] Clearly, however, the height of organization strength at the local level occurred during the late 1800s and early 1900s when political machines dominated such cities as New York, Boston, Chicago, and Kansas City (although political machines were not just an urban phenomenon). Under machine rule, the party boss controlled all aspects of the election process. The boss generally handpicked candidates, told the candidates the positions they would take on issues, made sure that the candidate would be supported on election day, and then ran the government. In fact, it was the party machine's manipulation of the democratic process that pushed Progressives to institute nonpartisan elections for many local offices, including judges.

Political reforms such as the Australian ballot, political primary, and the nonpartisan election; an increasingly educated American public; economic growth; and changes in national, state, and local laws regarding patronage all crippled the power of the party machine. That, along with weakened party affiliation of voters and the rise of candidate-centered elections,[15] made some begin to question the relevance of party organizations in general, much less those at the local level. As James Gibson and colleagues wrote in 1985:

> The last 20 years have not been kind to American political parties. Parties appear less able at performing their traditional functions than in the past: the ability to structure the vote is diminished as the partisan attachments of the electorate weaken; control over candidates' access to the party label is loosened as "democratization" opens primary processes to those with marginal party attachments; candidates eschew party election support and turn to political action committees and campaign consultants instead, thereby reducing the incentives to defer to the party; and the ability of parties to organize the government is waning.[16]

In other words, the party organization in the 1970s looked the exact opposite from that existing under the party machine of the early 1900s.

Or, at least that was the way it appeared. While party organizations certainly were not at the levels of strength that they enjoyed under machine rule, the research by Gibson and his colleagues set off a new wave of study that shows that local party organizations, while perhaps not bureaucratically organized, are active both in election and nonelection periods,[17] and that the strength of the party organization is increasing.[18] A later study by John Frendreis et al. finds that local parties are relevant electorally and are regularly involved in activities such as candidate recruitment and campaign planning with the party's candidates.[19]

Other analyses confirm these findings.[20] In their study of southern political party activists, John Clark and Charles Prysby write:

> Local party organizations help to recruit candidates for lower-level offices. They provide a base of possible volunteers for campaigns, especially local ones. They, along with local office holders, help to define the image that the party has at the local level. By their actions, grassroots activists can help to bring voters and activists into the party or they can drive them away.[21]

Overall, then, the literature on party organizations supports the view that they are an important part of campaigns. While a party-centered model cannot solely reflect what is happening in elections, neither can a candidate-centered model; as Frendreis and Alan Gitelson put it, local parties are the "spokes in a candidate-centered wheel."[22] None of these studies analyzes the role that county parties have in judicial elections; instead, they focus on congressional elections and other statewide and local offices. Because of the unique nature of judicial elections, one could argue plausibly that local parties take less of a role in these elections. However, because of the increasing importance of judicial elections, parties have a stake in getting like-minded candidates on the bench, even in nonpartisan elections. Simply because an election is nonpartisan does not mean that the parties do not care who wins the election; they benefit more from having "their nonpartisan candidate" on the bench than the other party's candidate. The results that follow indicate that, while the levels of involvement don't always reach that of other elections, parties perform many of the same activities. Furthermore, this involvement is not limited to partisan judicial elections.

The Study

During October–November 2005, I conducted an email survey of Democratic and Republican county party chairs in twenty-five states regarding their parties' involvement in trial court elections such as the superior court, circuit court, district court, or court of common pleas.[23] Each of these states selects its trial court judges by elections, either partisan or nonpartisan.[24] Some states, such as Indiana and Arizona, are not included in the sample because, as I note in chapter 1, counties in those states have different election formats.

I examine trial court elections as opposed to state supreme court or other appellate court elections for a few reasons. First, because only 100 Democratic and Republican state party chairs exist, and not all states elect their supreme court justices, the population is quite small. Including county chairs from the twenty-five states gave me more than 4,000 possible respondents.[25] Second, because trial court elections are not as prestigious as elections for the state supreme court, parties are less likely to be involved in them. In other words, the deck may be stacked against me. If I find partisan involvement at the local level, one can be relatively sure that parties are performing similar functions at the state level (and perhaps are even more involved than at the local level). The same cannot be said the other way around. Finally, most of the studies on judicial elections look at appellate-level elections. Because of data collection problems, few examine trial court elections.

There were 4,018 county chairs included potentially in the survey, but 164 of those seats were vacant at the time of the survey. One problem with conducting an email survey is that not everyone has an email account (especially in less-populated areas). Of the 3,854 party chairs, I obtained email addresses for 2,390. Of those chairs, 783 completed the survey, a response rate of 32.8 percent (20.3 percent of all chairs).[26] While survey researchers always hope to get higher response rates, one study finds that a response rate for mail surveys of roughly 25 percent produces accurate results.[27] Because of the fact that email addresses were significantly more accessible in more-populated counties than in less-populated counties (and the respondents reflected this fact), I weighted the data by county population.[28] Fortunately, Democrats were no more or less likely to fill out the survey than Republicans.

I modeled the survey after the Party Transformation Survey conducted in the late 1970s and a subsequent survey of party chairs sponsored by

Frendreis and Gitelson in the early 1990s, but respondents were queried specifically about their involvement in trial court elections.[29] Generally, I asked a series of questions about the wide variety of ways in which party committees may, or may not, be involved in judicial elections. From the recruitment of candidates to voter-mobilization efforts, county party chairs were asked to comment on the extent to which they engaged in each activity. Chairs were asked questions specifically regarding the recruitment of judicial candidates, money, campaign advertising, campaign strategy, the endorsement of candidates, and get-out-the-vote (GOTV) efforts.[30]

The Findings

There are some clear overall patterns in the results that relate to fundamental differences between partisan and nonpartisan elections. Not surprisingly, in every question examined, party organizations whose trial-court candidates ran in partisan elections were significantly more active than their counterparts whose candidates ran in nonpartisan races. Since partisan races are overtly partisan, this finding is not shocking (although the extent of the involvement in partisan contests might disturb some people). Perhaps the more interesting question is: How involved are party organizations in nonpartisan judicial campaigns? The answer appears to be that they are quite involved. While parties are not equally active in all aspects of nonpartisan judicial elections (and not necessarily active in every election cycle), they seem to be especially important in terms of GOTV efforts and increasing name recognition, candidate recruitment, candidate endorsements, coordinating campaigns with candidates, and even raising and contributing money. Furthermore, these results are relatively consistent with earlier studies that examined the role of county organizations in other local elections. Let us now look at specific activities.

Candidate Recruitment

County chairs regularly recruit candidates to run for elected offices. While certainly candidate recruitment is a major function performed by the parties' congressional campaign committees, it is often carried out on more local levels as well. In their study of county party chairs, Frendreis

TABLE 6.1

Percentage of County Organizations Involved in Recruitment of Judicial Candidates

	Partisan elections	Nonpartisan elections	All elections	N
Recruit candidates	68.32***	49.09	55.73	775

Note: Percentages are those who answered "very involved" or "somewhat involved."
  *** p < .001.

and his colleagues find that 94 percent of Republican county chairs and 87 percent of Democratic county chairs report being "very involved" or "somewhat involved" in the recruitment of candidates for county offices. They come across similar results for state legislative offices and less involvement for congressional and local offices. Roughly two-thirds of county party chairs said they were involved in the recruitment of congressional candidates; less than half (48 percent of Republicans and 42 percent of Democrats) said they were at least somewhat involved in candidate recruitment for city and local offices.[31] In a different study, Frendreis et al. find that counties with active party organizations are likely to have candidates running for lower-level offices.[32]

If parties are playing a part in judicial elections, we might expect, then, that they want to have input regarding who runs (even if a candidate's party affiliation doesn't appear on the ballot). The results of the survey indicate that county party involvement in candidate recruitment for judicial elections is similar to their involvement for city or other local offices. As Table 6.1 shows, roughly 56 percent of county chairs are at least "somewhat involved" in the recruitment of judicial candidates. Parties are more active recruiting candidates when the judicial election is partisan instead of nonpartisan, but still close to half of the chairs in counties with nonpartisan elections have a role in recruitment. In other words, nonpartisan elections are not keeping a significant number of party organizations from trying to get "their" candidates to run for judge.

The methods chairs use to recruit judicial candidates is not much different from the tactics they use for other offices. Many chairs report that they talk to local lawyers or members of the bar to get names of qualified candidates. Others create formal committees whose job is to search for possible candidates. Interestingly, because many county chairs are lawyers themselves and, therefore, have connections with the local legal community, they indicate having significant influence over which candidates run.

Campaign Contributions and Fundraising

Parties also raise money for candidates as well as donate to their campaigns. According to David Menefee-Libey, as elections became more candidate-centered, national parties switched from the "textbook party paradigm" in which a party controls most aspects of a candidate's campaign to the "accomodationist paradigm"—or, as Aldrich calls it, the "party in service"—where the party's role is to assist its candidates' campaigns.[33] The primary way in which the parties help the campaigns is by donating and raising money. National party fundraising led media consultant Raymond Strother to call parties "basically just banks—fundraising mechanisms."[34]

While the national party organizations are generally associated with fundraising and campaign donations, there is evidence that local parties are involved in these efforts as well. According to the Frendreis and Gitelson survey, roughly three-fourths of Democratic and Republican county parties arranged fundraising events or contributed to a state legislative candidate's campaign. In his study of southern party chairs, Robert Hogan uncovers results similar to those of Frendreis and Gitelson, although, in Hogan's study, chairs were more likely to say they contributed money and less likely to say they organized fundraisers.[35]

As Chris Bonneau and Deborah Goldberg indicate in chapters 4 and 5, respectively, money spent in a judicial election is extremely controversial. Judges are not supposed to be beholden to any donor, including political parties. According to my survey, that view hasn't stopped county parties from helping trial-court candidates raise money or kept parties from donating money to the candidates' campaigns. According to Table 6.2, more than half of the county chairs report arranging fundraising events for trial-court candidates at least "sometimes." Again, parties are significantly more involved in partisan judicial elections than in nonpartisan ones, but they are still very active in arranging fundraising events in nonpartisan trial court races as well (roughly 67 percent and 42 percent, respectively). Similar results are found regarding contributing money to a judicial candidate's campaign. Again, roughly half of all county party chairs say they sometimes give money to a judicial candidate (67 percent in partisan elections and 42 percent in nonpartisan elections). However, most of the donations are small. Only 7 percent of the respondents report that "on average" they give more than $1,000 to a trial-court candidate.

While the parties often arrange fundraising events, the chairs do not view their involvement as all that important. Only 22 percent say that their

TABLE 6.2
Percentage of County Organizations That Arrange Fundraising Events and Contribute Money

	Partisan elections	Nonpartisan elections	All elections	N
Arrange fundraising events	66.93***	41.75	50.66	603
Contribute money	66.73***	42.19	50.78	599

Note: Percentages are those who answered "always," "most of the time," or "sometimes."
*** p < .001.

party organization is "somewhat important" or "very important" to trial-court candidates and their campaign organizations regarding fundraising. Again, there are differences regarding whether the election was partisan. Roughly 25 percent of chairs whose counties hold partisan elections answer that their organization was at least somewhat important in candidate fundraising compared with roughly 20 percent of those chairs whose judicial elections are nonpartisan. Still, considering that many states don't allow parties to donate to candidates, these percentages are substantial.

Candidate Advertising

Political parties spend enormous sums of money on campaign commercials supporting their presidential, Senate, and House candidates, although, ironically, these ads often make no mention of the party.[36] However, it is not just these national offices on which parties decide to allocate large amounts of money. Frendreis and his colleagues find that 31 percent of Democratic and 24 percent of Republican local party organizations either bought television or radio time for the party or its state legislative candidates.[37] Even state supreme court elections have seen an increase in the amount of money spent on television ads by parties. In 2004, the Democratic and Republican Parties combined to spend almost $5 million on ads for their respective state supreme court candidates.[38]

Because of the immense cost of advertising on television (and, for that matter, on radio), it is unlikely that county party organizations—who have far less money than their state counterparts—will regularly run ads for their trial-court candidates on television or the radio. They may be more likely to promote the candidates in other less expensive ways, such as by handing out lawn signs or issuing press releases. The Frendreis and Gitelson study of county chairs found this to be the case. More than 50 percent of Democratic and Republican county chairs distributed mailings

TABLE 6.3
Percentage of County Organizations That Do Various Types of Advertising

	Partisan elections	Nonpartisan elections	All elections	N
Publicize candidate(s) by buying TV time	12.45*	7.56	9.20	639
Publicize candidate(s) by buying radio time	33.47***	13.86	20.49	649
Purchase billboard space	24.53***	14.21	17.70	635
Help candidates create webpage	27.38***	14.45	18.84	628
Distribute posters or lawn signs	85.29***	56.20	66.50	692
Sent mailings to voters	55.08***	31.99	40.08	678
Publicize candidate(s) through newspaper ads	58.47***	29.25	39.54	660
Publicize candidate(s) through press releases	58.53***	35.14	43.24	660

Note: Percentages are those who answered "always," "most of the time," or "sometimes."
  *** p < .001; * p < .05.

to voters, and more than 60 percent prepared press releases for the party or its candidates and bought newspaper ads. Roughly 90 percent of each party's county organizations distributed posters or lawn signs.[39]

County party organizations seem to be less involved in candidate advertising in trial court elections than they are for other local offices, but that doesn't mean that they are completely silent, either. Not surprisingly, few party chairs report buying television or radio ads, purchasing billboard space, or helping the candidate create a webpage. More than 90 percent respond that the county party "never" publicizes the candidate by buying TV time, and roughly 80 percent say the same about purchasing radio ads or billboards, or helping the candidate create a webpage (Table 6.3). However, slightly more chairs say that they purchased billboards at least "sometimes" in my survey than in the Frendreis/Gitelson survey (17.7 percent compared with less than 10 percent). Also, more chairs in my survey indicate that they help candidates with their webpages than in Hogan's study of southern party chairs (18.84 percent compared with roughly 10 percent).[40]

As I suspected, parties are more involved in other aspects of advertising. Close to 70 percent of all county organizations distribute posters or lawn signs at least sometimes, including approximately 85 percent of those parties whose candidates run in partisan elections; roughly 40 percent send out mailings to voters or purchase newspaper ads. As Table 6.3 shows, these forms of advertising are significantly more common in partisan than nonpartisan races. Press releases publicizing the parties' judicial candidates are released by almost 45 percent of the county parties; again, this is more common in partisan than nonpartisan races, although certainly not absent from the nonpartisan races.

Campaign Strategy

Parties regularly help candidates formulate their campaign strategy and measure the pulse of the nation, state, or district by conducting public opinion polls, although perhaps not to the extent that they once did. According to Paul Herrnson, state and local party organizations frequently assist congressional candidates by gauging public opinion.[41] Peter Francia and his colleagues find that, in campaigns for the state legislature, "parties often assist candidates with public opinion data by commissioning surveys" but "a very small percentage of state legislative candidates rely primarily on party organizations to manage their campaigns."[42] However, according to Frendreis et al., close to 60 percent of each party's county chairs said they were involved in the coordination of county-level campaigns.[43]

Once again, my survey has results similar to those of the Frendreis/Gitelson survey. Just over 60 percent of county chairs indicate that their party organization is at least sometimes involved in coordinating with trial-court candidate campaign organizations (Table 6.4). While close to 80 percent of those chairs whose judicial candidates run in partisan elections are active in the candidate's campaigns, roughly 50 percent of party organizations involved in nonpartisan elections say the same (and close to 16 percent say that they are "always involved."). What's more, 43 percent of county chairs think that their involvement in formulating a trial-court candidate's campaign strategy is at least "slightly important" (approximately 51 percent in partisan elections and 38 percent in nonpartisan elections).

Regarding polling, parties do not regularly help their judicial candidates. Only about 23 percent of party chairs indicate that they at least sometimes conduct public opinion polls, with similar results for those whose candidates run in partisan and nonpartisan elections. But the fact that more than one in five party organizations occasionally conduct polls

TABLE 6.4
Percentage of County Organizations that Coordinate with Campaigns and Conduct Public Opinion Polls

	Partisan elections	Nonpartisan elections	All elections	N
Coordinate with candidate campaign organization	78.64***	50.49	60.45	684
Conduct public opinion polls	25.64*	21.32	22.79	633

Note: Percentages are those who answered "always," "most of the time," or "sometimes."
*** p < .001, * p < .05.

for trial-court candidates is extraordinary, given the limited amount of information available in these races and the fact that judges are not supposed to be influenced by public opinion.

Candidate Endorsements

Obviously, political parties regularly endorse their candidates in the general election, although they are often reluctant to make endorsements during the primary. This is often the case even in elections that are officially nonpartisan. In California, for example, both the Democratic and Republican Parties in California consistently send mailers endorsing candidates in nonpartisan races.

This is one area where I cannot compare my survey results to the Frendreis/Gitelson survey. That survey asked county chairs whether they make "formal or informal preprimary endorsements"; they found that about 30 percent of the party chairs did so.[44] I ask simply whether the party organization endorses trial-court candidates. While many chairs wrote me to say that they do not endorse candidates in the primaries (most of this correspondence came from chairs in partisan jurisdictions), organizations are regularly making endorsements in the general election (although endorsements are not nearly as common as in, say, state legislative races in which I'd assume that close to 100 percent of county organizations make an endorsement).[45] Approximately 60 percent of county chairs report that their party organization at least sometimes endorses candidates. While about 71 percent of those chairs whose judicial candidates run in partisan elections are active in the candidate's campaigns, roughly 52 percent of party organizations involved in nonpartisan elections say the same (and close to 16 percent say that they "always" endorse judicial candidates) (Table 6.5).

Get-out-the-Vote Efforts

Finally, of all the aspects of partisan involvement examined here, one might expect political parties to be most involved in GOTV efforts. The party organization literature is filled with evidence that county party organizations regularly encourage people to go to the polls.[46] According to Francia et al, "Local party organizations . . . are the primary source of voter mobilization assistance,"[47] although the evidence is mixed regarding how effective parties are at actually mobilizing people to the polls.[48]

In their survey, Frendreis and Gitelson find that county organizations

TABLE 6.5
Percentage of County Organizations That Endorse Candidates

	Partisan elections	Nonpartisan elections	All elections	N
Endorse candidate(s)	71.33***	51.96	58.87	670

Note: Percentages are those who answered "always," "most of the time," or "sometimes."
*** p < .001.

TABLE 6.6
Percentage of County Organizations Engaging in Get-out-the-Vote (GOTV) Activities

	Partisan elections	Nonpartisan elections	All elections	N
Conduct GOTV efforts	82.43***	53.48	63.58	689
Organize campaign events	79.15***	48.02	58.91	673
Organize door-to-door canvassing	71.80***	47.07	55.59	670
Organize telephone campaigns	67.71***	42.49	51.22	670

Note: Percentages are those who answered "always," "most of the time," or "sometimes."
*** p < .001.

regularly engage in attempts to get out the vote. About 60 percent of Republicans and 70 percent of Democrats said they conducted GOTV efforts, while close to 80 percent of each party's chairs said they organized campaign events. Roughly 60 percent of the party organizations organized telephone campaigns, and slightly less participated in door-to-door canvassing.[49] All of these efforts are attempts to increase a candidate's name recognition and get supporters to the polls.

County party organizations appear equally active at doing these activities for trial-court candidates. Roughly 64 percent of chairs say they at least sometimes conduct GOTV efforts, and approximately 59 percent indicate they organize campaign events, such as rallies or forums. Another 56 percent organize door-to-door canvassing, while roughly 51 percent conduct telephone campaigns (Table 6.6).[50] Once again, organizations in partisan jurisdictions are more active in these types of events, but they are performed commonly by organizations whose candidates run in nonpartisan elections as well. Indeed, about 42 percent of the county organizations in nonpartisan elections still organized telephone campaigns, even though it is their least likely GOTV activity.

I also asked the chairs about their views on the importance of the county organization in terms of increasing a candidate's name recognition, organizing campaign events, providing volunteer workers, and getting voters to the polls on election day. In general, the chairs believed that their organizations have at least a "slightly important" role. Regarding providing volunteer workers for campaigns and organizing campaign events, approximately 58 percent and 51 percent of county chairs, respectively, said that the party organization is at least slightly important to trial-court candidates (again, significant differences exist based on whether the election was partisan or not). They are even more likely to believe that their efforts paid off. Roughly 65 percent say the party organization is at least slightly important in increasing the candidate's name recognition and getting voters to the polls on election day (with the regular statistical differences based on the type of election). Still, more than 55 percent of the chairs whose candidates ran in nonpartisan judicial races believe that they are at least slightly important in increasing a candidate's name recognition, while about 58 percent feel the same about getting voters to the polls. Again, these percentages indicate that parties may well be important even in nonpartisan judicial elections.

Conclusion

While most supporters of judicial elections believe that parties should take no role in them, these results indicate that just the opposite is true. Political parties are often involved in judicial elections in a variety of ways. Certainly this should not come as a complete surprise regarding partisan judicial elections, but these results may be disheartening to those who believe that nonpartisan elections severely limit party involvement. If you oppose partisan activity in judicial elections, nonpartisan elections serve your preference better than partisan elections. However, nonpartisan elections are not absent of party influence to the extent that you might prefer. Reformers may have to push for laws restricting partisan involvement in different ways, but, as Rick Hasen notes in chapter 2, these laws may no longer pass constitutional muster (and, in fact, some have already been struck down by federal and state courts).

How one views these findings likely depends on how one views judicial selection in general. Those who oppose judicial elections and instead back merit selection or some sort of other judicial selection plan likely will argue that these results provide evidence to support their view. Parties cannot be kept from being involved in judicial elections—whether the election is partisan or not. In their view, this is just another example of how judicial elections are becoming just like other elections (which, according to opponents of judicial elections, is not a good thing). Others may see the findings in a positive light, arguing that party involvement is needed in judicial elections because it gives voters a fighting chance to cast a somewhat informed vote, which will likely lead to greater voter turnout and more judicial accountability. Whatever a person's view, it is important that we learn more about the role that parties are taking in judicial elections. There is no evidence that parties are going to lessen their involvement, so supporters and opponents of judicial elections must engage in more empirical research to understand how parties affect judicial elections (for both the good and the bad).

These initial findings answer some of the questions regarding partisan activity in judicial elections, but much work remains to be done. I only examine differences in election type but do not look at whether one party is more active than the other or if there are some conditions that lead to greater partisan involvement. Does the closeness of the race matter? the quality of the candidates? the size of the county? whether the seat is for a trial court or an appellate court? Has partisan involvement increased in the past several years (as anecdotal evidence suggests that is has) or simply remained stagnant? Perhaps most important, how, if at all, does partisan involvement influence the election? I hope that scholars will continue to pursue these questions to provide more empirical evidence regarding the roles that parties have in the election of judges.

NOTES

1. I am deeply indebted to Barbara Burrell, Karen Schnite, and the Public Opinion Laboratory at Northern Illinois University for the implementation of the survey; Matt Barreto and Brian Schaffner for their suggestions on weighting the data; Jen Calanca for data input and research assistance; Barbara Burrell, Larry Baum, and Melinda Gann Hall for their comments on the construction of the survey; and John Frendreis for providing a copy of his survey of county party chairs in which he is the co-principal investigator with Alan Gitelson. Any errors are solely my own.

2. Justice at Stake Campaign, *Poll of American Voters.*

3. Nagel, "Political Party Affiliation and Judges' Decisions"; Champagne, "Political Parties and Judicial Elections"; Champagne, "Politics of Judicial Selection."

4. Dubois, *From Ballot to the Bench.*

5. Baum, "Explaining the Vote in Judicial Elections."

6. Squire and Smith, "Effect of Partisan Information on Voters."

7. Hall, "State Supreme Courts in American Democracy," p. 324.

8. Nagel, "Political Party Affiliation and Judges' Decisions," p. 850.

9. Cheek and Champagne, *Judicial Politics in Texas*.

10. Champagne, "Political Parties and Judicial Elections," p. 1421.

11. Ibid., p. 1426.

12. Eisenstein, "Financing Pennsylvania's Supreme Court Candidates."

13. Goldberg et al., *New Politics of Judicial Elections 2004*.

14. Aldrich, *Why Parties?* p. 124.

15. Wattenberg, *Rise of Candidate-Centered Politics*; Menefee-Libey, *Triumph of Campaign-Centered Politics*.

16. Gibson et al., "Whither the Local Parties?" p. 139.

17. Cotter et al., *Party Organizations in American Politics*.

18. Gibson et al., "Party Dynamics in the 1980s." For a competing view, see Lawson et al., "Local Party Activists and Electoral Linkage."

19. Frendreis et al., "Electoral Relevance of Local Party Organizations."

20. Herrnson, "Do Parties Make a Difference?"; Frendreis et al., "Local Political Parties and Legislative Races."

21. Clark and Prysby, "Studying Southern Political Party Activists," p. 6.

22. Frendreis and Gitelson, "Local Parties in the 1990s," p. 135

23. The states included in the survey are Alabama, Arkansas, California, Florida, Georgia, Idaho, Illinois, Kentucky, Michigan, Minnesota, Mississippi, Montana, Nevada, New York, North Carolina, North Dakota, Ohio, Oklahoma, Oregon, Pennsylvania, Tennessee, Texas, Washington, West Virginia, and Wisconsin. North Dakota has districts instead of counties, so, in this case, the district chairs were surveyed.

24. While Ohio technically holds nonpartisan judicial elections for courts of common pleas, it is included in this survey as holding partisan elections because candidates are nominated through partisan primaries.

25. However, a study that interviewed the state party chairs in more detail than can be obtained in a survey would certainly be a worthwhile project.

26. Because of the length of the survey, some people did not answer some parts of the survey.

27. Visser et al., "Mail Surveys for Election Forecasting?"

28. To create the weights, I divided the counties into five groups (low populated, medium-low populated, medium, medium-high populated, and high populated). Each group reflected 20 percent of the total counties. I then compared the percentage of sample counties that fell into these five groups. For example, only 10 percent of the sample came from low-populated counties and 30 percent of the sample came from high-populated counties (instead of the 20 percent one would want). Based on these percentages I created a weight for each county in the sample based on its population and used the "aweight" command in Stata 8.0. The weights reflect the true composition of what the sample should look like without the response bias.

Another possible concern is that because I aggregated the respondents from each state into one data set, it is possible that certain states will have a greater impact than others. For example, the states do not all have the same number of counties, and the probability that they would be included in the sample was not the same. For instance, email addresses were easier to obtain for the Democratic Party in Wisconsin than for the Republican Party in Minnesota. To address this concern, I used the ordered logit model with the partisan/nonpartisan variable as the main independent variable and controlled for each state (excluding one baseline state). Of the eighteen activities I examine in this chapter, the partisan/nonpartisan variable remained significant in all but two cases ("publicize candidate(s) by buying TV time" and "conduct public opinion polls"). In these two cases, the coefficient was still in the hypothesized direction. As a result, the difference in the number of respondents from each state does not appear to be a concern.

29. Cotter et al., *Party Organizations in American Politics*; Frendreis et al., "Local Political Parties and Legislative Races."

30. The actual question was "Please check how often your party organization engages in each of the following activities for trial-court candidates." The response alternatives were "always," "most of the time," "sometimes," "never, but it is legal according to state law," and "never, because it is illegal according to state law."

31. Frendreis et al., "Local Political Parties and Legislative Races."

32. Frendreis et al., "Electoral Relevance of Local Party Organizations."

33. Menefee-Libey, *Triumph of Campaign-Centered Politics*; Aldrich, *Why Parties?*

34. Quoted in Whitcover, *No Way to Pick a President,* p. 274.

35. Hogan, "Party Activists in Election Campaigns."

36. Franz and Goldstein, "Following the (Soft) Money."

37. Frendreis et al., "Local Political Parties and Legislative Races."

38. Goldberg et al., *New Politics of Judicial Elections 2004.*

39. Frendreis et al., "Local Political Parties and Legislative Races."

40. Ibid.; Hogan, "Party Activists in Election Campaigns." The differences between the results of my survey and the one used by Hogan may be because Hogan's survey was conducted in 2001. Since that time, candidate webpages have become more common, so parties may be taking a greater role in helping candidates create them.

41. Herrnson, "Do Parties Make a Difference?"

42. Francia et al., "Battle for the Legislature," pp. 179 and 177.

43. Frendreis et al., "Local Political Parties and Legislative Races."

44. Ibid.

45. Because Nebraska's state legislature is nonpartisan, I would guess that this percentage is likely less in that state.

46. For example, Herrnson, "Do Parties Make a Difference?"; Frendreis and Gitelson, "Local Parties in the 1990s"; Gibson et al., "Whither the Local Parties?"; Hogan, "Party Activists in Election Campaigns."

47. Francia et al., "Battle for the Legislature," pp. 181–182.

48. For evidence that party organizations are successful at mobilizing voters, see Wielhouwer and Lockerbie, "Party Contacting and Political Participation"; for an opposing view, see Hill and Leighley, "Party Ideology, Organization, and Competitiveness."

49. Frendreis et al., "Local Political Parties and Legislative Races."

50. I should note that the GOTV and canvassing efforts provided by the parties may not be solely for judicial candidates. When going door to door to solicit votes, for example, volunteers are likely to talk about several of the party's candidates for a variety of offices, not just for judge.

Chapter 7

Judicial Elections in the News

Brian F. Schaffner and Jennifer Segal Diascro

In chapter 6, Matthew Streb showed that political parties are taking active roles in judicial campaigns. However, it is not clear that their involvement has made people more informed about judicial candidates. In 2001, a national public opinion poll found that 29 percent of Americans who do not vote regularly or at all in state judicial elections give as their reason that they do not know enough about the candidates running for office.[1] Nearly three-quarters (73 percent) of respondents indicated that they had only some or a little information about candidates; 14 percent said they had no information at all about those in the race for positions on the state court bench.[2] These views buttress what scholars of the judiciary have suspected for some time: judicial elections tend to be low-information elections.[3] One often-repeated explanation for the low levels of information that citizens have about judicial elections is that the mass media do not report on these campaigns with any frequency or substance.[4] While there is good anecdotal evidence to support this contention, systematic examination of media coverage of judicial elections is scarce.[5]

In this chapter, we seek to strengthen our understanding of the informational character of judicial campaigns and elections and the part that the media play in providing information to voters in these contests. We begin by discussing briefly the ongoing debate about judicial elections and the lack of information citizens tend to possess in contests for seats on the bench. Next, we examine three aspects of coverage of these contests. First, we describe the nature of local newspaper reporting and how it influences the quantity of coverage devoted to state supreme court campaigns. Second, we analyze the quality of coverage by exploring the types of information that newspapers provide about judicial campaigns. Third, we attempt to explain variation in this coverage by accounting for differences in the types of newspapers covering these campaigns, as well as the context of the contests themselves. We conclude by summarizing our findings and considering their implications for reporting on and voting in judicial elections.

Judicial Elections: Information and Accountability

The debate about how to select justices is predominantly one involving the tradeoff between independence and accountability in the judiciary.[6] States that have instituted elections as their method of judicial selection presumably value a judiciary that is accountable to the public over one that is insulated from mass opinion. Justice Antonin Scalia argues as much for the U.S. Supreme Court in *Republican Party of Minnesota v. White*.[7] Scalia reasoned that judicial elections are not unlike legislative elections since state supreme court judges have the power to make policy from the bench. Thus, he suggests that judicial elections have the same purpose as legislative elections: to ensure the accountability of political officials (see chapter 2 for more on the *White* case). To fulfill this function, citizens must have meaningful information about candidates running for judge.

Yet, critics of judicial elections note that participation in these contests tends to be low. From 1980 to 1995, rolloff for the average state supreme court election was 27 percent.[8] In other words, more than one of every four citizens who had already bothered to show up at the polls did not cast a vote in the supreme court election. This low participation tends to be blamed on the lack of information most citizens have about judicial campaigns. For example, in 1986, Ohio voters were asked if there was enough information available about the campaign for governor, and 57.6 percent agreed that there was. When asked the same question about a race for the Ohio Supreme Court, only 38.8 percent said that there was enough information available about that race.[9] Likewise, a 1995 survey conducted in Washington found that two-thirds of voters said that they seldom had enough information to cast an informed vote in judicial elections.[10] Yet, if elections are to compel accountability by justices, then the ballots must be cast by an informed electorate.

Traditionally, the news media take a central role in providing the information citizens need to participate in the electoral process and hold public officials accountable[11] When voters need information about candidates for office or even about the courts, they turn to the news media as a primary source of that information.[12] Furthermore, citizens who are informed about judicial campaigns do participate in those contests and are able to do so intelligently.[13] Thus, if voters are lacking information about judicial elections, it may be because the news media fail to provide sufficient information on these contests.

Do the Media Cover State Supreme Court Elections?

Citizens are often criticized for having very little knowledge about politics,[14] but research demonstrates the power of the news media to increase political awareness.[15] People who pay more attention to the news have greater knowledge about politicians and political parties, even when controlling for other factors such as socioeconomic status.[16] In particular, newspapers are potent determinants of political knowledge. Both survey methodology,[17] and experimental methods[18] have confirmed that citizens who expose themselves to more newspaper coverage tend to have more political knowledge than those who pay attention to other mediums. In one notable study, a natural experiment revealed that citizens in Pittsburgh knew less about their House member in 1992 than those in Cleveland when the major Pittsburgh newspaper ceased publishing for eight months.[19] In another report, Michigan citizens exposed to more newspaper coverage about the 1984 Senate race were better able to recognize and rate the candidates.[20]

As these studies illustrate, newspapers have a critical role in providing citizens with the information they need to evaluate candidates for state and local offices.[21] This role may be particularly important for judicial contests where the candidates, and even the court itself, are less familiar to citizens. For example, a 1988 survey of Ohio citizens revealed that only 34.2 percent of respondents reported paying at least some attention to the Ohio Supreme Court. Most startling is that among these respondents who reported paying some attention to the court, fewer than 10 percent could correctly state the number of justices that sit on the court and fewer than 5 percent were able to correctly name the state's chief justice.[22] Thus, citizens appear to know little about state courts and are likely to need a great deal of information during judicial campaigns so that they can make informed choices on election day.

To what extent do local newspapers provide information about judicial campaigns to their readers? The propensity of these outlets to report on judicial campaigns is affected by the economic environment of the news industry. News organizations are business enterprises that are focused primarily on making a profit in the context of increasing competition in an ever-shrinking market.[23] The financial struggles of local newspapers have important consequences for the quantity and quality of their political news coverage.[24]

First, economics has spurred the shift toward consolidation, and fewer companies are beginning to own more of the print media in the United States. Several political scientists and mass communications scholars have considered the effect of consolidation on the quality of local news coverage. While the results are mixed,[25] at the very least, it appears that political coverage produced by chain-owned newspapers is less locally oriented than coverage produced by newspapers that are independently owned.[26] This may mean that local reporters are more drawn to local campaigns that have national implications, such as congressional elections, and they may be less concerned with more state-oriented contests such as judicial races.

Second, as revenues for many news organizations have declined, cost-conscious media owners have reduced the number of reporters and editors they employ. Some scholars have demonstrated that such cutbacks have seriously impaired the ability of local news organizations to produce quality news.[27] Those reporters who have not been laid off are also affected because they tend to be overworked and underpaid.[28] In fact, fewer than one-third of the reporters who cover the courts are considered full-time;[29] the others cover a number of beats, or are very specific in their focus; they are likely to have less expertise and fewer sources to rely on than the full-time regulars.

Peter Clarke and Susan Evans suggest that because of the economic pressures, local newspaper reporters do not have the time to "enterprise" stories of their own. This leads to a greater reliance on reactive news—that is, stories generated by common occurrences or staged events, like press conferences and debates. Reporters are attracted to these events because they provide most of the information needed to produce a news story and require little investigative or in-depth political reporting.[30] However, journalists reporting on the courts often lack such news events, as well as the additional challenge of lacking access to the justices themselves. Instead, court reporters rely on each other, sources outside the judiciary (like interest groups, lawyers and law professors, and officials from other branches), and public documents to inform their coverage of the court. This can make the job of reporting on the court quite difficult and helps explain why coverage of courts is limited compared to the other branches of government.[31] These patterns may be particularly acute for local news reporters, who face greater resource constraints than their national counterparts.

Just as journalists face several difficulties in reporting on the activities of the courts, judicial campaigns are unique in their propensity to limit the ability of candidates to provide journalists with newsworthy information. While many states have opted for judicial elections as the method for selecting justices to their highest courts, these states have also established rules about how judicial campaigns and elections are conducted to preserve some judicial independence (see chapter 2).[32] For example, most states maintain codes of ethics designed to discourage candidates from sharing some types of information during campaigns (e.g., how a judicial candidate will rule in particular cases from the bench).[33] For instance, a candidate for Ohio's Supreme Court explained to one reporter, "The canons don't permit us to make any promise. I have decided I am not announcing any of my personal views."[34] If they are prohibited or reluctant to speak about certain issues, then there is little for reporters to write about. In fact, when reporters do write about these contests, they often note the lack of information that the candidates are able to reveal. One reporter for the *Birmingham News* explained to readers, "Because of ethical and other campaign guidelines, the judgeship candidates have been limited in what they can say. Thus their ads and campaign rallies have not been filled with fusillades."[35] While there are methods of obtaining information about candidates and their views independent from the candidates themselves, we have noted that reporters tend to have neither the time nor the inclination to find this information.[36] Therefore, with reporters reluctant to spend a great deal of effort producing stories, and judicial candidates constrained in what information they can provide to reporters, it is likely that judicial campaigns will receive little attention from local newspapers.[37]

Reporters also know that even if they produce stories on judicial campaigns, editors may not be inclined to publish these stories. As several scholars have noted, the "news hole," or the space in a newspaper or broadcast designated to the reporting of news, is shrinking as the needs of advertisers increase while audiences appear to desire less political news.[38]

These trends are particularly true for local news outlets, including newspapers.[39] As a result, the choice of what to report—what is newsworthy—is paramount to reporters and editors. Doris Graber outlines five criteria that journalists generally use to determine what is newsworthy: conflict, proximity, timeliness, impact, and familiarity.[40] Because we know that most people have very little information about the judiciary, it is reasonable to expect that stories about courts, candidates, and campaigns do not inherently meet the familiarity standard. It is also difficult to imagine that judicial elections have the type of impact that attracts reporters because most citizens do not even know very much about what state courts do and how they affect their daily lives.[41]

Graber argues that conflict, proximity, and timeliness are the most important criteria for determining whether something is newsworthy. Proximity refers to the propensity of audiences to prefer news that is relevant to their communities.[42] State supreme court elections, because they are statewide affairs, may be considered more proximate than national politics to readers of local newspapers, but they are not as proximate as local campaigns. Timely events are also more likely to be reported, which may mean judicial elections will be increasingly newsworthy as the day of the election nears. Ultimately, however, reporters place a premium on conflict when reporting on politics.[43] While conflict is an inherent part of most elections, the competitive nature of judicial campaigns cannot be taken for granted. Indeed, many races for seats on the supreme court are not meaningfully contested, and nearly half are not contested at all.[44] Even in competitive campaigns, codes of ethics may prevent judicial candidates from making claims about their opponents, thus limiting the amount of conflict that reporters can write about. And if judicial campaigns do not involve conflict, they are more likely to take a back seat to those campaigns that do.

Because of the constraints faced by reporters and the traits that make judicial campaigns less newsworthy, we would expect to find minimal coverage of these contests. In one of the few studies examining news coverage of judicial campaigns, Joseph D. Kearney and Howard B. Eisenberg found that in covering Wisconsin's judicial elections, newspapers "served less as interpretive intermediaries between the candidates and the general public, and more as occasional conveyors of unfiltered information, or as suppliers of information on how voters could acquire that unfiltered information through their own efforts (e.g., by attending one of the numerous public forums)."[45] In the following section, we expand on this work.

Quantity of Coverage of State Supreme Court Campaigns, 2000–2004

To examine local coverage of judicial elections, we examined local newspaper coverage of fifty-one state supreme court campaigns in sixteen states from 2000 through 2004 (Table 7.1). In particular, we tracked coverage during the last two months of each campaign in each state's capital city newspaper, when that paper was available.[46] We examined the frequency of coverage, as well as a number of structural characteristics of the reporting, including the format, placement, focus, and timing of the stories.

TABLE 7.1
Newspapers Coded for Analysis of Coverage

State	Newspaper	Year	Seats	Type
AL	*Birmingham News*	2000	1	Partisan
		2002	1	Partisan
AR	*Arkansas Democrat*	2000	1	Nonpartisan
GA	*Atlanta Journal*	2004	1	Nonpartisan
KY	*Louisville Courier-Journal*	2000	1	Nonpartisan
		2004	1	Nonpartisan
MI	*Lansing State Journal*	2004	1	Partisan
MN	*Minneapolis Star Tribune*	2000	4	Nonpartisan
		2002	1	Nonpartisan
		2004	1	Nonpartisan
MS	*Jackson Clarion-Ledger*	2000	3	Nonpartisan
		2002	1	Nonpartisan
MT	*Great Falls Tribune*	2000	3	Nonpartisan
		2002	1	Nonpartisan
		2004	2	Nonpartisan
NV	*Las Vegas Review Journal*	2000	1	Nonpartisan
		2002	1	Nonpartisan
		2004	3	Nonpartisan
NC	*Greensboro News & Record*	2000	2	Nonpartisan
		2002	2	Nonpartisan
		2004	2	Nonpartisan
OH	*Columbus Dispatch*	2000	1	Partisan
		2004	3	Partisan
OR	*Salem Statesman Journal*	2000	1	Nonpartisan
TX	*Austin American Statesman*	2000	3	Partisan
		2002	5	Partisan
		2004	1	Partisan
WA	*The Olympian*	2002	2	Nonpartisan
WV	*Charleston Daily Mail*	2000	1	Partisan
		2004	1	Partisan
WI	*Madison Capital Times*	2000	1	Nonpartisan
		2003	1	Nonpartisan

Note: "Seats" is the number of contested seats in that year.

Our data yielded 501 news stories across the fifty-one campaigns, with the average judicial contest covered in 9.8 stories. How does this amount of coverage compare with that of other statewide elections? Similar research by Brian F. Schaffner and Michael W. Wagner examined newspaper coverage of Senate campaigns in 2000 and found that the average Senate campaign received coverage in 81.4 stories, more than eight times as much coverage as state supreme court campaigns.[47] Thus, newspapers appear to devote far less attention to judicial elections than they do to Senate races.

We might be more sanguine about the low frequency of coverage if the reports were likely to reach and educate potential voters. This is not the case, however. Table 7.2 presents information on the balance of news versus editorials in these stories, the location of these reports within the newspaper, and the prominence of the judicial coverage within the article. Overall, as illustrated in the table, even daily readers of local newspapers will find little information about state supreme court contests. First, one of every four stories covering judicial campaigns appeared on the editorial page. While editorials can be valuable for readers interested in learning more about the issues at stake in the campaign, they may also present less detailed information about the contests. Additionally, they tend to provide less balanced accounts of the campaign since the primary purpose of an editorial is to take a position. Finally, many readers pay little attention to the editorial page of their newspaper, particularly if they tend to disagree with the opinions expressed by the editors.

Second, when print reporters do cover judicial campaigns, the stories do not hold a particularly prominent place in the newspaper. Since most people do not read the entire newspaper every day of the week, it becomes less likely that they will have seen a story on a judicial campaign when that story was not on the front page or in the front section of the paper. Only 14.4 percent of the stories covering supreme court contests appeared on the first page of the newspaper, and fewer than half of the stories even appeared in the front section of the newspaper.

Third, in many cases the judicial contest was not the primary focus of the news articles. Newspapers frequently discussed several campaigns in the same story, and news about the judicial campaign would simply be a small part of the longer article. The last two lines in Table 7.2 illustrate this point. In over one-third of the stories we coded, the judicial campaign was not a prominent enough part of the story to be mentioned in the headline or first (lead) paragraph of the text. The difference between these types of stories can be very important. For example, in the *Olympian*'s coverage of

TABLE 7.2
Types of Stories Devoted to Judicial Campaigns

Type of coverage	Number of stories	Percentage of stories
Type of story		
News	379	75.6
Editorial	122	24.4
Location of story		
Front page	67	14.4
First section	125	26.9
Other section of paper	272	58.6
Prominence		
Mentioned in headline or		
lead paragraph	304	60.8
Mentioned further in story	196	39.2

Note: Total number of stories, 501

the Washington Supreme Court election, one article presents only a few lines of information on different campaigns. The first part of the story publicizes a forum for candidates for countywide office; it is not until after this announcement that the report presents a three-sentence notice of an upcoming debate for the candidates for the supreme court.[48]

A story like this stands in stark contrast to one that focuses solely on the judicial election, like the 1,435-word article published by Salem's (OR) *Statesman Journal* that centered entirely on the campaign for Oregon's vacant supreme court justice position.[49] The story not only revealed extensive information about the candidates but also presented a question and answer format with the candidates and provided a detailed explanation of what the supreme court does and how it affects the lives of citizens. These examples underscore the important differences between articles that simply mention a supreme court contest and those that focus and elaborate on that campaign.

It is also instructive to understand the timing of coverage in these contests. For instance, news coverage is most valuable to citizens when it appears closer to the election. Figure 7.1 presents the percentage of coverage appearing on each of the sixty days prior to the election; bars on the left represent coverage closer to the election. The data reveal that most of the coverage of judicial campaigns appears at the very end of the campaign. In fact, over half of the total coverage of supreme court contests appeared during the final two weeks of the campaign period. Thus, what little coverage there is of judicial campaigns does appear close to election day, perhaps when citizens are in greatest need of election information.

The analysis of newspaper coverage of state supreme court elections

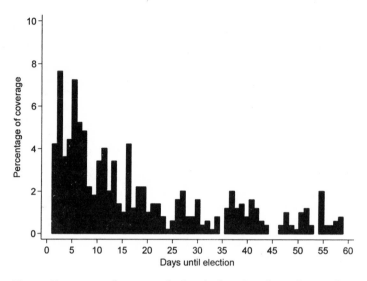

Fig. 7.1. Frequency of coverage during the last sixty days of campaign

demonstrates some impediments to learning about judicial elections. Put simply, coverage of these campaigns is likely to be difficult for readers to find. Even though half of the coverage appears within two weeks of the election, stories are still infrequent and often buried within the newspaper. Of course, newspapers do devote some coverage to judicial elections. In the following section, we explore what information is available in these articles.

Is News Coverage of Judicial Campaigns Informative?

While judicial coverage is sparse, particularly when compared with coverage of contests like campaigns for the U.S. Senate, citizens may still receive information they can use to make reasonable voting decisions when they cast their ballots. Among the most instructive knowledge for voters is that about substantive issues and the candidates' qualifications. After all, these pieces of information tell citizens who incumbents are and how they have performed in office, and who challengers are and how they may perform in office. It is this type of information that is at the core of accountability. Yet, issue and candidate coverage of campaigns is often lacking, particularly when compared with the amount of attention that reporters devote to covering the "horse race" aspect of the contest.[50] This coverage tends to focus on the competitive aspects of the race—who is ahead or behind and the strategic aspects of the campaign. When campaign news focuses more on the contest itself rather than the issues and candidates involved, voters are provided with less useful information for decisionmaking. Nevertheless, the horse race aspects of the campaign are those that reporters and editors tend to find more newsworthy, particularly compared with detailed coverage of issues, which many journalists perceive as being uninteresting to readers. The emphasis on horse race rather than issue coverage may be particularly prevalent in judicial elections since the ethical constraints on candidates reduces the amount of issue information that reporters may be able to cover easily.

While citizens may be best served by thorough discussion of issues and candidates, scholars have learned that voters may still make reasonably informed choices by using heuristics, or information "shortcuts."[51] By acquiring small pieces of information, a voter may learn (or at least assume) a great deal about candidates and issues and use this information in their voting calculus.[52] For example, knowing the party affiliation of a candidate may convey valuable information about that candidate's views on some issues. If the candidate is a Republican, the voter might reasonably assume that the candidate favors a more punitive approach to criminal punishment than a Democrat, who might favor a more rehabilitative approach. When voters know little else about the candidates in an election, simply telling them which party the candidates affiliate with greatly increases the odds that they will cast a vote in that election.[53]

Other common heuristics include political ideology and endorsements from interest groups or other politicians. Ideology can be used by citizens in a similar way as party affiliation to extrapolate a candidate's positions on a wide array of issues.[54] Endorsements are another cue that newspapers can convey that may provide the reader with a great deal of information about a candidate.[55] For example, the *Birmingham News* ran a story during the 2000 campaign noting that the U.S. Chamber of Commerce's Institute for Legal Reform had endorsed several state supreme court candidates. Most readers likely know that the Chamber of Commerce represents businesses and would likely assume that the candidates they endorsed are more favorable toward business interests. The article provides additional information about the organization, noting that "the institute's mission is to reduce the number of excessive and frivolous lawsuits."[56] Thus, readers may learn a great deal about the candidates in this campaign from the short 145-word story announcing these endorsements.

Finally, in low-information elections, knowing whether candidates are, for example, judges, defense lawyers, prosecuting attorneys, or plaintiffs' lawyers may provide citizens with one way to judge their competence to hold judicial office and potentially their views on relevant issues. Indeed, citizens are more likely to vote in low-information contests when they know the candidates' occupations because it allows them to cast a ballot for the candidate whose occupation suggests a higher degree of experience for the job.[57] While assumptions based on heuristics may occasionally be incorrect, more often they will lead citizens to correct conclusions about the candidates.[58]

Citizens are often not well educated about judicial campaigns as it is. The news media's propensity to not cover these contests adds another hurdle for voters attempting to make an informed decision. However, the media can aid voters by using what little space they devote to judicial elections to discuss the issues involved or even just to provide readers with information shortcuts that will allow them to make a better informed decision.

Information Provided in Judicial Campaign Coverage

To examine the types of information presented in stories covering supreme court elections, we coded news stories for the types of information discussed above. Figure 7.2 presents the percentage of stories that provided each of these types of information. Fewer than half of the stories (48.5 percent) covering these contests mentioned the substantive issues involved in the campaign, while more than three-fourths (78.8 percent) of the stories referred to the horse race aspects of the campaign. When citizens find coverage of state judicial contests, that coverage is much more likely to inform them about who is likely to win or lose the contest than it is to tell them where the candidates stand on the issues. Compare this with the study of U.S. Senate campaigns mentioned earlier. In that study, the authors found that 57.8 percent of the stories mentioned issues involved in the contest and only 42.0 percent focused on the horse race. Thus, not only is coverage of judicial campaigns more sparse than that for other contests, but also it is less focused on the issues.

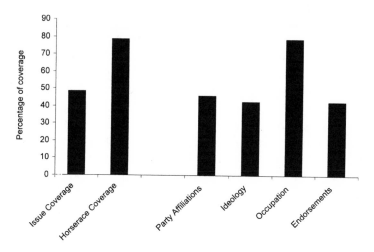

Fig. 7.2. Type of information provided in judicial campaign coverage

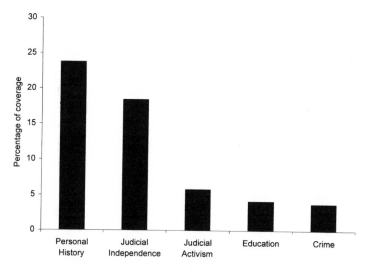

Fig. 7.3. Issues mentioned in judicial campaign coverage

When newspapers did address issues in their judicial coverage, what subjects did they discuss? For each story, we coded up to four different subjects addressed by the reporter. Figure 7.3 presents the percentage of stories that reported the five most commonly covered topics—the candidates' personal histories, judicial independence, judicial activism, crime, and education.

Two issues appeared to capture the attention of reporters more than the others. The most frequently mentioned was personal history—these were stories in which a candidate's background or traits were discussed. Nearly one-fourth of the coverage of judicial campaigns fell into this category. This is not surprising since state ethical codes often keep judicial candidates from talking about little more than their background and qualifications for a seat on the court. The second most covered topic was judicial independence, the degree to which sitting judges represent or have been unduly influenced by special interests. Accounting for 18.4 percent of the stories that reported issues, it is surprising that judicial independence is covered so little, and that it is second in coverage to personal traits. The issue of judicial independence is a hot topic in many jurisdictions as the increased sophistication of judicial campaigns and the influx of campaign funds has heightened concerns about equity and due process in state courts.[59]

The other issues—judicial activism, education, and crime—were each covered in fewer than 6 percent of the stories. The topic of judicial activism—a complex concept, but one that is often understood as the practice of judges legislating from the bench—is particularly familiar to those who follow judicial selection at the federal level and has been reported by both national and state news papers in a variety of judicial contexts.[60] The topic is exceptionally controversial and the subject of much debate; it would appear to meet the standards for newsworthiness, yet it is essentially not discussed in reports about judicial elections. Education issues are particularly salient at the state level since they comprise the single largest expenditure in state budgets.[61] State courts are loci for cases dealing with public school finance, an issue that was particularly salient in Ohio's campaigns in 2000 and 2004.[62] Yet, outside of Ohio, education issues garnered little attention in judicial campaign coverage.

More surprising in its absence from judicial campaign coverage is crime, which is one issue that should make the court a newsworthy topic for reporters.[63] Many readers may have direct knowledge of criminal activity, and most people are concerned with their personal safety, as well as the safety of their communities. To the extent that staffing the courts is related to criminal justice policy, we would expect journalists to report on judicial elections in the context of criminal justice issues. Yet, of the five most mentioned issues in judicial election coverage, crime is the least reported (the subject of fewer than 5 percent of the campaign stories).

While substantial issue coverage was mostly lacking for the coverage of judicial campaigns, citizens may learn a great deal about candidates even if they only garner small pieces of information such as the candidates' party affiliations, ideologies, endorsements, and even their occupations. Returning to Figure 7.2, we present the extent to which coverage of judicial campaigns conveys these cues to citizens. The most commonly mentioned information was a candidate's occupation—more than three of every four (78.8 percent) stories revealed the occupation of at least one of the candidates in the race. At a minimum, this information may allow citizens some basis on which to judge each candidate's credentials for sitting on the supreme court and provide clues to the positions that candidates may have on important issues such as crime or tort reform.

The other three heuristics we measured were reported in fewer than half of the stories. We might take some comfort in knowing that a particularly useful heuristic, occupation, was included in the vast majority of stories; however, given the ease with which party affiliation, particularly, but even ideology and endorsements could be included in local newspaper coverage of the races, it is striking that such basic and potentially useful information is so infrequently reported.

Overall, our examination of the content of coverage does not improve on the conclusions drawn about the quantity of coverage. In what coverage the media do provide on judicial campaigns, the emphasis is on the horse race rather than issues. When issues are discussed, the articles are less substantive and focus more on the personal histories of the candidates. Nor is coverage of judicial campaigns particularly effective at conveying basic heuristic information about the candidates. Even if a citizen does come across a story covering a supreme court campaign, he or she is more likely to read about the horse race component than to learn the candidates' ideological leanings or their perspectives on judicial activism.

Variation in Coverage

To this point in the chapter, we have discussed the coverage of state supreme court campaigns. On average, coverage of these campaigns appears to be lacking in both magnitude and substance. Considering only the average amount of coverage masks important variation across campaigns and newspapers, however. For example, the *Columbus Dispatch* devoted forty articles to one of the Ohio State Supreme Court campaigns in 2000, while in the same year two Texas races received coverage in only one story in the

Austin American Statesman. Why do some judicial campaigns receive more coverage than others? In this section, we consider this question.

One reason that some races may receive more coverage than others may be influenced by the type of ballot used. The primary difference among judicial elections is whether they are partisan or nonpartisan. Thirteen of the twenty-one states that elect supreme court justices do so on a nonpartisan ballot (one that does not identify the candidates' party affiliation), while the remaining eight states have partisan ballots.[64] Reporters may cover nonpartisan elections less often than partisan campaigns for two reasons. First, it may be easier for reporters to discuss partisan judicial campaigns in the context of the conflict between Democrats and Republicans that characterizes the coverage of other elections being held at the same time. A nonpartisan campaign may be more difficult to fit into this existing narrative and may receive less coverage as a result. Second, there may be fewer campaign activities for reporters to cover when those campaigns are held on nonpartisan ballots. As Matthew Streb explains in chapter 6, party organizations are less involved in campaigns for nonpartisan judicial offices than they are for partisan campaigns, and that reduction in activity may be mirrored in the coverage of the race.

Another factor that may explain why coverage varies from election to election is how competitive the contest is. As noted earlier in this chapter, reporters and editors determine what is news based on several criteria. Conflict is one of these criteria, and conflict is likely to be more pronounced in campaigns that are competitive. In addition, competitive campaigns are more interesting because the outcome is in doubt, which makes for more compelling stories than a campaign where one candidate is certain to win. Finally, it may simply be easier for reporters to gather information about competitive campaigns. In these contests, more vigorous campaigning occurs and more interest groups mobilize to influence the outcome. The involvement of so many forces in competitive contests produces a wealth of information that is easier for reporters to collect than it may be in uncompetitive contests. Therefore, newspapers may devote more coverage to campaigns that are competitive and also provide more substantive information about those campaigns.

Finally, as we discussed above, reporting on state supreme court elections may vary depending on whether the newspaper is owned by a large media conglomerate or by a smaller, independent company. Chain newspapers may be more likely to use stories that are produced in a way to be relevant to many of their newspapers, which precludes the need to employ as many reporters for each individual newspaper. In addition, reporters may frequently move from one paper to another within the same corporation and, by doing so, may be less familiar with the politics in the state they are reporting on. Therefore, reporters for chain newspapers may pay less attention to state and local political campaigns, such as those for the supreme court, while devoting more attention to national politics.

Explaining the Variance in Coverage

In this section, we attempt to explain some of the variation in coverage of judicial contests by comparing partisan and nonpartisan elections, competitive and uncompetitive campaigns, and chain- and independently owned newspapers. Two-thirds of the campaigns in our dataset were nonpartisan contests, while the remainder were partisan elections. We defined a competitive campaign as one that was decided by 10 percent of the vote or less. Twenty-two of our fifty-one campaigns qualified as competitive under this criterion, while the remainder were classified as uncompetitive. In addition, we compared coverage produced by the four independently owned papers in our sample (the *Arkansas Democrat-Gazette, Charleston Gazette, Columbus Dispatch,* and *Las Vegas Review Journal*) to that published by the other twelve newspapers that were each part of a corporate chain.[65]

Figure 7.4 shows how coverage varies depending on these three factors. First, the type of ballot used in the election appeared to have an important effect on how much coverage the campaign received. Partisan elections received coverage in 13.8 stories, on average, while newspapers devoted an average of just 7.8 stories to nonpartisan campaigns for the bench. This difference of six stories is substantial considering that judicial elections receive little coverage in the first place. In addition, reporters tend to honor the spirit of nonpartisan contests by rarely mentioning the party affiliations of candidates in these contests. While 75.7 percent of the articles covering partisan judicial contests mentioned the candidates' party affiliations, only 19.9 percent of those focusing on nonpartisan campaigns did so. Of course, if reporters do not mention candidates' party affiliations in a story, they may still convey similar information by using ideological labels instead. However, stories on nonpartisan contests were only slightly more likely to attach ideological labels to the candidates; though not nearly enough to make up for the reduction in partisan information that

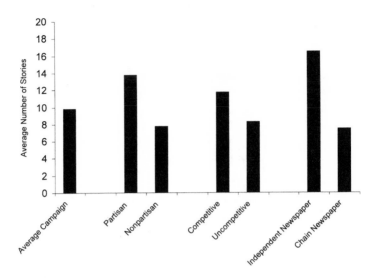

Fig. 7.4. Explaining variance in campaign coverage

the stories provided. Thus, nonpartisan elections not only receive less coverage from newspapers, but they also include substantially less information about the candidates' party affiliations.

In addition to ballot type, the extent to which a campaign was competitive also affected the amount of coverage that contest received. Figure 7.4 indicates that, on average, competitive campaigns received coverage in 3.4 additional stories compared with uncompetitive contests. It is not surprising to find that reporters devote more coverage to competitive campaigns, considering that these contests are likely to offer more conflict and to be more newsworthy because of the uncertainty of the outcome. Of course, it is important to recall that compared with the average U.S. Senate campaign, even competitive judicial elections receive very little coverage. While citizens are more likely to encounter news on a judicial campaign when the contest is close, such coverage is still rather sparse compared with that of other elections.

Finally, whether a newspaper was independently owned or part of a chain was also an important factor in how much coverage that paper devoted to a state supreme court campaign. As the findings in Figure 7.4 indicate, independent newspapers produced more than twice as much coverage of judicial campaigns as those papers owned by chains. As noted earlier, one of the fears held by critics of media consolidation is that newspapers owned by large corporations will be less attentive to state and local news. Our findings appear to be consistent with this criticism. Independently owned newspapers produced far more coverage than chain newspapers. In fact, chain newspapers produced an average of just 7.5 stories on state supreme court campaigns. Furthermore, what stories chain newspapers did publish were less likely to feature the campaign prominently in the story, and a higher percentage of these stories were editorials rather than regular news accounts.

Two newspapers provide particularly good examples of these differences between chain and independently owned papers. It was particularly common for Texas's *Austin American-Statesman,* a newspaper owned by Cox Enterprises, to present information in the form of endorsements that were one-line descriptions of the *Statesman*'s preferred candidates. In 2004, there was one race for a seat on the Texas Supreme Court, and in three of the six reports published on this race, the text simply listed the candidate's name, party affiliation, and status as incumbent. The three remaining reports included an endorsement that included some additional background information on the incumbent endorsed by the paper and basic facts about the supreme court, a few letters to the editor about the two candidates in the race, and, a 367-word editorial that included four paragraphs about the race and an endorsement of the incumbent.

In contrast, the *Columbus Dispatch,* an independent locally owned newspaper, covered the three judicial races during the 2004 election season in twenty reports, with each race addressed in at least fifteen stories. In other words, the *Dispatch* reported on each of its judicial contests more than twice as frequently as the *Statesman* did for Texas's judicial contest during the same year. Additionally, the nature of these stories was dramatically different. Fourteen of the twenty reports were news stories that focused exclusively on one or more of the three campaigns and ranged from 356 to 1,243 words. The remaining six reports included an editorial; a series of brief stories; a brief, four-line endorsement; and a letter to the editor. Overall, the *Columbus Dispatch*'s coverage of the Ohio Supreme Court contests was not only more prevalent than the *Statesman*'s coverage of the Texas campaign, but also the articles provided far more information to readers.

Our analysis indicates that much of the variation in coverage of state supreme court campaigns can be explained by understanding the type of contest, the competitiveness of the campaign, and the type of newspaper covering the election.[66] Based on our analysis, state supreme court campaigns receive the least amount of coverage when they are uncompetitive, held on a nonpartisan ballot, and covered by a chain newspaper. When all of these conditions hold, we would expect the campaign to receive coverage in fewer than seven news articles. Alternatively, when a partisan judicial election is competitive and covered by an independent newspaper, that campaign receives coverage in more than fourteen stories, on average. It is important to note that nearly two-thirds of states with judicial elections use nonpartisan ballots, most judicial campaigns are uncompetitive, and most large daily newspapers are owned by media conglomerates. Thus, while our analysis indicates that higher levels of coverage are possible under the right circumstances, the conditions that generate the least amount of coverage are most common to judicial elections.

Conclusion

The analysis we present in this chapter suggests that we should not be surprised to find citizens lacking information about judicial elections. Indeed, citizens turning to newspapers for information on state supreme court campaigns will find a dearth of coverage on these contests. Reporting on judicial campaigns may present challenges for reporters and newspaper editors, and they typically respond to these challenges by producing less coverage than for other statewide campaigns. Recall that the average supreme court campaign received coverage in fewer than ten newspaper articles, while an average contest for the U.S. Senate received more than eight times as much coverage. To further put this into perspective, consider several points about this coverage. First, of the 9.8 stories covering the average judicial campaign, 2.4 were editorials. Thus, the average contest was actually covered in only 7.4 news articles. Second, of the noneditorial stories, only one-third appeared in the first section of the newspaper. Thus, most coverage of judicial elections was placed deeper in the newspaper where readers may not have always found it. Third, one of every three of these news stories did not even mention the judicial campaign at the beginning of the article. In these articles, coverage of the supreme court campaign was buried further within the story itself. Once all of these factors are taken into account, the picture of coverage becomes fairly bleak—the typical judicial campaign may receive as little as two news stories that both appear in the front section of the paper and mention the contest prominently.

The actual content of what little coverage there is also presents cause for concern. As with most campaigns, reporters tend to rely on the types of stories that are easier to produce—those focusing on the horse race aspect of the campaign. In fact, fewer than half of all stories covering state supreme court campaigns addressed issues at all. And even when newspapers did produce issue coverage, the issues discussed dealt more with the candidates' personal histories than with their views on judicial activism or crime. Thus, even if citizens are able to find coverage of judicial campaigns, that coverage may not present a sufficient amount of useful information about the candidates.

At the beginning of this chapter, we noted that the states that have chosen to select their judges through the electoral process value accountability in the judiciary. However, to hold elected officials accountable, citizens must have access to information about them, particularly during campaigns. The analysis in this chapter indicates that this information is clearly lacking for most judicial contests. What are the consequences of this lack of coverage for judicial accountability? To hold judges accountable, the public must have at least some information about the candidates in judicial elections before they go to the polls. When citizens lack this information, they tend to abstain from voting or base their choices on what little information they are able to collect from news coverage, campaign materials, or even the ballot itself. As a result, when the electorate goes to the polls with less information, the prospects for judicial accountability decline.

This is not to suggest that judicial elections are inherently unable to produce accountability. To the contrary, they may serve their purpose well if reporters and candidates conducted themselves somewhat differently during these campaigns. As we noted above, reporters tend to find reporting on judicial campaigns difficult. Furthermore, many journalists likely question the news value of judicial campaigns compared with other contests. To some extent, both points relate to the constraints under which candidates operate during campaigns. As one team of political scientists suggested in their analysis of voter information in judicial contests:

> It seems clear . . . that public education about the courts, better media coverage of judicial races and more interesting and informative contests for judicial office are all within reach if only the candidates for judicial office and their lawyer associates had a little more accurate view of who it is that is listening, watching and casting ballots in judicial races.[67]

Perhaps journalists are underestimating the latent interest that citizens have in judicial elections. If they are to be taken at their word, citizens do want more information on these contests. In addition, perhaps judicial campaigns will become more newsworthy in the wake of the U.S. Supreme Court's *White* decision. Now candidates for judge are legally free to express their views on any subject. While ethical limits still exist, candidates may be more likely to speak out on a wider array of topics during campaigns, a dynamic that would produce more news for reporters to cover. Ultimately, increased news coverage and a more informed electorate are critical if judicial elections are to compel accountability in the judiciary.

NOTES

1. Justice at Stake Campaign, *Justice at Stake Frequency Questionnaire.*
2. Ibid.
3. Baum, "Electing Judges"; Baum, "Judicial Elections and Judicial Independence"; Dubois, *From Ballot to the Bench*; Iyengar, "Effects of Media-Based Campaigns on Candidate and Voter Behavior"; Klein and Baum, "Ballot Information and Voting Decisions in Judicial Elections"; Solimine, "False Promise of Judicial Elections in Ohio."
4. Baum, "Electing Judges"; Dubois, *From Ballot to the Bench.*
5. One notable exception is the thorough set of case studies about newspaper coverage of Wisconsin elections held in 1999. See Kearney and Eisenberg, "Print Media and Judicial Elections."
6. Champagne and Haydel, *Judicial Reform in the States.*
7. *Republican Party of Minnesota v. White*, 536 U.S. 765 (2002).
8. Hall, "Ballot Roll-off in Judicial Elections."
9. Ohio Political Survey, November 1986.
10. Walsh Commission, *The People Shall Judge.*
11. For example, Arnold, *Congress, the Press and Political Accountability.*
12. Ibid.; Cook, *Governing the News.* A national survey conducted by the Indiana Public Opinion Laboratory for the State of Washington indicated that more than 80 percent of the public sometimes or regularly received their information about the courts from newspaper coverage. Office of the Administrator of the Courts, *How the Public Views the Courts).*
13. Lovrich et al., "Citizen Knowledge and Voting in Judicial Elections."
14. Converse, "Nature of Belief Systems in Mass Publics"; Delli Carpini and Keeter, *What Americans Know about Politics.*
15. Patterson and McClure, *Unseeing Eye.*
16. Delli Carpini and Keeter, *What American Know about Politics.*

17. Robinson and Davis, "Television News and the Informed Public"; Berkowitz and Pritchard, "Political Knowledge and Communication Resources"; Weaver and Drew, "Voter Learning in the 1990 Off-Year Election."

18. DeFleur et al., "Audience Recall of News Stories."

19. Mondak, "Newspapers and Political Awareness."

20. Goldenberg and Traugott, "Mass Media in Legislative Campaigns."

21. While newspaper readership increases citizen knowledge about politics, watching television news does not have a similar effect. See Delli Carpini and Keeter, *What Americans Know about Politics.*

22. Ohio Political Survey, December 1988.

23. Cook, *Governing the News*; Graber, *Mass Media and American Politics*; Yeric, *Mass Media and the Politics of Change.*

24. The constraints discussed here are even more severe for local television news and, as a result, we expect the coverage of judicial elections by this medium to be even more limited in its coverage than it is for local newspapers.

25. For research claiming that newspaper consolidation does adversely affect coverage, see Bagdikian, *Media Monopoly.* For research providing less conclusive results, see Demers, "Corporate Newspaper Bashing."

26. Schaffner and Sellers, "Structural Determinants of Local Congressional News Coverage."

27. Just et al., "Thinner, Cheaper, Longer."

28. Kaniss, *Making Local News.*

29. Davis, *Decisions and Images*, p. 63.

30. Clarke and Evans, *Covering Campaigns*; Kaniss, *Making Local News.*

31. Slotnick and Segal, *Television News and the Supreme Court.*

32. Caufield, "In the Wake of *White.*"

33. Goldberg and Sanchez, *New Politics of Judicial Elections 2002.*

34. Quoted in Craig, "O'Neill Seeks to Unseat Appointee O'Donnell."

35. Gordon, "Amendments, Court Races Lead State Ballot."

36. Research by Kearney and Eisenberg substantiates this in the context of judicial elections. They found that newspapers appeared unwilling to use their resources to investigate beyond the information provided by the candidates themselves (Kearney and Eisenberg, "Print Media and Judicial Elections," pp. 752, 762).

37. However, as Rick Hasen notes in chapter 2, with the Court's recent ruling in *White* and other judicial canons coming under attack, it is possible that journalists will find it easier to report on judicial campaigns in the future.

38. Cook, *Governing the News*, p. 173; Graber, *Mass Media and American Politics*, p. 102.

39. Graber *Mass Media and American Politics*, p. 104

40. Discussed in ibid., pp. 99–102.

41. According to the *Justice at Stake Frequency Questionnaire* (2001), fewer than one-quarter of respondents (22 percent) said that they knew a great deal about

what courts and judges do in their states; more than three-quarters (77 percent) said they knew some, just a little, or nothing at all about their states' judiciary (Q21).

42. Graber, *Mass Media and American Politics*, p. 101.

43. Manheim, "News Shapers."

44. Hall, "State Supreme Courts in American Democracy."

45. Kearney and Eisenberg, "Print Media and Judicial Elections," pp. 749–750.

46. We began the coding process by identifying the candidates for each contested supreme court election in sixteen states from 2000 through 2004. We used newspapers available through Lexis-Nexis to search for coverage. When available, we used the newspaper from the state's capital city since that newspaper would be most proximate to the supreme court. However, for five states, we used an alternative newspaper because the capital newspaper was not available. In each case, we used the most prominent newspaper available through Lexis-Nexis. The newspapers we used in the analysis are listed in Table 7.1. Once we identified the newspaper, we searched variations on all candidates' names for the last two months of the general election campaign. We had a trained research assistant code each article along several criteria and eliminate articles that were unrelated to the judicial campaign. If a single article covered more than one judicial campaign in the same state, we coded that article separately for each race.

47. Schaffner and Wagner, "Buy One Get One Free?"

48. "Campaign Trail."

49. Davies, "Supreme Court Has One Contested Seat."

50. Patterson, *Mass Media Election*; Just et al., "Thinner, Cheaper, Longer."

51. Sniderman et al., *Reasoning and Choice.*

52. Schaffner and Streb, "Partisan Heuristic in Low-Information Elections." See also, for example, Klein and Baum who examine the effect of ballots in judicial elections and find that providing party affiliation on the ballot helps voters in their decision about whether to vote and for whom to vote (Klein and Baum, "Ballot Information and Voting Decisions").

53. Schaffner and Streb, "Partisan Heuristic in Low-Information Elections."

54. Sniderman et al., "Reasoning Chains."

55. Brady and Sniderman, "Attitude Attribution"; Sniderman et al., *Reasoning and Choice.*

56. "Institute Backs GOP Candidates for High Court."

57. McDermott, "Candidate Occupations and Voter Information Shortcuts."

58. Popkin, *Reasoning Voter.*

59. Champagne, "Interest Groups and Judicial Elections"; Goldberg et al., *New Politics of Judicial Elections 2004.*

60. A Lexis-Nexis search of the four categories of regional newspapers, conducted on February 3, 2006, revealed 384 articles that included the phrase "judicial

activism" in the headline or leading paragraph during the time frame of our analysis, 2000–2004.

61. *2003 State Expenditure Report.*

62. Bosworth, *Courts as Catalysts.* The issue at stake in Ohio's 2000 and 2004 judicial campaigns related to the Supreme Court's recent rulings that the state's funding of public schools was inadequate.

63. For an extensive discussion about local media coverage of crime, see Graber, *Mass Media and American Politics*, pp. 291–295.

64. American Judicature Society, *Judicial Selection in the States.* Technically, only six states elect their judges on a true partisan ballot. In Michigan and Ohio, candidates run in the general election without partisan affiliation listed on the ballot. However, in Michigan general-election candidates are nominated at political party conventions, and in Ohio general-election candidates are chosen in partisan primary elections. As a result, we categorized each as partisan contests because we believed that since the candidates won partisan nominations it is more likely that reporters would be able to frame the contest in the running partisan narrative with which they report on other races.

65. We used the *Columbia Journalism Review*'s online database of media conglomerates (http://www.cjr.org/tools/owners/) to determine whether a newspaper was part of a chain. Of the twelve chain newspapers in our sample, Gannett owned six, Cox Enterprises owned two, and McClatchy Company, Landmark Communications, Lee Enterprises, and Advance each owned one.

66. We tested the three explanations simultaneously using ordinary least squares regression analysis with the number of stories as the dependent variable and ballot type, competitiveness, and ownership as the independent variables. All three independent variables had statistically significant effects of similar magnitude to those we discuss in this section. The three variables explained 38.5 percent of the variation in coverage.

67. Lovrich et al., "Citizen Knowledge and Voting in Judicial Elections," p. 33.

Chapter 8

Voter Responses to High-Visibility Judicial Campaigns

Lawrence Baum and David Klein

As several of the chapters in this book have made clear, election campaigns for judgeships have changed.[1] In the last decade, levels of spending for and against candidates have grown substantially. Sitting judges are more likely to face attacks on their records, and campaign rhetoric has become more heated. Across the states, most campaigns are still in the quieter mode of earlier eras, but departures from that quieter mode have become considerably more common. This is especially true of contests for seats on the state supreme courts.[2]

As commentators have emphasized, these changes in the character of judicial elections may have significant effects on the judiciary. Indeed, there is widespread concern about perceived negative consequences, especially for judicial independence.[3] Judges' need for campaign contributors may compromise their impartiality. Fears of triggering electoral opposition may deter judges from making unpopular decisions.

To a considerable extent, the consequences of changes in judicial elections depend on the voters. If few voters are aware of heated campaign rhetoric, for instance, that rhetoric will have little effect on election outcomes. Yet we know little about how voters have responded to the larger and more contentious campaigns of recent years, primarily because of the dearth of surveys of voters in judicial elections. As a result, our understanding of the effects of the changes in judicial campaigns is limited.

In this chapter we address this issue. In recent years, election campaigns for seats on the Ohio Supreme Court have varied considerably in their size and level of contention. For example, the campaigns in 1998 were relatively quiet, while those in 2002 were quite noisy. Using several sources of information, including surveys of Ohio voters, we compare the very different kinds of campaigns in those two years and voter responses to them, probing the effect of the larger and noisier[4] judicial elections that have become more common.

Voters in Judicial Elections

From the voters' perspective, the outstanding characteristic of judicial election campaigns in their traditional form is that they supply little information. The small scale of campaigns and limited coverage by the mass media make it difficult for voters to learn much about the candidates. This is especially true because the great majority of states hold elections to judgeships at the same time as other contests that garner far more attention—campaigns for president, governor, and the Senate, among others. In this respect, judicial elections are not unique. Rather, they are similar to contests for many other elected offices. Citizens typically face the same kinds of difficulties in learning about candidates for state auditor or county engineer that they do with candidates for judgeships.[5]

Voters who lack much information about candidates for a particular office may choose not to cast a vote. "Rolloff" of voters from the highest offices to lower-level offices such as judgeships is often substantial.[6] When voters do choose between candidates about whom they know little, they rely heavily on the information that is provided on the ballot itself. If the ballot lists the candidates' party affiliations, voters who feel more positively about one party than the other may make their choice on that basis alone. Information that can be gleaned from the candidates' names, such as gender and ethnicity, may also affect voters' choices.[7] For that matter, recognition of a candidate's name in itself can benefit the candidate— even when name recognition is false in the sense that only the name, not the candidate, is familiar. There is a long history of success for judicial candidates who benefited from a familiar name even though the candidates themselves were unknown.

Perhaps the most important piece of information that appears on some ballots is candidates' party affiliations. Among the states that elect judges, about one-third use partisan elections in which candidates are identified by party. In those states, voters are likely to give heavy weight to partisan considerations in their choices. In states with nonpartisan elections, voters may not be able to identify the candidates with a party, and partisanship will play a substantially smaller role in their choices (although as Matthew Streb shows in chapter 6, partisan activity is not entirely absent in these elections).[8]

When voters who are starved for information rely on what the ballot tells them, they are not basing their decisions on information about judges' work on the bench, whether the past performance of a judge in office or the prospective performance of a nonincumbent. At best, they can infer candidates' positions on judicial issues from information such as party affiliation and gender. One effect is to limit the accountability of judges for the quality of their work and the content of their decisions.

Judicial campaigns that are larger in scale and that attract more attention from the mass media have the potential to change all this. There is no guarantee that voters will actually receive and assimilate the information they are provided about candidates for judgeships. But if they do, they will go to the polls in a different position from voters in traditional judicial elections.

For one thing, they will be more likely to participate in those elections. The more that voters know about the candidates for a judgeship, the less likely they are to skip over that contest in the election booth. Thus rolloff from the highest offices to judicial elections would decline.

Further, the voters who do participate in judicial elections will be less reliant on the ballot itself for information. Armed with information they obtained from the campaigns and the media, voters can base their choices on an array of considerations. Most important, voters may be in a position to assess the actual or prospective performance of candidates for judgeships. One result would be to increase judges' accountability for their decisions, no matter whether that is a good thing, a bad thing, or a mix of the two.

As we noted, the increased volume of available information in high-profile judicial contests does not guarantee that voters will make use of that information. Most citizens give limited attention to political information of any type. Moreover, even relatively large-scale judicial campaigns must compete for voters' attention with other election contests. Thus the effect of such campaigns in enhancing the information that voters bring with them to the polls and ultimately on voter behavior is quite uncertain.

The Setting: Elections to the Ohio Supreme Court

The Ohio Supreme Court is a seven-member court. It stands at the top of the three-level judicial system that exists in most states: a set of trial courts, an intermediate appellate court, and a supreme court. The Ohio Supreme Court's jurisdiction is mostly discretionary, meaning that the court can decide which cases it will hear from those that are brought to it.

Justices on the court hold six-year terms. Elections are staggered, so that each two years two or three of the seats on the court are on the ballot. Ohio does not use districts in supreme court elections, so candidates for each seat on the court run statewide.

Ohio uses an unusual mixed election system: candidates are nominated for the supreme court on partisan ballots, but the two parties' candidates (and any other candidates) run in the general election without party labels.

Until the 1980s, elections to the Ohio Supreme Court were generally small in scale and quiet.[9] Ohio began to depart from that traditional form before most other states. The primary trigger for the change was the court's innovations in tort law, the law of personal injuries. After the court gained a Democratic majority in 1978, it changed a number of rules to favor individuals who sought compensation for their injuries. In doing so, the court was participating in a nationwide trend, but the speed and extent of the legal changes aroused opposition from the business community and professionals such as doctors who are defendants in personal-injury suits.

In 1986 a challenger defeated the Democratic chief justice, restoring a Republican majority to the court, after a campaign that was unprecedented in the level of spending and media attention. But the Republican majority did not translate into a conservative majority, because one and later two Republicans on the court generally took liberal positions on economic issues such as tort law. The supreme court elections following 1986 varied widely in their character, depending primarily on whether Republicans and conservatives had an opportunity to win additional seats on the court.

The 1998 supreme court elections were relatively quiet, even though three seats on the court were contested. Three incumbents were running for reelection, and all were in a strong position to win, so the campaigns were fairly small. The 2000 elections were quite different.[10] No incumbent justice had been defeated since 1986, but business groups perceived that a

Democratic incumbent was vulnerable, and defeating her would finally create a conservative majority on economic issues. Operating a campaign independent of the Republican challenger, the U.S. and Ohio Chambers of Commerce spent several million dollars on television commercials attacking Democratic incumbent Alice Robie Resnick (see chapter 5). That campaign created something of a backlash. Resnick won by a moderately large margin, and a Republican incumbent who had seemed safe won by a smaller margin.

Having failed in 2000, business groups and other conservatives saw the 2002 elections as a better opportunity. A Republican justice who had taken liberal positions on economic issues was retiring, and a victory for the Republican in the contest for that seat could be expected to tilt the balance on the court. Ohio and national interest groups recognized the stakes in that contest, and the result was a massive campaign effort that extended to the other supreme court contest in the state. Thus, as in 2000, Ohio was a prime example of the growth in the scale and visibility of judicial elections that was occurring around the country.

Table 8.1 provides an overview of the 1998 and 2002 contests. The three contests in 1998 and one of the two contests in 2002 pitted incumbents against challengers who sat on lower courts. In the other contest, a trial judge ran against the state's lieutenant governor, who had once sat as a trial judge. In 1998, each incumbent justice won by a substantial margin: all achieved more than 60 percent of the vote, the two Republicans more than 70 percent. The contests were closer in 2002, with incumbent Evelyn Stratton winning 55 percent and lieutenant governor Maureen O'Connor

TABLE 8.1
Candidates in the 1998 and 2002 Contests for the Ohio Supreme Court

Name	Party	Status/Occupation	Percentage share of vote
1998			
Thomas J. Moyer	Republican	Incumbent chief justice	72.2
Gary Tyack	Democrat	Court of appeals judge	27.8
Stephen W. Powell	Republican	Court of appeals judge	38.5
Francis E. Sweeney	Democrat	Incumbent justice	61.5
Paul E. Pfeifer	Republican	Incumbent justice	71.4
Ronald Suster	Democrat	Trial judge	28.6
2002			
Tim Black	Democrat	Trial judge	42.7
Maureen O'Connor	Republican	Lieutenant governor	57.3
Janet Burnside	Democrat	Trial judge	44.7
Evelyn Stratton	Republican	Incumbent justice	55.3

TABLE 8.2

*Campaign Expenditures by Ohio Supreme Court
Candidates, 1998 and 2002*

Name	Expenditures (dollars)
1998	
Thomas J. Moyer	688,000
Gary Tyack	346,000
Stephen W. Powell	159,000
Francis E. Sweeney	474,000
Paul E. Pfeifer	512,000
Ronald Suster	261,000
Mean for all candidates	407,000
2002	
Tim Black	1,306,000
Maureen O'Connor	1,610,000
Janet Burnside	1,166,000
Evelyn Stratton	1,704,000
Mean for all candidates	1,447,000

Source: Campaign finance reports filed with office of Ohio Secretary of State.

winning 57 percent. The victories by both Republicans maintained the 5–2 Republican majority on the court and were expected to produce a conservative majority on the economic issues that had long divided the court.

The difference in the scale of the campaigns between the two election years is made clear by the levels of the candidates' expenditures, shown in Table 8.2. In 1998 the mean expenditure among the candidates was about $400,000, and in each contest one of the candidates (the incumbent and winner) greatly outspent the other. Each challenger spent less than $350,000.

The picture was quite different in 2002. The mean expenditure was about $1,447,000, three-and-a-half times the mean in 1998. Every candidate, winner or loser, spent over a million dollars. Even this contrast fails to fully capture the differences between the two years in the scale of the campaigns. In 1998, there were no substantial efforts on behalf of the candidates by groups independent of their campaigns. In contrast, alongside the almost $6 million spent by the candidates in 2002, independent interest groups spent considerable amounts on their own. According to one report, four groups spent about $1.83 million on television commercials, and a group associated with the Ohio Chamber of Commerce raised about $1 million for the supreme court contests.[11] Altogether, the four supreme court candidates aired about 9,000 television commercials, and independent groups aired another 4,000 on their behalf. The total of 13,000 was more than three times the total in any another state in 2002.[12]

The low levels of expenditures in 1998 reflected the perception that the three incumbent justices were invulnerable, which made it especially difficult for the challengers to raise money. Recognizing their disadvantage, all the challengers sought to give the voters a basis for voting against the incumbent. In the contest for chief justice, Gary Tyack attacked incumbent Thomas Moyer primarily on issues involving administration of the court and the court system. Tyack gave particular emphasis to a proposed relocation of the supreme court to a renovated building, which he depicted as excessively expensive.

The two incumbent associate justices were both part of the 4–3 majority that typically took liberal positions on economic issues, the same majority that had struck down the state's system for funding of public education as a violation of the Ohio Constitution in 2000.[13] Their challengers attacked them for engaging in "judicial activism." The attack took an unusual form in the contest between incumbent Paul Pfeifer and challenger Ronald Suster, since Pfeifer was a Republican. Indeed, some Republican activists had hoped to deny him renomination to the court because of what they regarded as his excessive liberalism. The challengers' low levels of expenditures and the election results suggest that these attacks, like those on Chief Justice Moyer, had only limited effect on the voters.

The candidates' heavy expenditures in 2002 were possible because of massive contributions from groups with an interest in the court's decisions on economic issues. The Democrats received the largest share of their funding from labor unions and lawyers who represent personal injury plaintiffs, while business and professional groups—especially physicians and insurance companies—were the leading financial supporters of the Republicans.

The candidates' campaigns presented a mix of issue-related appeals and other messages. For the most part the candidates emphasized personal qualities that they thought would appeal to the voters. They maintained this stance despite the June 2002 decision of the U.S. Supreme Court that gave judicial candidates greater freedom to discuss issues (see chapter 2).[14] To a degree, however, the candidates issued messages reflecting the concerns of their contributors by referring to their leanings on economic issues. For instance, a commercial for Judge Burnside said she "received no contributions from big insurance companies."[15] A fund-raising letter for Justice Stratton from the Republican attorney general called her the supreme court's most pro-business justice.

On a largely separate track were the independent campaigns, which strongly emphasized policy issues and which had a much harder edge than the candidates' own campaigns. A commercial supporting Justice Stratton implied that she was holding the line against frivolous lawsuits. Another commercial argued that the supreme court's support for medical malpractice plaintiffs was driving insurance costs up and forcing doctors out of their practices, thus making it difficult for pregnant women to find doctors for their deliveries. Two commercials attacked Justice Stratton for a vote to limit the liability of drug companies for damages from a drug taken by pregnant women and for her dissent from a ruling favorable to an injured worker. Another commercial charged that the Republican candidates put "large corporations ahead of working families," while the Democrats "will hold large corporations accountable for wrongdoing."[16]

Meanwhile, some medical doctors actively campaigned for the Republican candidates, holding a demonstration at the state capitol in the last week of the campaign and distributing literature to patients. On election night, O'Connor emphasized "the influence of the medical community" in bringing about her victory.[17]

Mindful of the backlash to the anti-Resnick campaign in 2000, the candidates generally distanced themselves from the television commercials produced by the independent campaigns and sometimes denounced even the commercials that supported them. Whatever the candidates might say about these commercials, however, they provided voters with more information about the candidates' positions on judicial issues than did the candidates' own messages.

News coverage of judicial contests typically reflects the scope and content of the campaigns, and this was true of the 1998 and 2002 supreme court contests. In both years, Ohio newspapers reported primarily what the candidates and their supporters said and did. Because much more was said and done in 2002, the newspapers reported considerably more about the contests in that year.

Table 8.3 summarizes stories about the supreme court contests in the *Cleveland Plain Dealer* and the *Columbus Dispatch,* the Ohio newspapers with the largest circulations. The table shows that these newspapers provided twice as many stories about the contests in 2002, even though there were only two contests rather than three. Some features of the coverage were similar in the two years. In both 1998 and 2002, stories routinely referred to candidates' current occupations and party affiliations, the latter noteworthy because of the absence of those affiliations on the ballot.

But in some other respects the content of stories differed considerably.

TABLE 8.3

Coverage of the 1998 and 2002 Ohio Supreme Court Contests in the Cleveland Plain Dealer *and* Columbus Dispatch

Newspaper	Candidate stories	Occupation	Background	Qualification	Party	Issue	Ideology	Group support	Campaign candidate	Evaluation independent
1998										
Columbus	25	23	6	12	21	11	0	9	4	1
Cleveland	33	27	8	23	32	11	5	24	1	1
Total	58	50	14	35	43	22	5	33	5	2
2002										
Columbus	51	45	16	7	43	23	0	30	12	21
Cleveland	66	58	5	9	64	22	2	46	13	23
Total	117	103	21	16	107	55	2	76	25	44

Note: "Candidate stories" counts a newspaper story once for each supreme court contest that is mentioned in the article. For each category of coverage, figures are based on candidate stories. Thus, in the *Columbus Dispatch* in 1998, there were 25 candidate stories, 23 of which referred to the candidate's occupation. In 1998, the total number of newspaper articles in which these stories appeared was 34—16 in the *Dispatch*, 18 in the *Plain Dealer*. In 2002, the total was 70—33 in the *Dispatch*, 37 in the *Plain Dealer*.

In the relatively quiet campaigns of 1998, the two newspapers gave greater attention to the candidates' backgrounds and qualifications. In 2002 a higher proportion of stories referred to policy issues and interest-group support for candidates. Although ideological differences underlay the issues and group lineup, few stories specifically referred to the candidates' positions on a liberal-conservative scale. Not surprisingly, the biggest difference was in the frequency with which newspapers reported evaluations of the campaigns, including their own—and especially the campaigns that were independent of the candidates. One of the most important things that the newspapers did was to report and amplify on the charges and countercharges that were contained in and spurred by campaign commercials.

Studying Voter Responses to the Contests

In 2002, Ohio voters were presented with far more information about their supreme court candidates than they had received in 1998. The content of the information they received gave them a better opportunity to respond to the candidates in terms of judicial issues and interest-group alignments. Thus, voters who wanted to choose candidates on the basis of their likely positions on judicial issues had a better basis for doing so in 2002.

The broad question to be considered is the extent to which differences in the volume and content of information in the two election years affected voter responses to the contests and candidates. First, we ask whether the higher volume of information in 2002 increased voter participation by reducing rolloff from the race for governor to the supreme court contests. Second, we ask whether the mix of people who chose to vote in supreme court contests was different in 2002 from 1998. Finally, we ask whether the influences on voters' choices of candidates differed from one election to the next.

To answer the first of these questions, we can look at the election returns themselves. To address the other two questions, we make use of two post-election Ohio Political Surveys, conducted at Ohio State University. The samples of interest are the 537 respondents who reported turning out to vote in the 1998 Ohio general election and the 547 people who said they voted in the 2002 general election. The voting question for each race took this basic form: "In the contest between Candidate A and Candidate B, did you vote for Candidate A or for Candidate B, or did you not vote in this contest?" (As part of a separate research project, in each survey some respondents were provided with information about candidates' parties in the questions asking them whether and how they had voted. In this chapter, respondents who were given party information for a particular contest are excluded from all analyses of voting in that contest.)

The results that we report from these surveys must be approached with some caution. For one thing, we are relying on self-reports of respondents' voting behavior. Self-reports are never entirely reliable, as respondents may forget what they did or they may lie.[18] This would be a major concern if our aim were to estimate rolloff and candidate shares of the vote accurately. But our focus is on the relationships between voting behavior and other variables, and there is less reason to think that misreports will lead to serious mistakes in inferences about those relationships. In any event, our task is to compare two election years, and there is no reason to think that voters' misreports would differ between the two years. Still, the fact that our analyses rely on self-reports should be taken into account.

For another thing, we will not be able to make as many direct comparisons of the 1998 and 2002 elections as we would like, because some important questions asked in one survey were not asked in the other or were asked in a different form. Finally, it is always necessary to bear in mind that we are comparing only two election years. Any differences or similarities we find may not hold for other campaign years.

Voter Participation: The Extent of Rolloff

In 1998 and 2002, the Ohio ballot included a contest for governor. In 1998 there was a Senate race as well. The contest for governor was closer in 1998, thus generating more interest. Because of that interest and the presence of a Senate race, turnout was somewhat higher in 1998—50 percent of registered voters, compared with 47 percent in 2002.[19]

Our first question is whether the relatively high level of information directed at voters in 2002 produced lower rolloff. Of the citizens who went to the polls and voted for governor, did a higher proportion choose candidates for the supreme court?

The answer is clearly yes. In 1998 the rolloff from the contest for governor to the supreme court contests was quite similar across the three judicial races, and it averaged 18 percent. (The Senate contest attracted more voters than the contest for governor; the average rolloff from Senate to supreme court contests was 20 percent.) That proportion was fairly typical for Ohio elections over the last two decades. In 2002, in contrast, the rolloff was 11 percent in the contest between Burnside and Stratton and 8 percent in the Black-O'Connor contest, for an average of 9 percent. That 9 percent average rolloff was the lowest in the period from 1984 to 2004. The two 2002 contests had the second and third lowest rolloff of any supreme court contests in that period, ranking behind only the very heated contest for chief justice in 1986.[20] The enormous difference in the volume of information from the campaigns and the news media had a very substantial effect on voters' participation in the supreme court races.

Voter Participation: Who Voted?

People who turn out to vote in elections are typically somewhat unrepresentative of the general population: for example, they tend to have higher incomes, be better educated, and be more interested in and knowledgeable about politics.[21] We would normally expect the smaller pool of people who go on to vote in judicial contests to be still less representative in some of these respects.[22] Realistically, high-visibility judicial campaigns cannot attract a pool of voters who look just like the general population, since only those who make it to the voting booth can participate in the judicial contests. But it is realistic to think that the gap between all voters and judicial-contest voters might be smaller in years where the judicial races are particularly visible. We explore that possibility in this section.

We begin by examining the relationships between the decision to vote in a judicial contest and five variables that were included in both surveys and that could be expected to influence the decision to vote. Our measure of voting comes from the question given earlier. Respondents who said they voted for one candidate or the other are coded as having voted (a score of 1). Those who said they did not vote or could not remember were coded as not voting (0). Respondents who refused to answer were excluded from the analysis.

The five explanatory variables of interest are:

1. *Strength of partisanship.* This is a four-point scale. People calling themselves independents without any party leanings score 0; independents who reported leaning toward one party or the other score 1; respondents who reported a party affiliation but did not feel a strong attachment to the party score 2; respondents who are strong party identifiers score 3. We expect that people with stronger party ties will tend to have a greater interest in all campaigns and tend to have greater access to political information, therefore will be more likely to vote.

2. *Strength of ideological leanings.* This is also measured on a four-point scale, created by folding a seven-point ideology scale onto itself: those assigning themselves a value of one or seven, the most liberal and most conservative positions, get scores of 3. People with a score of two or six on the measure of ideology receive a 2 on the measure of ideological strength. Those with a three or five on ideology score a 1 on ideological strength. Pure moderates (four on the seven-point scale) score 0. The logic here is the same as for partisanship.

3. *Income.* Our measure separates people into four quartiles, based on their reported incomes. Those in the highest 25 percent score 4, those in the lowest 25 percent score 1. We suspect that those with higher incomes will be more likely to vote in supreme court races— partly because they probably follow politics more closely in general, partly because they may see more connection between decisions of the supreme court and their own interests.

4. *Education.* Our measure of education has five values: (1) not a high school graduate; (2) high school graduate only; (3) some college; (4) college graduate; (5) some postgraduate education. We expect voting rates to be higher among people with more education, since they are likely to have more interest in and information about politics.

5. *Political knowledge.* For the same reason, we expect levels of political knowledge to be associated with participation in the judicial contests. Respondents in each survey were asked four questions about political facts, such as the party controlling the U.S. House of Representatives. Respondents get one point for each question answered correctly, yielding a measure with scores ranging from 0 to 4.[23]

We wish to compare voting in 1998 to voting in 2002. There were three separate contests in 1998 and two in 2002. One way to conduct our analyses would be to look at the six individual comparisons separately (first 1998 contest versus first 2002, first 1998 versus second 2002, etc.). But the result would be a blizzard of data that would require far more time and energy from our readers than we have a right to request. It makes more sense to combine information from the different contests into two sets of observations to compare, one for 1998 and one for 2002. The simplest way to do this would be to treat each voting decision in each year as a separate observation. But if we proceeded in this way, some respondents would be double-counted or even triple-counted, depending on what questions they were asked and how they answered them. This would cause serious problems for interpreting the data.

Our solution is to combine information from the different contests in each year, but to use information from only one contest per respondent. Specifically, if we have information for a particular respondent for only one contest, we use the information from that contest. If we have information from a respondent for more than one contest, we randomly choose which contest to count, so that in the end, the three 1998 contests each account for roughly the same number of observations in the 1998 data and the 2002 data is about equally divided between the two 2002 contests. To make sure that we are not missing anything important happening in individual races, we have carried out all the analyses discussed below (and more) for each of the contest-by-contest comparisons. But with the exception of the discussion in the next section of differences between the Suster-Pfeifer race and the other contests in 1998, we do not present results from those analyses here. Rather, we focus on results from the samples combining contests.

Turning to those results, the first question to ask for each variable is whether it has an effect on rolloff in either election year. If not, there is no point in exploring it further. If it does, then we can look for differences in its effects across years.

TABLE 8.4
*Voting in 1998 and 2002 Ohio Supreme Court Contests,
by Strength of Party Identification*

	Strength of party identification			
	No preference	*Independent leaner*	*Weak partisan*	*Strong partisan*
Percentage voting	55.0	59.3	65.9	61.2
Total number of respondents	60	189	229	314

Note: Percentages are of those respondents who reported going to the polls.

TABLE 8.5
*Voting in 1998 and 2002 Ohio Supreme Court Contests,
by Strength of Ideological Identification*

	Strength of ideological identification			
	Weak	*Fairly weak*	*Fairly strong*	*Strong*
Percentage voting	58.3	68.4	58.1	59.6
Total number of respondents	132	275	255	94

Note: Percentages are of those respondents who reported going to the polls.

TABLE 8.6
Voting in 1998 and 2002 Ohio Supreme Court Contests, by Income

	Income			
	Lowest quartile	*Second quartile*	*Third quartile*	*Highest quartile*
Percentage voting	58.9	61.5	57.8	68.0
Total number of respondents	175	174	180	181

Note: Percentages are of those respondents who reported going to the polls.

As Tables 8.4, 8.5, and 8.6 show, strength of partisanship, strength of ideology, and income appear to have little effect on the decision whether to vote in judicial contests once at the voting booth. Note, for instance, that strong party identifiers vote at marginally lower rates than weak party identifiers and only slightly higher rates than pure independents.

Political knowledge and education both had significant effects on voting, even when both are included in a logistic regression model so that the influence of the other variable is controlled for. To avoid cluttering this chapter with tables, we will not show those results but instead will proceed directly to comparisons between 1998 and 2002. The results for political knowledge, shown in Table 8.7, are striking. Voting rates are substantially higher in 2002 at all levels of political knowledge, but the differences between 1998 and 2002 are far greater at lower levels of political knowledge. To take one comparison, among respondents able to answer all four political knowledge questions correctly, the percentage voting in a 2002 contest

TABLE 8.7
*Percentage Voting in 1998 and 2002 Ohio Supreme Court Contests at
Different Levels of Political Knowledge*

	0 correct	1 correct	2 correct	3 correct	4 correct	Overall
1998	23.1	41.4	46.0	50.8	70.0	50.7 ($N = 408$)
2002	66.7	67.1	70.9	72.8	86.8	73.0 ($N = 385$)
1998–2002 increase	43.6	26.3	24.9	22.0	16.8	

Note: Percentages are of those respondents who reported going to the polls.

TABLE 8.8
*Percentage Voting in 1998 and 2002 Ohio Supreme Court Contests at
Different Levels of Education*

	Some high school	High school grad	Some college	College grad	Postgraduate	Overall
1998	35.3	45.8	46.0	57.1	64.6	50.7 ($N = 408$)
2002	52.9	72.2	73.2	72.4	81.0	73.0 ($N = 385$)
1998–2002 increase	17.6	26.4	27.2	15.3	16.4	

Note: Percentages are of those respondents who reported going to the polls.

is about 17 percentage points higher than the percentage voting in a 1998 election; among respondents unable to answer any questions correctly, the difference between 1998 and 2002 is more than 43 percentage points. Another way to look at this is that the gap in participation rates between those with the least information and those with the most is much smaller in 2002 (20.1 percentage points) than in 1998 (46.9 percentage points). This is strong evidence that, in terms of political knowledge, the pool of voters in the more-visible judicial contests is more representative of the general population than the pool of voters in the less-visible contests.

The story told by the results for education, shown in Table 8.8, is neither quite the same nor quite as clear, but it is still intriguing. The 1998–2002 voting gap is about the same (roughly 17 percentage points) for respondents with the least education as for those with the most. But if we ignore the first column of figures, we see a pattern similar to the one observed for political knowledge. The 1998–2002 gap is above 26 percentage points for respondents who finished with a high school diploma and those who took some college classes, below 17 for those with college degrees. Here again is evidence—not so strong this time—that high-information contests increase voting more among those who are less likely to vote in typical judicial elections, making the pool of voters a better reflection of the general population.

We are inclined to believe that the differences in rolloff and patterns of rolloff found here are attributable to the greater amount of information available to voters in 2002. But other explanations are possible. For instance, the 2002 campaign surely made people more aware of the state supreme court contests than they were in 1998 and might have made the contests seem more important. Voting could have increased for these reasons, regardless of the amount of information voters possessed. We could feel surer of our interpretation if we had evidence that (a) possession of information about candidates had a powerful influence on the decision to vote and (b) Ohioans who went to the polls had more information about candidates in 2002 than in 1998. As we will show shortly, there is strong evidence for the importance of candidate information. Unfortunately, because of major differences between the candidate information questions asked in the 1998 and 2002 surveys, we cannot draw any conclusions about the relative levels of voter information in the two years.

In 1998, for each race, respondents were asked either to identify the candidates' parties or identify which one candidate of the two was the incumbent. The 2002 questions were harder to answer correctly in two ways. First, they asked respondents about either candidates' ideologies or whether labor or business groups had supported them, information that is typically harder to come by. Second, the 2002 survey asked about each candidate separately. So, for instance, a respondent who recalled that Maureen O'Connor was aided by business groups but not that Tim Black got support from labor would not get full credit for contest information in 2002, whereas a 1998 respondent who recalled that Thomas Moyer was a Republican could answer the contest information question correctly without knowing anything about Gary Tyack.

With these caveats in mind, we can consider what the data show, beginning in 1998. In the Suster-Pfeifer race, about 27 percent of respondents were able to identify the candidates' parties; 43 percent knew that Pfeifer was the incumbent. (In this instance and all others discussed here, a large majority of those not answering correctly said "Don't Know"; few gave wrong answers.) In the Sweeney-Powell race, 24 percent correctly identified Sweeney as a Democrat, and 38 percent knew he was the incumbent. In the chief justice race, 29 percent of respondents got the parties right, and 41 percent identified the incumbent.

Turning to 2002, 8 percent (21 of 262) of respondents knew that Black had been supported by labor groups and O'Connor by business. Another 11 percent (28) answered correctly for one candidate but gave no answer for the second. (A few others got one candidate right and one wrong. We suspect that most such combinations arise from guessing, so we do not count them as correct.) So 8 percent of respondents were entirely correct, and 19 percent had at least partial information about outside support for the candidates. For the other 2002 contest, respondents were asked about ideology. Arguably the best answers were that Stratton was conservative and Burnside was either moderate or liberal. But there are no unassailable grounds for rejecting the view that Stratton was moderate. What we can insist on to label a respondent as well informed is that he or she recognized that Stratton was to Burnside's ideological right. Counting as correct any combination in which Stratton was characterized as conservative and Burnside as moderate or liberal or in which Stratton was characterized as moderate and Burnside as liberal, we find a correct response rate of about 18 percent (48 of 271).[24]

Because the 2002 questions were harder to answer correctly, had we found a similar or higher rate of correct answers in 2002, it would have been powerful evidence that Ohioans learned more about the candidates in the more visible election of the two elections. The lower rates that we actually found are inconclusive.

However, we can still use the measures to test the importance of campaign information. In each of the five contests, campaign information has a strong effect on voter participation. In fact, the effect of campaign information in multivariate analyses is the largest of any variables we have investigated. A few numbers are enough to illustrate. In an analysis of the combined 1998 elections, the voting rate in judicial elections among those able to answer the pertinent candidate information question correctly, as described above, is 38 percentage points higher (77.5 vs. 39.6) than among those unable to answer correctly. In 2002, the gap is 26.5 points (94.5 vs. 68.0). Recall that these comparisons, like all others in this chapter, include only respondents who claimed that they turned out to vote in the general election.

Because the effect of campaign information on voting is so powerful, it is hard to imagine that greater access to information did not have an important role in the higher participation rates of 2002. But without direct evidence that voters actually knew more in 2002, we cannot consider the issue settled.

Influences on Voters' Choices

So far we have found differences between 1998 and 2002 in the rates of participation in judicial elections and, to an extent, in the patterns of participation across groups. Were there also important differences between the two elections in the factors influencing voters' choices of candidates? To answer this question, we need to focus on possible influences that could have significant implications for thinking about methods of judicial selection. Four variables that were measured in both surveys satisfy this criterion: party identification, ideology, income, and ratings of the Ohio Supreme Court.[25]

Our expectations for three of these variables are straightforward. Voting on the basis of ideology, one's views of the current Ohio Supreme Court, or one's economic interests (as reflected in income) requires information that is not available to many voters in low-information races. Since more information was available in 2002 than 1998, if there is any difference in the strength of these voting influences across the elections, it should be that they are stronger in 2002.

Making a prediction for party identification is not as simple. We suspect that party identification, too, had a stronger effect on voting in 2002 than 1998, for the simple reason that many voters in judicial contests (and other elections) like to vote for the candidate from the party he or she prefers. The more voters there are who know the candidates' party affiliations, the more there are who can vote their party preferences. But there are plausible alternatives. It might be that when voters learn more about candidates, they are less prone to rely on party information, because they can now vote on the basis of more substantive concerns such as ideology or economic interests. So we could find that party identification mattered less in 2002. Or the two kinds of information usage might cancel each other out, so that no change is evident.

Party identification is measured on a five-point scale, with strong Democrats scored 1, strong Republicans scored 5, and independents scored 3. Ideology is a seven-point scale, with 1 most liberal and 7 most conservative. For income, as in our analysis of participation, we divided respondents into four quartiles. The measure of Ohio Supreme Court ratings was created by combining slightly different questions that were asked of different respondents into one three-point scale, where 1 is a low rating, 2 is medium, and 3 is high. The dependent variable for this set of analyses is whether the respondent voted for the Republican candidate (1) or the Democratic candidate (0).

The effects of income and supreme court ratings do not approach statistically significant levels in any contest or set of contests. Before we discard these variables, it is important to consider the possibility that the effects of greater information are limited to a certain set of people who are more likely to receive that information. Even in presidential elections, some voters know far more than others—and even highly visible judicial contests do not rise to the level of presidential contests. The additional information they provide likely reaches only more aware and interested voters. For this reason, we examined our data to see whether income or court ratings affected the votes of better-educated or more-informed voters. They did not. Let us focus, then, on ideology and party.

The picture for ideology is more complicated. Beginning by considering all respondents together, we find that ideology, taken alone, has fairly strong positive effects in each campaign year—in fact, in each contest except the Suster-Pfeifer race in 1998. But once we control for party identification (in a logistic regression), ideology is no longer significant. So we cannot conclude that ideology mattered more in 2002 than 1998 for voters generally. However, when we isolate different groups of voters, we do find a significant difference, whether or not we include votes from the Suster-Pfeifer race. (We will discuss the complications associated with this contest shortly.) Among voters who answered all four political knowledge questions correctly, even controlling for party, ideology has a stronger effect on voting in 2002.

We will illustrate using figures from the logit model. Logit results allow one to estimate the probability of a vote for one candidate or the change in that probability associated with a change in one or more of the independent variables. Here, using data from all of the contests except Suster-Pfeifer, we hold party constant by limiting consideration to independents and ask how the probability of voting for the Republican candidate is expected to change as we move from someone scoring a 2 on ideology to someone scoring a 6. The estimate for 1998 voters is 0.13; that is, fairly strong conservatives should be about 13 percentage points more likely to vote for the Republican than fairly strong liberals. The estimate for 2002 voters is much higher, 59 percentage points.[26] As interesting as this result it, we should note that we do not find this same effect for ideology at any of the higher levels of education, indicating that the result should be treated with some caution.

TABLE 8.9

*Proportion of Voters Choosing Republican Ohio Supreme Court Candidates,
by Party Identification*

Party identification	1998	2002
Strong Republican	71.4	81.2
Weak/Leaning Republican	66.7	67.8
Independent	60.0	65.0
Weak/Leaning Democrat	65.3	47.6
Strong Democrat	52.8	40.0
Difference between strong Republicans and strong Democrats	18.6	41.2

Note: For 1998, $N = 286$; for 2002, $N = 298$.

TABLE 8.10

*Proportion of Voters Choosing Republican Ohio Supreme Court Candidates,
by Party Identification, Omitting Votes in the Suster/Pfeifer Contest in 1998*

Party identification	1998	2002
Strong Republican	77.1	81.2
Weak/Leaning Republican	55.7	67.8
Independent	56.5	65.0
Weak/Leaning Democrat	38.8	47.6
Strong Democrat	29.2	40.0
Difference between strong Republicans and strong Democrats	47.9	41.2

Note: For 1998, $N = 260$; for 2002, $N = 298$.

A first look at differences between 1998 and 2002 in the effect of party identification yields interesting results, as shown in Table 8.9. Party seems to matter much more in 2002. For instance, the difference between strong Republicans and strong Democrats in support for Republican candidates is about 41 percentage points in 2002 versus almost 19 percentage points in 1998. A logit model in which we test for the difference in the effect of party identification between 1998 and 2002 confirms that this difference is statistically significant.[27] On closer inspection, the story is a bit more complicated. When we examine contests individually, we find that party identification has a strong effect on voting for the Republican candidate in four of the five elections. In the Suster-Pfeifer contest, it has no effect at all.

Table 8.10 is the same as Table 8.9, except that now all Suster-Pfeifer votes are eliminated from the analysis. Note how similar the results for 1998 and 2002 now are. In fact, now the difference between strong Democrats and strong Republicans is actually slightly greater (about 48 percentage points) in 1998 than in 2002.

The lesson of these results seems clear: the Suster-Pfeifer contest was different from all of the others and is responsible for the observed differences between 1998 and 2002. There are two reasonable ways to interpret this finding. One is that information differences across campaigns have no role in our results for vote choice; the Suster-Pfeifer contest was simply a strange race, perhaps because of the ambivalence of some party leaders toward their own candidate, and the fact that it occurred in 1998 is just coincidence. The other interpretation accepts the premise that the Suster-Pfeifer race was unusual, perhaps more confusing or less interesting than others, but holds that had it occurred in the 2002 environment, the greater visibility of the race could have overcome some of its deficiencies and allowed more voters to base their votes on the same criteria they employed in other races. In a sense, the idea behind this interpretation is that a low-information campaign climate is an enabling condition that allows confusing or uninteresting races to remain so.

The conclusions that we can draw about the determinants of voters' choices between the candidates in 1998 and 2002 depend in part on which of these interpretations is more appropriate. However, it seems clear that, for the electorate as a whole, those determinants did not differ radically between the two election years. The emphasis given to economic policy issues in the 2002 campaigns might have elevated the importance of voters' ideological positions as a basis for their choices. With the apparent exception of one highly knowledgeable group of voters, however, it did not.

Similarly, if one unusual 1998 contest is left aside, the influence of voters' party identifications on their choices was about the same in 1998 and 2002. As suggested earlier, the reasons for party-line voting might have differed between the two years. Voters in 1998, lacking much information about the candidates, may have voted for the candidates of their own party (if they could identify the candidates' affiliations) simply because no other basis for decision was available. In contrast, voters in 2002 might have had other bases for their choices, but the greater availability of information about the candidates' party affiliations made it easier for voters to cast party-line votes. However, the lack of impact for voters' economic status and their ratings of the Ohio Supreme Court and the similar impact of ideology across the two election years weigh against this interpretation. In any event, the quite different setting of the 2002 elections did not greatly change the extent of partisan voting.

Conclusions

For many people who care about the courts, changes in the character of judicial elections that have occurred in the past decade are a cause for concern. Some sources of that concern are independent of voters' reactions to election campaigns. One example is the possible effects of campaign contributions on judges' behavior as decisionmakers. But most potential effects of the more visible and issue-oriented campaigns that have become more common depend at least in part on the voters. And how the voters react to those campaigns can help in assessing the benefits and drawbacks of the new-style campaigns.

The contrast between the 1998 and 2002 contests for the Ohio Supreme Court gave us an opportunity to probe these issues. Like most judicial elections, the three 1998 contests were relatively quiet: the campaigns were relatively small in scale, and coverage by the news media was limited. In contrast, the two 2002 contests featured large-scale campaigns and an unusual level of media coverage. Moreover, the campaigns and the media in 2002 told voters far more about how the candidates might decide cases than they did in 1998.

As we have noted, there are substantial limits to what can be concluded from our study of voters in the two election years. Within those limits, however, the findings are noteworthy. The primary effect of the higher levels of information available in 2002 was on participation in the supreme court contests. The election returns themselves show a dramatic difference between the two years: rolloff from the gubernatorial contest to the supreme court contests was twice as high in 1998 as it was in 2002. A good many people who ordinarily would skip the judicial races when they were in the voting booth chose not to skip them in 2002.

Those people were not a random sample of voters. Rather, our surveys showed, they were disproportionately among those with limited political knowledge. To a lesser degree, they tended to have low levels of education. One could conclude that this effect was desirable (in that it made the judicial electorate in 2002 more representative of the citizenry) or undesirable (in that it brought more people with limited knowledge into the choice of judges). Whatever one's evaluation of the effect, the set of people who voted for supreme court candidates in 2002 was somewhat different from the set in 1998.

In contrast with patterns of participation, the determinants of choices between the candidates did not seem to differ very much between the two election years. On the whole, voters' party identifications had similar effects in 1998 and 2002. The 2002 campaigns had the potential to make voters' economic status and their ideological orientations more salient to their choices, but they did not. While our probe of the determinants of the vote was limited by the content of the election surveys, our findings suggest that the differences in scale and content of the campaigns had no radical effect on how voters chose between candidates.

If this conclusion is accurate, what we learned about voters' knowledge of the candidates in 2002 helps to explain it. Only one in five of the respondents correctly identified Janet Burnside as more liberal than Evelyn Stratton, and some of those responses undoubtedly were lucky guesses. Only one in ten correctly indicated that Tim Black was supported by labor groups and Maureen O'Connor by business.

The voters should not be condemned for their lack of knowledge about these matters, since fairly close attention to the judicial campaigns and (especially for ideology) a degree of political sophistication was required to gain that knowledge. However, that lack of knowledge underlines the limits in what the 2002 campaigns communicated to voters. The candidates' campaigns, the independent campaigns, and coverage of both by the news media could convey to the voters that the supreme court contests were important. They were not so successful in conveying *why* the contests were important.

This is not always the case. Even in the absence of surveys, we have good reason to conclude that some campaigns against judicial incumbents effectively inform voters of the incumbent's unpopular position on the death penalty.[28] But the more complicated messages that the candidates and their supporters presented in 2002 are not as easy to communicate.

Taken as a whole, our findings raise the possibility that the large-scale judicial campaigns of recent years are not quite as consequential as some observers have thought. Perhaps the most important lesson of this study is that those consequences should not be taken for granted. Especially when our concern is the influence of campaigns on the voters, that influence needs to be probed rather than assumed.

NOTES

1. For conducting surveys of Ohio voters and providing data from those surveys, we are grateful to the Survey Research Center, Department of Political Sci-

ence, and College of Social and Behavioral Sciences at Ohio State University and to Herbert Weisberg, Dean Lacy, and Matthew Courser. We appreciate Jim Gibson's comments on a draft of this chapter.

2. A good summary of current developments in changes in the character of judicial elections is in Goldberg et al., *New Politics of Judicial Elections 2004*.

3. For instance, Reid, "Politicization of Judicial Retention Elections," and Geyh, "Why Judicial Elections Stink."

4. In an oft-quoted remark, legal scholar Roy Schotland said in 1988 that "judicial campaigns are getting noisier, nastier, and costlier" (quoted in Woodbury, "Is Texas Justice for Sale?").

5. Byrne and Pueschel, "But Who Should I Vote for For County Coroner?"; Mueller, "Choosing among 133 Candidates."

6. Wattenberg et al., "How Voting Is Like Taking an SAT Test." Rolloff in state supreme court elections is also discussed in Dubois, "Voter Turnout in State Judicial Elections."

7. McDermott, "Voting Cues in Low-Information Elections."

8. Dubois, "Voting Cues in Nonpartisan Trial Court Elections." See also Schaffner et al., "Teams without Uniforms."

9. Elections to the Ohio Supreme Court in earlier eras are discussed in Barber, "Judicial Politics in Ohio," and Tarr and Porter, *State Supreme Courts in State and Nation*.

10. The 2000 contests are discussed in Glaberson, "Spirited Campaign for Ohio Court," and Bradshaw, "Special-Interest Money Dominates O'Donnell-Resnick Race."

11. Bischoff, "Races for the Court Raised Millions."

12. Goldberg and Sanchez, *New Politics of Judicial Elections 2002*, p. 8.

13. *DeRolph v. State*, 728 N.E.2d 993 (Ohio 2000).

14. *Republican Party of Minnesota v. White*, 536 U.S. 765 (2002).

15. Quoted in Craig, "Other Ad Campaigns."

16. Quoted in Richey, "GOP: Justice Race TV Ad 'Misleading.'"

17. Stratton added that "their efforts will pay off," which she later agreed was a poor choice of words ("Cheers and Jeers").

18. Weisberg, *Total Survey Error Approach*, ch. 5. Certainly voters who are interviewed after an election might forget some of what they knew on election day. But we found that the proportions of voters who correctly recalled information about the supreme court candidates declined only slightly between the interviews conducted shortly after the election and those conducted later.

19. All data on voter participation in this section are taken from *Ohio Election Statistics*, compiled by the office of the Ohio Secretary of State each two years.

20. It is difficult to compare rolloff between years with and without presidential contests. In presidential years, many voters appear at the polls with an interest only in the presidential contest, so rolloff to offices such as judgeships is

substantially higher than in other election years. In 2000, another year with a high level of information about the supreme court candidates, the average rolloff from the presidential contest to the supreme court contests was 16 percent. That was the lowest rolloff of any presidential year in the 1984–2004 period.

21. Leighley and Nagler, "Socioeconomic Class Bias in Turnout"; Shields and Goidel, "Participation Rates, Socioeconomic Class Biases, and Congressional Elections"; Timpone, "Ties That Bind."

22. Wattenberg et al., "How Voting Is Like Taking an SAT Test," pp. 243–247.

23. The other questions are whose responsibility it is to determine if a law is constitutional, which party is more liberal, and what job or political office is held by William Rehnquist.

24. Because information about the candidates' party affiliations would affect respondents' responses to these questions, we excluded from these figures respondents whom we informed of the candidates' affiliations.

25. On the determinants of voters' choices between candidates, see Flanigan and Zingale, *Political Behavior of the American Electorate,* ch. 8.

26. The gap between 1998 and 2002 is slightly greater if we include the Suster-Pfeifer contest. The changes in predicted probabilities were calculated using the CLARIFY program in Stata, developed by Michael Tomz, Jason Wittenberg, and Gary King (King et al., "Making the Most of Statistical Analyses"). Standard errors for the estimates are 0.20 for 1998 voters and 0.16 for 2002 voters.

27. Specifically, we analyzed a logit model that included an interactive term, Party ID x 2002.

28. Reid, "Politicization of Judicial Retention Elections."

Chapter 9

Competition as Accountability in State Supreme Court Elections

Melinda Gann Hall

This chapter examines the exact nature of electoral competition in all 877 supreme court elections from 1980 through 2000 in the thirty-eight states using partisan, nonpartisan, or retention elections to staff their high court benches.[1] The primary goal of this inquiry is to address one fundamental question: Can supreme court elections serve to create important linkages between citizens and the bench? In other words, do judicial elections appear to have any of the qualities necessary to promote the accountability function inherent in elections?

This issue is enormously complex. Not only can accountability can be defined in numerous ways, accountability is not necessarily dependent on elections. Consider, for example, a judge appointed to the bench for a lifetime term who, quite apart from ever having faced voters to become a judge or ever needing to seek voter approval to continue in office, nonetheless takes public opinion into account when deciding the most controversial political issues embodied in the cases being litigated. Such a situation might be the product of the judge's previous career experiences in elective office outside the judiciary, or it might reflect a broader role orientation toward politics that places a high priority on representation in public institutions, including courts.

Generally, however, accountability is equated with citizen control of the bench through elections in two fundamental ways. First, accountability is manifested simply by virtue of the fact that citizens have formal control over who holds office, including the ability to oust sitting judges who fail to meet citizen expectations. Thus, this highly symbolic form of accountability is present in any situation where judges must seek voter approval to retain their seats, regardless of any other features of these contests.

Second, accountability can be seen as a product of electoral competition, produced by the willingness of challengers to enter the electoral arena and the propensity of the electorate not to give their full support to incumbents. Indeed, there is perhaps no better device for forging linkages between citizens and government. Electoral competition enhances the ability of voters to voice disapproval of incumbents and remove unpopular ones, thereby bringing the judiciary better in line with citizen preferences. Moreover, competition serves to structure the decisions of judges once on the bench when judges' preferences are inconsistent with those of their constituencies.

Consider first the effect of challengers and electoral coalition size on democratic incentives. Without challengers in nonpartisan and partisan elections, incumbents cannot be defeated. Thus, the symbolic ideal of citizen control over the composition of the bench cannot be realized in its most basic element under these conditions, regardless of the extent to which the electorate disapproves of the incumbent. Similarly, even when incumbents win, voters in the absence of challengers cannot signal incumbents that there are preferred alternatives for sizeable proportions of the electorate. Instead, incumbents, however unworthy, are reelected with 100 percent of the vote.

Further, heated campaigns between opponents stimulate voter interest, provide information about candidate qualifications, and mobilize the electorate to vote.[2] Without the excitement generated by hard-fought campaigns from contending candidates, information upon which to cast votes is poor, and voters are disinterested and unmotivated to participate. Finally, slim margins of victory produced by close races between candidates increase the likelihood of future electoral challenge, setting into motion another cycle to enhance the accountability function.[3] Thus, the presence of challengers, which are necessary to produce narrow vote margins for incumbents and electorate defeats, become important mechanisms for promoting accountability.

In retention elections, the functional equivalent of challengers is the ever-present ballot option not to retain. In effect, retention elections always provide choice which, in turn, has the potential to produce the same tight margins and defeats as nonpartisan and partisan elections. Of course, campaigns in this context are directed exclusively toward the incumbent rather than on the relative merits of the challengers and incumbent.

From a different perspective, the process of having to face voters, particularly under competitive electoral conditions, affects judicial decisions by creating incentives for judges to pay attention to citizen preferences when deciding highly visible and publicly salient issues.[4] In effect, the extent to which incumbents are challenged in their bids for reelection and the resulting degree of support given to incumbents by voters become important devices for producing public policies that better represent the citizenry. Indeed, even in retention elections where challengers are precluded, large percentages of votes not to retain the incumbent can serve to strengthen the important nexus between the electorate and the bench.

Of course, elected public officials, including judges, can fear serious challenge and ultimate defeat even if there is no realistic possibility of either event occurring. For example, the odds of being ousted from the United States House of Representatives are not high. From 1980 through 2000, only 246 of 4,354 House incumbents seeking reelection were defeated, for an overall defeat rate of 5.6 percent.[5] However, we know that House members vigorously engage in numerous activities to improve their prospects for reelection, including the use of voting strategies to appease their constituencies.[6] Thus, the reality of electoral competition should serve as a strong incentive for public officials to be responsive to citizen preferences and should facilitate meaningful choices by the electorate about the composition of political institutions.

Moreover, each of the judicial election systems is designed to produce varying levels of electoral accountability. Retention elections, which preclude challengers and partisan labels for incumbents, are least attached to the principles of accountability by formal design. Nonpartisan elections are somewhere between retention elections and partisan elections by allowing challengers but no partisan labels for candidates. Finally, partisan elections are the same in form to elections for the political branches of government and thus have the greatest capacity to connect citizens to the bench, at least in theory.

Recognizing this inextricable linkage between electoral competition and accountability and the variations inherent in the different types of judicial elections, this chapter seeks to ascertain the extent to which challengers take on incumbents and the degree to which voters support them, both in terms of the proportions of the vote cast in favor of incumbents and in the extent to which incumbents are unseated. Without challengers in nonpartisan and partisan elections, voters cannot affect the composition of the bench, even though the electorate formally has control over the institution. Likewise, in all elections, if the electorate consistently favors incumbents with significant proportions of the vote, we have at least some reason to question whether voters are seeking to control the selection process, and we know that incumbents chosen under these conditions will have no incentive to defer to their constituencies on those issues where such strategies otherwise would be prudent for minimizing future opposition and retaining office.

Why the need to ask these fundamental questions? Remarkably, there have been few empirical studies of judicial elections, and the only study national in scope of state supreme courts ends with the 1994 elections.[7] Therefore, it is imperative to update this work, especially with a view toward recent trends.

More importantly, however, the prevailing wisdom about these contests, particularly partisan elections which most often are disfavored by court reform advocates, is that incumbents are "rarely challenged and infrequently defeated"[8] or, more broadly, that judicial elections are "uniquely different"[9] and "inadequate to promote judicial accountability."[10] Indeed, the alleged failure to achieve the accountability function is "the most fundamental and damning of the criticisms leveled against popular judicial elections."[11] These claims, which go the heart of the debate over judicial selection, merit careful scientific scrutiny.

In addressing these claims, I begin by acknowledging that the issues surrounding the merits or demerits of elections are exceptionally complicated and cannot be reduced to a single set of arguments or one simple set of tests. This is particularly true of controversies involving accountability. Some might start with the proposition that electoral accountability is a highly undesirable goal for the judiciary. Thus, under no conditions would elections, especially those highly competitive, be an acceptable method of judicial selection. At the same time, others might think that accountability is important only to the extent that it does not interfere with the legitimacy of the institution or the impartiality of judges. Thus, issues like campaign financing become paramount concerns in choosing among alternative selection systems using this criterion. Finally, others might believe that judges are elected public officials who should be held to the same standards of review as all other officeholders, particularly given the discretion inherent in appellate decisionmaking and the policymaking function of courts. In this context, competitive elections become the only effective means for staffing the state court bench.

This chapter does not address these intensely divisive issues surrounding the desirability of electoral accountability for the American judiciary or offer any overall judgments about whether elections are an appropriate means for selecting judges. Instead, I examine one significant portion of the case underlying arguments about accountability and ask whether the critics' claims are empirically sound. The results of this inquiry then can be included with all other relevant evidence to make better-informed choices in the judicial selection debate.

Overall, this chapter proceeds from a basic set of assumptions, grounded firmly in the larger body of scientific literature about the nature of courts and judicial decisionmaking.[12] First and foremost is the proposition that courts are vitally important political institutions with the awesome power to resolve some of the most significant and divisive issues on the American political agenda, and in deciding these questions judges have substantial discretion. Moreover, judges have well-developed political preferences and seek to enact these preferences into public policy, while clearly understanding the effect of their decisions on the distribution of wealth and power in the United States. Third, judges, like all other political actors, are constrained in their ability to make decisions solely on the basis of their preferences. Among these constraints are the law relevant to each case, forces defining the state political environment, and the institutional arrangements surrounding the court that serve to structure the range of opportunities available to judges, as well as the sanctions possible against them. Particularly important among these is selection method. Finally, there is no perfect system for staffing the bench. Appointive systems can be plagued by elitism, cronyism, and intense partisanship; legislative selection systems can inhibit the exercise judicial review,[13] and election systems can interject representative politics into the judicial decisionmaking process.[14] In short, each selection system has advantages and disadvantages and, in large measure, reflects underlying preferences about who should control access to the bench and monitor judicial performance, along with beliefs about the role of the judiciary in American democracy.

Measuring Electoral Competition

Because of the importance of electoral competition to the accountability function, this chapter evaluates state supreme court elections to assess the extent to which competition is evidenced in these races. Specifically, these elections are evaluated using three separate measures of competitiveness:

TABLE 9.1
Various Indicators of Competition (as Percentages) in the
U.S. House of Representatives, 1980–2000

Year	Incumbents challenged	Average vote for incumbents	Defeat rates
1980	86.9	65.5	9.3
1982	86.0	64.1	9.9
1984	83.7	65.9	4.6
1986	81.9	68.2	2.0
1988	80.9	68.2	1.7
1990	79.1	63.5	3.9
1992	91.0	63.1	11.7
1994	86.6	62.8	9.8
1996	95.8	63.3	6.0
1998	76.6	63.3	1.7
2000	85.0	65.1	2.2
Total	84.9	64.8	5.6 (246/4,354)

Note: These data are taken from Abramson et al., *Change and Continuity in the 2004 Elections*. Average vote for incumbents are for contested elections only. Data for all elections are not available.

the presence of challengers, the narrowness of vote margins, and electoral defeats. In doing so, elections in which incumbents are seeking reelection are analyzed separately from open seat races. Theoretically, the focus of greatest interest in this chapter is on incumbent accountability, particularly with respect to challenger and voter responses to their reelection bids, rather than on how justices gain accession to the bench when incumbents are not running. Practically speaking, open seat races are highly competitive and to include these elections would unduly inflate competition rates.[15]

Overall, the standard for evaluating whether conditions for accountability are evidenced in state supreme court elections is this: Do significant proportions of the justices seeking reelection face challengers, win by tight margins, or lose their seats? The critical baseline used in this chapter to gauge these patterns will be elections to the U.S. House of Representatives, arguably the most accountable institution by function in the nation.

To begin this exploration of competition and accountability, Table 9.1 presents information about the extent to which House members seeking reelection from 1980 through 2000 were challenged, built sizable electoral coalitions, or lost their seats. Looking first at contestation, we see that most House members faced challengers during this period. The overall contestation rate for the two decades is 84.9 percent. However, these rates vary somewhat over time. Contestation rates were at their lowest at 76.6 percent in 1998, compared with the overall high of 95.8 percent just two years earlier, for a difference of 19.2 percent. Moreover, while most House members were forced to confront challengers in their bids for reelection, about one of every six did not.

Similarly, as Table 9.1 demonstrates, the average percentage of the vote received by House incumbents from 1980 through 2000 was just under 65 percent, an average that remains relatively consistent over time. The difference between extremes (62.8 percent to 68.2 percent) is only 5.4 percent. However, these figures exclude uncontested races, or seats won with 100 percent of the vote. To include these races would increase average vote margins significantly, particularly in years when contestation was below average.

Finally, as Table 9.1 illustrates, while some House members seeking re-election were ousted from office from 1980 through 2000, the seats were safe about 94 percent of the time. As with contestation, however, defeat rates vary over time, from 1.7 percent to 11.7 percent.

Evidence about Electoral Competition in State Supreme Courts

With these figures for the U.S. House of Representatives firmly in mind, consider state supreme court elections, beginning with the presence of challengers in these races. Table 9.2 presents these data for nonpartisan and partisan elections. Retention elections are excluded because they always preclude challengers.

TABLE 9.2
State Supreme Court Incumbents Challenged for Reelection,
by Type of Election System, 1980–2000

Year	Nonpartisan elections			Partisan elections			All elections		
	Running N	Challenged %	N	Running N	Challenged %	N	Running N	Challenged %	N
1980	23	56.5	13	19	52.6	10	42	54.8	23
1982	20	60.0	12	24	41.7	10	44	50.0	22
1984	19	42.1	8	16	56.3	9	35	48.6	17
1986	24	16.7	4	18	61.1	11	42	35.7	15
1988	15	33.3	5	19	73.7	14	34	55.9	19
1990	24	37.5	9	18	72.2	13	42	52.4	22
1992	22	54.5	12	20	65.0	13	42	59.5	25
1994	17	52.9	9	11	81.8	9	28	64.3	18
1996	23	65.2	15	11	100.0	11	34	76.5	26
1998	17	70.6	12	12	91.7	11	29	79.3	23
2000	25	68.0	17	11	90.9	10	36	75.0	27
Total	229	50.7	116	179	67.6	121	408	58.1	237

Contestation in State Supreme Court Elections

As Table 9.2 indicates, state supreme court justices running for reelection from 1980 through 2000 were more likely than not to face challengers in their bids for reelection, although certainly not at the levels observed for the House of Representatives during this period. While the overall contestation rate in the House was 84.9 percent, the same rate in supreme courts was only 58.1 percent. However, the results are mixed with respect to partisan supreme court elections, which most closely resemble House elections in form. In 1988, 1990, and 1994, contestation rates in partisan supreme court elections come close to those for the House, and, beginning in 1996, actually exceeded them. In contrast, only the 1998 results in nonpartisan elections resemble those for the House.

In fact, contestation in supreme court elections is increasing. In the last three election cycles examined in this chapter (1996, 1998, and 2000), at least three of every four incumbents up for reelection faced the possibility of being ousted from office by challengers. Thus, broadly speaking, while a sizable proportion of justices have no chance of being unseated in partisan and nonpartisan elections, the large majority does, particularly in recent years.

Moreover, as Table 9.2 reveals, competition in the form of contestation has ebbed and flowed over time, ranging from an overall low of 35.7 percent in 1986 to a high of 79.3 percent in 1998. In fact, there have been two election cycles (1984 and 1986) in which most justices seeking reelection were not challenged.

These temporal variations also are evident within election systems. In fact, contestation rates in nonpartisan elections range from 16.7 percent in 1986 to 70.6 percent in 1998, for a difference of almost 54 percent. Similarly, contestation rates in partisan elections vary over time, from 41.7 percent in 1982 to 100 percent in 1996, for a difference of just over 58 percent.

Looking specifically at differences between nonpartisan and partisan elections, Table 9.2 indicates that competition is far keener on average overall, by almost 17 percent, in partisan than nonpartisan elections. Specifically, the contestation rate is 50.7 percent for all nonpartisan elections and 67.6 percent for all partisan elections during this period. Moreover, partisan elections produced only one of eleven election cycles (1982) in which challengers were absent in a majority of races, while nonpartisan elections produced four (1984–1990). Similarly, while in the two earliest election cycles (1980 and 1982) contestation rates were higher in nonparti-

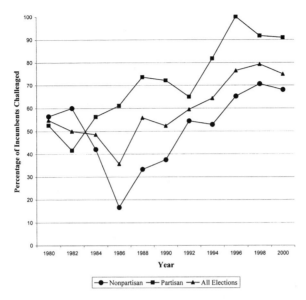

Fig. 9.1. State supreme court incumbents challenged for
reelection, 1980–2000

san elections than in partisan elections, partisan elections have attracted
challengers over nonpartisan elections at rates that range from 11 percent
to 44 percent. In fact, in more recent years, competition in the form of
challengers has become almost a certainty in partisan elections but simply
remains more likely than not in nonpartisan races.

Figure 9.1 illustrates these trends quite well by providing a graphical de-
piction of contestation rates over time and by selection system. In fact, the
increases in supreme court contestation rates from 1980 to 2000, particularly since 1990, are obvious. Looking specifically from the perspective of
the decades, the average rate of contestation in nonpartisan elections in
the 1980s (1980–1990), or the first half of the time series in this chapter,
was 40.8 percent, but increased to 62.5 percent in the 1990s (1992–2000).
Similar changes between the decades are evidenced in partisan elections,
with contestation rates increasing from 58.8 percent to 83.1 percent.[16]

Given these facts, what inferences about accountability in state supreme
court elections can we accurately derive? Generally, while voters in sizable
proportions of these races will have no opportunity to express dissatisfaction with incumbents because of the absence of challengers, these opportunities have increased substantially in recent years and, in the case of

partisan elections, now exceed those for the House of Representatives. In essence, partisan state supreme court elections now seem to have about the same capacity to promote accountability as House elections, while nonpartisan elections continue to fall short of this goal but are moving closer to it over time. Further, while it is most understandable why many would have questioned the democratic nature of supreme court elections in the 1980s, these criticisms seem misplaced since the mid-1990s, although less so for nonpartisan elections than partisan elections.

Vote Totals for Incumbents in State Supreme Court Elections

Table 9.3 looks at a second measure of electoral competition: the average percentage of the vote received by supreme court incumbents seeking reelection. On this measure, higher values indicate less competition and the corresponding reduced opportunities for citizen control of the bench. As discussed earlier, huge wins reduce the probability that justices will face future electoral challenge or defer to their constituencies in publicly salient cases once they are on the bench.

Practically speaking, this measure taps a threshold effect, wherein we can identify the approximate level at which justices will or will not face future electoral pressures or engage in strategies to promote their reelection. Studies of elections have identified this threshold at 60 percent—the cutoff point for distinguishing between competitive and noncompetitive elections, or safe from unsafe seats.[17]

As Table 9.3 indicates, state supreme court justices on average receive substantial support from the electorate. Overall, the average percentage of the vote for incumbents in state supreme court elections from 1980 through 2000 was 73.1 percent, an average considerably above the mark for competitive, or unsafe, seats. Moreover, nonpartisan, partisan, and retention elections look quite similar overall in the extent to which voters favor incumbents. Overall averages are, respectively, 77.7 percent, 70.1 percent, and 71.5 percent. In fact, it is quite interesting that partisan elections and retention elections look remarkably alike in this regard. Further, when individual election cycles are considered, retention elections actually are more competitive than partisan elections in five of eleven cycles (1980–1986, and 1992).

For a different perspective, consider the statistics in Table 9.3 for contested races only. As we would expect, when uncontested races are removed, average election margins for incumbents fall sharply and almost

TABLE 9.3

Average Vote (in Percentages) for Incumbents in State Supreme Court Elections,
by Type of Election System, 1980–2000

Year	Nonpartisan elections		Partisan elections		Retention elections	All elections	
	All races	Contested races	All races	Contested races	All races	All races	Contested races
1980	77.8	63.3	75.3	53.0	72.4	74.7	58.8
1982	74.8	58.0	82.6	58.3	74.4	77.3	58.1
1984	81.5	58.3	76.6	58.5	75.4	77.6	58.4
1986	91.2	55.7	71.9	54.0	69.9	77.2	54.4
1988	86.2	58.7	69.8	59.0	75.9	76.5	58.9
1990	82.7	59.5	65.3	52.7	67.1	71.8	55.8
1992	73.7	54.0	71.1	55.5	69.2	71.3	54.8
1994	76.6	55.8	61.4	52.8	66.3	68.5	54.3
1996	70.6	55.0	54.4	54.4	67.8	66.4	54.7
1998	72.7	63.6	57.6	53.8	74.6	71.2	58.9
2000	68.1	55.9	64.6	61.0	72.0	69.2	57.8
Total	77.7	58.0	70.1	55.8	71.5	73.1	56.9

always result in averages below the 60 percent threshold for marginal, or unsafe, seats. Total averages for all contested nonpartisan and partisan elections are, respectively, 58.0 percent and 55.8 percent, with a total average for all contested elections of 56.9 percent. Similarly, looking at each election cycle, only two nonpartisan election cycles and one partisan election cycle produced average vote margins that exceed the 60 percent standard. Thus, generally speaking, when challengers decide to take on incumbents, they have much more than a superficial effect on the electoral performance of incumbents.

Figure 9.2 graphs these rates over time for each selection system generally and for contested nonpartisan and contested partisan elections. On the whole, we see the relative stability of electoral support for incumbents in retention elections but a decline in nonpartisan and partisan elections, though certainly not like the trends evidenced in Figure 9.1 for contestation. Taken together, we can attribute these declines, at least in part, to the increasing presence of challengers. Regarding contested elections, Figure 9.2 illustrates overall stability in the ability of incumbents to garner votes when challengers are present. In the face of opponents, incumbents perform fairly consistently on average across systems and election cycles.

Now compare these results about the electoral fortunes of supreme court justices to U.S. House members. Looking at all supreme court elections combined, or within systems where contested races are not excluded, one simply might conclude that House elections are much more competi-

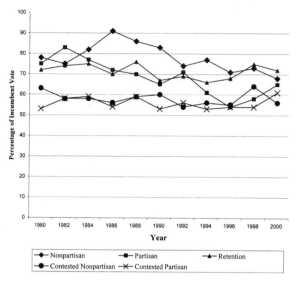

Fig. 9.2. Average vote for incumbents in state supreme court elections, 1980–2000

tive. However, a closer examination of the data reveals that this conclusion is not entirely satisfactory. Even with uncontested races included in the calculations for supreme court elections, average margins reached House levels in nonpartisan elections in 1998 and in partisan elections in 1986, 1988, and 1990. Moreover, competition in partisan judicial elections exceeded House races during the last four election cycles discussed in this chapter (1994–2000). Likewise, election results in retention elections, on average, resemble House races in five of eleven elections (1986 and 1990–1996), even when most of the legislative elections were contested.

In this same manner, when uncontested elections are removed, state supreme court elections are more competitive than House elections in every election cycle in both nonpartisan and partisan elections. Thus, supreme court elections, particularly when challengers are present, show a remarkable capacity for fulfilling the accountability function.

Ousting Incumbents: Defeats in State Supreme Courts

Table 9.4 looks at the most extreme form of electoral competition: incumbent defeats. As the data clearly indicate, a number of supreme court justices seeking to retain their seats from 1980 through 2000 were unsuccessful in doing so. Overall, 64 of 735 justices were removed from office, for a defeat rate of 8.7 percent. Compared with the U.S. House of Representatives, state supreme court seats are quite competitive from this perspective.

However, defeat rates vary sharply across election systems and over time. As Table 9.4 demonstrates, retention elections are the least likely to result in electoral defeat, while partisan elections are the most likely. In fact, defeats in retention elections are quite unlikely. Of the 327 incumbents facing voters and the possibility of being removed from office, only six (or 1.8 percent) have lost over a twenty-year period. And, of eleven election cycles, only three have produced defeat. Of course, 1986 is the most atypical election cycle—the one in which three justices were removed from the California Supreme Court in nationally visible campaigns. Overall, however, we have reason to question whether retention elections effectively promote accountability, at least on this one measure.

Nonpartisan elections fall in the middle, with an overall defeat rate from 1980 through 2000 of 7.4 percent. Of course, defeat rates in nonpartisan elections vary considerably over time, ranging from a low in 1998 of no defeats among the seventeen justices seeking reelection to a high in 1982 of 20.0 percent. Even so, by this standard nonpartisan supreme court elections are more competitive than elections to the U.S. House.

TABLE 9.4

State Supreme Court Incumbents Defeated, by Type of Election System, 1980–2000

	Nonpartisan elections			Partisan elections			Retention elections			All elections		
	Incumbents running	*Incumbents defeated*		*Incumbents running*	*Incumbents defeated*		*Incumbents running*	*Incumbents defeated*		*Incumbents running*	*Incumbents defeated*	
Year	N	%	N	N	%	N	N	%	N	N	%	N
1980	23	4.3	1	19	26.3	5	35	0.0	0	77	7.8	6
1982	20	20.0	4	24	4.2	1	28	0.0	0	72	6.9	5
1984	19	15.8	3	16	0.0	0	26	0.0	0	61	4.9	3
1986	24	4.2	1	18	22.2	4	33	9.1	3	75	10.7	8
1988	15	6.7	1	19	15.8	3	28	0.0	0	62	6.5	4
1990	24	4.2	1	18	33.3	6	34	0.0	0	76	9.2	7
1992	22	9.1	2	20	25.0	5	23	4.3	1	65	12.3	8
1994	17	5.9	1	11	36.4	4	27	0.0	0	55	9.1	5
1996	23	4.3	1	11	36.4	4	23	8.7	2	57	12.3	7
1998	17	0.0	0	12	33.3	4	41	0.0	0	70	5.7	4
2000	25	8.0	2	11	45.5	5	29	0.0	0	65	10.8	7
Total	229	7.4	17	179	22.9	41	327	1.8	6	735	8.7	64

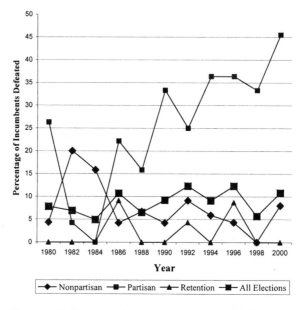

Fig. 9.3. Defeat rates in state supreme court elections, 1980–2000

With respect to partisan elections, not only are they the most competitive of the three election systems, the overall defeat rate is startling. In fact, partisan elections manifest a defeat rate of almost 23 percent, or a situation in which one of every four to five justices loses a seat on the high court bench to challengers. What also is quite fascinating is that defeat rates in partisan elections, with the exceptions of the 1982 and 1984 races, are high over time. Indeed, by this measure, state supreme court partisan elections are considerably more competitive than the U.S. House of Representatives. In short, supreme court justices in states using partisan elections have a great deal to fear from voters and do not fare nearly as well as their colleagues in the House.

Figure 9.3 clearly documents the differences across systems in defeat rates and illustrates the increasing competitiveness of partisan elections. In retention elections, defeats peaked in 1986 and again in 1996 but otherwise look fairly flat over time. Nonpartisan elections show a spike in 1982 but basically return to a flat average over the next two election cycles. In contrast, after experiencing declines from 1980 through 1984, defeats in partisan elections have skyrocketed.

Partisan Transformation of the South

These striking patterns in partisan elections, not only with respect to defeats but also contestation as discussed earlier, certainly beg explanation. Perhaps the most obvious and easiest explanation to consider relates to the partisan transformation of the American South, which essentially has moved from domination by the Democratic Party to two-party competition or, in some states, Republican control. Because most partisan elections occur in the South, we can compare rates of contestation and defeats between regions to ascertain whether changes in partisan elections seemingly relate to regional partisan change or, alternatively, to national trends making supreme court elections more competitive generally. If the partisan transformation hypothesis is the predominant factor explaining these trends, we should see increases in contestation and defeats in the South that are not mirrored in the rest of the nation.

Table 9.5 addresses this intriguing question and produces some fascinating and surprising results that raise doubts about the partisan transformation hypothesis. Clearly, regardless of region, challengers in state supreme court elections have increased considerably over time, both inside and outside the South. Regardless of region, challengers now are the norm in these races and, in fact, contestation rates converge for Southern and

TABLE 9.5

Challengers and Defeats in State Supreme Court Elections, by Region, 1980–2000

Year	Non-Southern states			Southern states[a]		
	Number running	*Challenge rate*	*Defeat rate*	*Number running*	*Challenge rate*	*Defeat rate[b]*
1980	25	56.0	8.0	17	52.9	23.5
1982	20	60.0	20.0	24	41.7	4.2
1984	20	50.0	15.0	15	46.7	0.0
1986	21	19.0	4.8	21	52.4	19.0
1988	14	50.0	14.3	20	60.0	10.0
1990	23	39.1	8.7	19	68.4	26.3
1992	22	54.5	9.1	20	65.0	25.0
1994	13	61.5	7.7	15	66.7	26.7
1996	18	72.2	5.6	16	81.3	25.0
1998	17	70.6	5.9	12	91.7	25.0
2000	20	75.0	10.0	16	75.0	31.3
All Years	213	54.5	9.9	195	62.1	19.0

[a] Southern states are Alabama, Arkansas, Florida, Georgia, Louisiana, Mississippi, North Carolina, Tennessee, and Texas. Virginia and South Carolina, also Southern states, do not elect judges. Non-Southern states are all others.

[b] Defeats in the primaries in Southern states occurred in Mississippi in 1992, North Carolina in 1994, Tennessee in 1990 (two cases by state party committee), and in Texas in 1980 (two cases), 1982, and 1986.

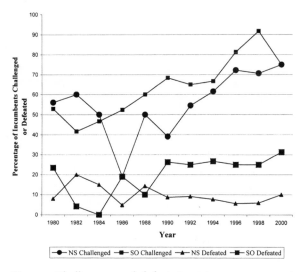

Fig. 9.4. Challengers and defeats in state supreme court elections, by region, 1980–2000 (NS, non-Southern; SO, Southern)

non-Southern elections at numerous points in the time series. The only unusual result is the substantial and unexplained dip in contestation for non-Southern elections in 1986.

But, defeats are harder to interpret. Defeat rates clearly have increased in the South, exceeding 20 percent since 1990. However, in 1980, well before the Southern states began to manifest a pronounced preference for the Republican Party, the supreme court defeat rate was 23.5 percent, a level very consistent with the most recent years. Making matters more complicated is that in the next two elections (1982 and 1984) only one of thirty-nine incumbents seeking reelection was defeated in the South. Moreover, outside the South, defeat rates remain relatively stable, if not declining, over the time series.

Figure 9.4 illustrates these trends. Thus, we see obvious increases in contestation both within and outside the South, but a considerable increase in electoral defeats only in the South and only in contrast to 1982–1984. In essence, for whatever reason, challengers in the South simply are much more successful than their counterparts outside the region. These intriguing patterns, and a fuller exploration of the partisan transformation hypothesis, certainly merit greater attention in future research.

Open Seats: Contestation and Electoral Margins for Winners

So far, this chapter has examined only those elections in which incumbents were seeking reelection. But what about elections in which no incumbents are running? Table 9.6 displays rates of contestation for open seats in state supreme courts from 1980 through 2000. Immediately apparent is the fact that it is rare for these elections not to attract at least two candidates, regardless of whether the election is nonpartisan or partisan. Overall, the contestation rate is 92.3 percent for all open seats, and 90.9 percent and 93.1 percent for nonpartisan and partisan elections, respectively. Similarly, in seven of eleven election cycles in nonpartisan elections, and eight of eleven in partisan elections, all of the elections drew more than one candidate. In short, when incumbents are absent, competition in the form of alternative candidates is a virtual certainty in state supreme court elections.

Table 9.7 illustrates open seat races from a second perspective: the margins of victory for winners of these contests. As with contestation, these data indicate that open seat elections are very competitive, with an overall average margin across elections and over time of 59.3 percent. Interestingly, by this standard nonpartisan elections appear to be slightly more competitive on average than partisan elections, with average vote margins at 60.0 percent and 58.3 percent, respectively.

TABLE 9.6
Contestation in Open Seat Races for State Supreme Courts,
by Type of Election System, 1980–2000

Year	Nonpartisan elections			Partisan elections			All elections		
	Total elections N	Elections contested %	N	Total elections N	Elections contested %	N	Total elections N	Elections contested %	N
1980	5	100.0	5	12	100.0	12	17	100.0	17
1982	4	75.0	3	8	87.5	7	12	83.3	10
1984	5	100.0	5	6	100.0	6	11	100.0	11
1986	4	75.0	3	5	100.0	5	9	88.9	8
1988	4	100.0	4	8	100.0	8	12	100.0	12
1990	3	100.0	3	11	72.7	8	14	78.6	11
1992	6	100.0	6	6	100.0	6	12	100.0	12
1994	7	85.7	6	7	100.0	7	14	92.9	13
1996	6	100.0	6	10	80.0	8	16	87.5	14
1998	6	66.7	4	5	100.0	5	11	81.8	9
2000	5	100.0	5	9	100.0	9	14	100.0	14
Total	55	90.9	50	87	93.1	81	142	92.3	131

TABLE 9.7
Average Vote (in Percentages) for Winners of
Open Seat State Supreme Court Elections,
by Type of Election System, 1980–2000

Year	Nonpartisan elections	Partisan elections	All elections
1980	52.3	58.1	56.4
1982	66.6	61.1	62.9
1984	55.2	59.7	57.7
1986	71.3	58.9	64.4
1988	56.4	57.7	57.2
1990	53.4	68.5	65.2
1992	52.0	55.0	53.5
1994	57.3	52.5	54.9
1996	61.7	65.5	64.1
1998	63.5	53.9	59.1
2000	53.3	60.3	57.8
Total	58.3	60.0	59.3

Without question, we see democracy in action in elections for open seats on state supreme courts. Challengers are present, voters have choice, and winners establish tenuous electoral coalitions, on average. In fact, the winners of these elections are brought onto their courts after having experienced the democratic process at its extremes. Alternatively, political scientists have documented a sophomore surge effect, in which justices do much better in subsequent elections than their first.[18] Thus, gaining entry to the court by way of an open seat may not produce the same pressures on judicial voting behavior as marginal elections for established incumbents. Such investigations would be an important goal for future research.

Conclusion and Implications for the Controversy over Electing Judges

This exploration of competition in state supreme court elections reveals some fascinating ways in which democratic processes are present in these races. While challengers did not enter supreme court elections as often as U.S. House elections from 1980 through 2000, justices seeking reelection were more likely, at least on average, to be challenged than not. Moreover, challengers in nonpartisan and partisan elections increasingly have been active since the 1980s. In fact, challengers now are more likely in partisan supreme court elections than in House elections, and it appears that partisan elections have an even greater capacity to promote accountability than House elections by this standard. Similarly, since 1990 in nonpartisan elections, about two of every three justices have been forced to confront challengers in their bids for reelection. In sum, the assertion that justices are "infrequently challenged" now is incorrect.

From the perspective of electoral support for incumbents, supreme court elections in all three forms are less competitive on average than House races, when both uncontested and contested seats are aggregated for courts. However, these differences are not great in either retention or partisan elections. Recall that the overall vote average for House members was 64.8 percent, while the averages for retention and partisan elections were, respectively, 71.5 percent and 70.1 percent. Of course, the gap for nonpartisan elections is wider. Also along these lines, in some election years, retention, nonpartisan, and partisan judicial elections look fairly similar to House elections. Even more so, however, when we remove the uncontested judicial elections from consideration to render the averages more comparable with the statistics reported for the House, both nonpartisan and partisan elections are more competitive with respect to the size of incumbents' electoral coalitions than their legislative counterparts. Again, all things considered, evidence suggests that criticizing supreme court elections for their incapacity to promote accountability in the form of reduced support for incumbents seems misplaced.

Finally, while defeats of sitting justices in supreme court retention elections are rare, defeat rates for justices in nonpartisan and partisan elections are higher than those in the House. In fact, the defeat rate in partisan supreme court elections is almost four times higher than that in the House. Although retention elections reasonably can be questioned for their ability to oust incumbents, justices in nonpartisan and partisan election states are far from being "rarely defeated."

In short, when we consider tangible indicators of electoral accountability, we see that, under most situations, supreme court elections perform quite well, particularly in the last decade or so. The only glaring exception is retention elections, which show a pronounced tendency against incumbent defeat relative to other types of elections. Of course, in large measure, this is precisely the result intended by proponents of retention elections, and why the plan continues to be advocated by those who view electoral accountability as an undesirable feature of the judiciary. At the same time, however, incumbents' approval ratings in retention elections seemingly are about on par with other elections. Along these same lines, we certainly can see evidence in nonpartisan, partisan, and retention elections that rightfully would have caused court observers to question the accountability possible in judicial elections in the 1980s

Looking more broadly at supreme court elections, including temporal trends, we find a more refined conclusion about these elections, especially since about the mid-1990s: they really do not conform to their negative stereotype. Indeed, generally speaking, democratic politics appears to be alive and well in elections to the state high court bench, leaving us to question the accuracy of assertions about the incapacity of these races to promote meaningful connections between citizens and the bench. Similarly, in many regards, state supreme court elections look quite similar to elections for other important offices.

In fact, we reasonably can expect to see these trends toward greater competitiveness to continue in state supreme court elections, given the U.S. Supreme Court's landmark decision in *Republican Party of Minnesota v. White* (2002) that removed restrictions on campaign speech in judicial elections.[19] However, it should be emphasized that competition began to escalate in supreme court elections long before the *White* decision. Thus, *White* will be contributing to, not causing, the long-term rise in supreme court competition that might continue in these elections beginning in 2002.

As mentioned earlier, whether electing judges is desirable and whether one type of election system is better than others are considerations beyond the scope of this chapter and will remain, at least to some extent, normative in foundation. But obviously, much more empirical work is needed to understand the exact nature of each selection alternative and to evaluate the consequence of each system on the politics of courts. Only then can we reach sound and informed conclusions about the best means for recruiting and retaining judges in the American states. However, beliefs about the failure of judicial elections to promote accountability should not be part of that calculation, unless the charge is directed specifically toward retention elections. Otherwise, nonpartisan and partisan elections appear to fulfill their goals.

NOTES

1. This chapter draws extensively on my previous work, especially Hall, "State Supreme Courts in American Democracy," and also on the collaborative work

cited herein with Chris Bonneau. I am grateful to Chris for his contributions to this project. Also, I gratefully acknowledge the contributions of Paul Abramson for providing data on U.S. House elections described herein, and Jeffrey VanSlette and Frederick Wood for their excellent research assistance.

2. Hall, "Mobilizing Voters in State Supreme Court Elections."

3. Hall, "Voluntary Retirements from State Supreme Courts"; Bonneau and Hall, "Predicting Challengers in State Supreme Court Elections."

4. Brace and Hall, "Interplay of Preferences, Case Facts, Context, and Rules"; Hall, "Constituent Influence in State Supreme Courts"; Hall, "Electoral Politics and Strategic Voting"; Hall, "Justices as Representatives."

5. Abramson et al., *Change and Continuity.*

6. For example, Miller and Stokes, "Constituency Influence in Congress."

7. Hall, "State Supreme Courts in American Democracy."

8. Dubois, *From Ballot to the Bench,* p. 33.

9. Rottman and Schotland, "What Makes Judicial Elections Unique?" p. 1369.

10. Geyh, "Why Judicial Elections Stink," p. 43.

11. Dubois, *From Ballot to the Bench,* p. 28.

12. For a more detailed discussion of these assumptions, see Hall, "State Judicial Politics."

13. Brace et al., "Judicial Choice and the Politics of Abortion"; Langer, *Judicial Review in State Supreme Courts.*

14. For example, Brace and Hall, "Interplay of Preferences, Case Facts, Context, and Rules"; Hall, "Constituent Influence in State Supreme Courts"; Hall, "Electoral Politics and Strategic Voting"; Hall, "Justices as Representatives."

15. Hall, "State Supreme Courts in American Democracy."

16. In comparing 1980–1988 to 1990–2000, the same dramatic changes are apparent. In nonpartisan elections, rates of contestation increase from 41.6 percent to 57.8 percent, and in partisan elections, from 56.3 percent to 80.7 percent.

17. Weber et al., "Vanishing Marginals in State Legislative Elections."

18. Hall, "State Supreme Courts in American Democracy"; Hall and Bonneau, "Does Quality Matter?"

19. *Republican Party of Minnesota v. White,* 536 U.S. 765 (2002).

Chapter 10

Judicial Selection Methods and Capital Punishment in the American States

Paul Brace and Brent D. Boyea

Until now, the contributors to this book have examined the actual judicial election process as it relates to such things as money, partisan activity, news coverage, and voting. However, no contribution has looked at the *actual* effects of those elections on judges' rulings. In this chapter, we address this issue, specifically regarding the reversal of capital punishment cases.

When it comes to capital punishment, the question of judicial selection and judicial impartiality is literally a matter of life and death; therefore, it is reasonable to ask whether state supreme courts act impartially or are swayed by public opinion. In the 1990s, public support for the death penalty reached a contemporary high, with almost 80 percent supporting the punishment in national surveys. Could a state supreme court judge risk ignoring this support when they were faced with a capital appeal?

Capitalizing on data collected by the National Science Foundation (NSF) State Supreme Court Data Project and recent developments in the measurement of state public opinion and other critical variables, this study considers both the direct and indirect effects that public opinion has on judges' votes in capital punishment cases. We examine the frequency with which state supreme court judges voted to overturn capital sentences in states with elected and nonelected state supreme court judges, controlling for a host of influences, including case characteristics, judge ideology, nearness of judicial elections, whether a judge was retiring, and regulations on the conduct of elections. We find that elected judges were sensitive to public opinion and electoral pressures and were substantially less likely to vote to overturn capital convictions than their appointed counterparts.

We also consider indirect effects of public opinion on decisions in capital punishment cases. Specifically, we examine the connection between public support for the death penalty and judge ideology in states with and without capital punishment and states that elect or appoint their supreme court judges. As anticipated, the linkage between public support for the death penalty and judge ideology is strongest in states that elect their judges and where support for capital punishment is highest. We believe that capital punishment provides voters with a strong cue that has promoted a more conservative judiciary. When there is a salient issue that cuts across partisan cleavages, judicial elections serve to link both the decisions of courts, and the composition of courts, to public opinion.

The Practice of Electing Judges

Among the most significant reforms in nineteenth-century American politics involved the popular election of state appellate and inferior court judges.[1] Observers from Alexis de Tocqueville to James Bryce and from Roscoe Pound to Sandra Day O'Connor have all bemoaned the practice of subjecting judges to popular election.[2] As Rick Hasen notes in chapter 2, in the contemporary era, concerns with the deleterious effects of unfettered electoral competition led many states to regulate the politics of judicial elections. Nine states adopted guidelines promulgated by the American Bar Association that restricted aspirants for judgeships from making announcements about "his or her views on disputed legal or political issues."[3] Another twenty-six elective states adopted American Bar Association guidelines that restricted judicial candidates from making statements that commit candidates to positions on cases or issues that are likely to come before their courts.[4] In 2002, campaign speech limitations within nine states that restricted general announcements were declared unconstitutional by the U.S. Supreme Court in *Republican Party of Minnesota v. White*.[5] Notably, in her concurrence, Justice O'Connor reasoned that if a "state has a problem with judicial impartiality, *it is largely one the State brought upon itself by continuing the practice of popularly electing judges*" (emphasis added).[6]

Justice O'Connor's observations summarize the widely held belief that has taken on the status of a truism: elections influence judicial decision-making. By tying the holding of judicial office to success in elections, many observers fear that judges bend to public opinion rather than follow the rule of law. While this belief is pervasive, to date there has been no direct test of the effects of public opinion on judge decisionmaking in state courts, the very courts to which many judges are elected. Given the U.S. Supreme Court's invalidation of state efforts to regulate conduct in judicial elections in the *White* case, the issue is as important as ever. Is it unreasonable to think elected judges operate any differently? In their study of criminal trial judges in Pennsylvania, Gregory A. Huber and Sanford C. Gordon provide persuasive support that elected judges become more punitive as reelection approaches, punishing criminal defendants more severely.[7] Therefore, it is reasonable to expect that elected judges operate quite differently from appointed judges where the electoral mechanism does not exist.

As is clear in several other chapters in this book, many judicial elections have become more visible during the last two decades. Observers of these contests have commented on a new style of judicial campaign with heated races focused on hot-button issues.[8] Traditionally these races were "low-information affairs" with little voter attention and limited participation, similar to the 1998 Ohio State Supreme Court elections that Lawrence Baum and David Klein discussed in chapter 8.[9] Increasingly, many contestants gain attention in these otherwise staid contests by capitalizing on the public's fear of crime generally and support for capital punishment specifically. As noted by Baum elsewhere, "in this climate of opinion, creating the impression that a judge is soft on crime can have great electoral impact. Convincing voters that a judge is unwilling to impose or uphold death sentences is uniquely effective because capital punishment is especially salient and easy to understand."[10] In fact, Huber and Gordon present convincing evidence that sentencing becomes more punitive as elections near.[11] This occurred even though the elections in Huber and Gordon's study were low-information, nonpartisan retention elections. In state after state, supreme court judges that voted to overturn death sentences have faced opponents that labeled them as soft on crime, even if these votes were based on findings of egregious error.[12] It is hard to imagine that other judges were unaware of these races.[13]

It should come as no surprise that capital punishment is particularly salient in contests for state supreme court seats. As a procedural matter, state supreme courts review all death sentences given in their state when they are appealed by the criminal defendant. In many states, death penalty appeals constitute one-fourth or more of state supreme court dockets.[14] These cases force state supreme court justices to review what are often very heinous crimes that have had substantial media coverage. The public, moreover, has shown strong support for capital punishment. Various annual polls document a dramatic increase in support for capital punishment from the 1970s through the late 1990s.[15] When it comes to capital punishment, state supreme court judges confront very visible cases involving an issue that is extremely salient to the public. This issue, then, is an ideal place to examine the linkage between public opinion and judicial decisionmaking.

In this heated political climate, it is fair to wonder whether state supreme court justices retreat from finding reversible error in death penalty appeals for fear of political reprisals. There is circumstantial evidence to support this conclusion. An authoritative study of error rates in capital cases from 1973 to 1995 reveals that nearly seven in ten contained reversible, prejudicial error.[16] However, the same study indicates that the rate of overturning cases on reversible error in state supreme courts declined from 63 percent in 1979 to 30 percent in 1994. In other words, due to reinstatement and expansion of the death penalty, capital convictions went up more than 500 percent, while the rate of reversal in state supreme courts dropped by over 50 percent in these two decades. Although part of this trend could be accounted for by tightening standards for appeals emanating from the U.S. Supreme Court, reversal rates in life-tenured federal courts did not decline at a parallel rate.[17]

Impartiality versus Responsiveness

When it comes to courts, we commonly prize impartiality. When it comes to elections, we value democratic responsiveness. When judges are elected, then, we have a clash of values. Do judicial elections serve to link public opinion to judicial outcomes? Ultimately, the question of judicial responsiveness to public opinion must be nested within the more general debate regarding the linkage between public opinion and public policy. Clearly, if more general claims about the connections between opinion and policy in legislative bodies are subject to debate or criticism, the expectation that judges follow public opinion must confront those same criticisms.

There are three broad schools of thought about the opinion-policy nexus. Some are highly critical of the notion that the public exerts influence on policy outcomes, citing decades of survey research illustrating the common lack of knowledge the public holds about politics and politicians.[18] Clearly, policy is likely to be nonresponsive to public opinion if the public has few clear and consistent views that political leaders might meaningfully follow.

In stark contrast are those who hold that policy is strongly tied to public opinion. Most notably, the early work of Miller and Stokes examined the relationship between opinions of voters in congressional districts and the behavior of House members while in office, reporting some modest (though variable) links.[19] Other studies of constituency opinion, employing a variety of methodological assumptions and different measures of opinion and behavior, have extended the foundation Miller and Stokes established, generally reporting stronger evidence of a persisting link across general policy indices or specific policies.[20]

A third perspective views the effects of public opinion in a contingent manner. The most prominent advocate of a contingent view of the linkage between opinion and policy was V. O. Key. To Key,

> Mass opinion may set general limits, themselves subject to change over time, within which government may act. In some instances opinion may be permissive but not directive of specific action. In others opinion may be, if not directive, virtually determinative of particular acts.[21]

More recently Geer makes the simple but powerful point that political actors are more likely to respond to public opinion when they are confident they know what opinion the public holds.[22] From this contingent perspective, the degree to which opinion exists may vary across issues, time, or space. On a given issue, public awareness may change over time, or it may differ between constituencies.[23]

Judicial Decisions on the Death Penalty: Testing for Linkage on a Salient Issue

A contingent perspective on the effects of death penalty opinion on judicial decisionmaking would seem ideally suited to the American states. While national polls revealed strong support for capital punishment throughout the 1980s and 1990s, recent research also reveals that this support varies substantially across the states and is strongly tied to capital punishment laws within the states.[24] The lopsided support for capital punishment evident in many states may, in Key's terms, virtually determine the act of voting to uphold a capital conviction. Seated justices who wish to retain their position would be reluctant to ignore this opinion where it is very pronounced. Moreover, prospective candidates for the bench that had reservations about the punishment should be disinclined to seek office in such political climates. In other states, opinion may be less well formed, offering more latitude in the kinds of judges on courts and more discretion in their decisionmaking.

Claims that policy is linked to public preferences rest on the assumption that political elites derive benefit from pursuing policies that accord (or appear to accord) with the wishes of citizens.[25] In this way, policy corresponds with public sentiment either because elites fear losing office or because the elite shares the public's opinion.[26] Following the classic argument of Miller and Stokes, the public's support for the death penalty may operate *directly* and lead seated judges to alter their voting behavior to align with public opinion, or *indirectly* by helping to recruit judges that share the public's sentiments.[27] Given the gravity of a death sentence, it is easy to imagine a state supreme court justice that was morally opposed to the death sentence retiring from the bench in a political atmosphere where capital punishment had taken center stage. Overall, the most reasonable place to look for linkage (or judicial dependence) is where the public holds strong opinions, where judges remain committed to retaining their seat, and where elective selection systems can intersect public preferences with judge reelection ambitions.[28]

We hypothesize that the following conditions should promote connections between public opinion and judicial decisions: (1) public opinion on an issue is strong, (2) judges are elected, (3) judges want to be reelected, and (4) candidates are not restricted from campaigning on the issue by state laws governing campaign conduct. Conversely, when opinions on an issue are weaker, judges aren't elected, judges plan on retiring, or candidates are restricted from raising the publicly salient issue in their campaigns, there should be less connection between the public and judicial decisionmaking.

State Death Penalty Opinion

While support for capital punishment was very high in general in the 1990s, this support was not distributed uniformly across the states. As illustrated in Figure 10.1, there was wide variation in public sentiment about

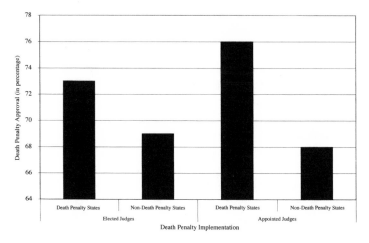

Fig. 10.1. Public opinion, death penalty implementation, and method of selection

capital punishment among the states, depending on the method of judicial selection and whether the state allows for capital punishment. Seemingly, a judge voting to overturn a death sentence in Texas had more to worry about than a judge in New York if they were going to stand for election.[29]

The critical question for our purposes is whether the practice of electing supreme court judges affected voting in capital punishment cases. The patterns in Figure 10.2 suggest it did. As we would expect, the lowest rate of capital punishment reversal voting occurred in states that elected their judges and where support for the punishment was highest.[30] In those states, judges voted to reverse death sentences 20 percent of the time. Contrast this with states that appointed their judges and where support for the death penalty is greatest. In those states, reversal votes occurred 29 percent of the time, almost 50 percent more frequently than in states with elections and with greater death penalty support.

If elections and public opinion are influencing judges, perhaps their political ambitions reinforce or modify this influence. Like legislators, elected judges may exhibit changing levels of responsiveness to their constituents, based on their decisions to stay or retire. Among political actors, "shirking" represents a lack of responsiveness by political representatives to their constituency. Rather than pursuing the policy interests of his or her constituency, a political representative, or a judge, shirks when acting solely on their personal ideological preferences.[31] We would expect elected

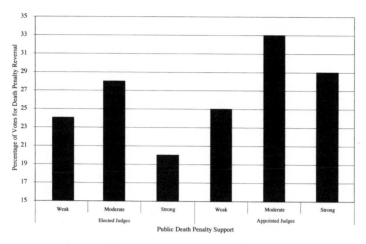

Fig. 10.2. Effect of public opinion on judges' votes in reversing capital punishment cases

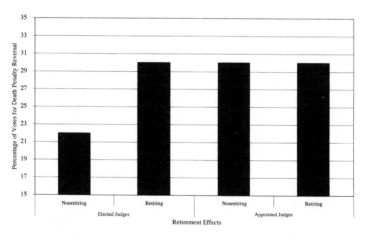

Fig. 10.3. Effect of retirement on judges' votes in reversing capital punishment cases

judges to be less constrained by public opinion in the year they retire from state supreme courts. No longer facing the prospect of an election campaign to retain their judgeship, these justices may thus shirk their obligations to follow constituency preferences and should be more inclined to find reversible error, ceteris paribus.

The patterns in Figure 10.3 conform to our expectation. Appointed judges and judges that are retiring all exhibit a higher propensity to vote to over turn capital convictions than elective judges that are not retiring. There is a remarkable similarity of the frequency of reversal voting between retiring judges and judges in appointive courts. Once freed from the pressures of election, it appears that judges vote in remarkably similar patterns. Nonretiring elective judges voted to reverse capital punishment 22 percent of the time, while the other justices voted to reverse 30 percent of the time, which is about one-third more often.

If judges are retiring, they no longer need to be concerned about elections. For judges who plan to stay on the court, the proximity of an impending election could heighten their concern about voter retribution for an unpopular judicial vote. Because of this, we would expect judges to be less likely to vote to overturn a capital decision as their election nears.

The patterns in Figure 10.4 again confirm our expectations. Elected judges provide substantially different patterns of behavior when elections are pending or concluded. There is a remarkable dissimilarity between elected judges facing electoral pressures and those who are relatively secure within their office. The patterns reinforce this finding when looking at time periods both before and after an election. In both instances, judges are seemingly less responsive to electoral pressures and vote to reverse the death penalty more frequently.

Before they were partially invalidated in a recent U.S. Supreme Court case, many states placed a variety of restrictions on judicial candidates.[32]

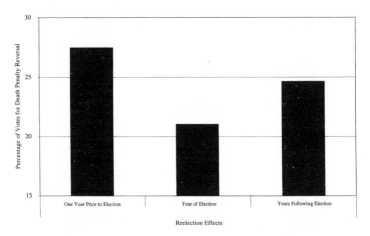

Fig. 10.4. Effect of reelection on judges' votes in reversing capital punishment cases

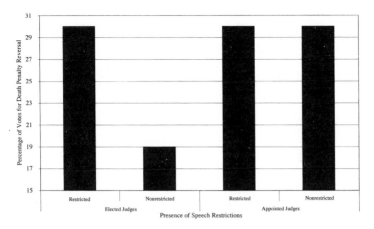

Fig. 10.5. Effect of campaign speech restrictions on judges' votes in reversing capital punishment cases

Presently, twenty-six states continue to place speech restrictions on judicial candidates.[33] Commonly known as the "commit clause," these states apply the 1990 American Bar Association *Model Code of Judicial Conduct* to their state judicial elections.[34] The commit clause restricts candidates from making "statements that commit or appear to commit the candidate with respect to cases, controversies or issues that are likely to come before the court."[35] Our hypothesis here is straightforward and follows the logic of these restrictions. Specifically, we expect that where such restrictions exist, judges are better insulated from potential attacks on their death penalty votes and arguably have less need to be responsive to public opinion. Alternatively, in states without these restrictions, incumbent judges and their opponents may publicly articulate their views on the death penalty, thereby making the punishment an explicit campaign issue. Under these circumstances, judges' votes in capital cases can come back to haunt them at election time, and we would expect this to reduce the number of reversal votes.

The evidence shown in Figure 10.5 supports our expectation. Judges elected in states without campaign restrictions voted to reverse capital convictions 19 percent of the time. Contrast this with elected judges protected by campaign restrictions and with appointed judges, where, respectively, reversal votes occurred 30 percent of the time and 60 percent more often.[36] It is notable that rates of reversal voting are effectively equal in appointed states and in states with commit clauses. The striking contrast between these states and the significantly lower reversal rates in elective states without the commit clause provides yet additional evidence of the effects of judicial elections on death penalty voting in state supreme courts.

Capital cases often involve heinous and unspeakable acts of violence and cruelty that arouse public ire and make these cases uncommonly salient to the public. Where state supreme courts may commonly operate in quiet anonymity on the vast majority of cases that come before them, capital cases may move their actions to the forefront of public attention. Because of this possibility, we would expect elected judges to be the most sensitive to the aggravating circumstances involved in a capital case. We classified capital cases as having unusually high numbers of aggravating circumstances involved in the case, contrasted with relatively low numbers in other cases.[37] The patterns presented in Figure 10.6 conform to our expectation. Elected judges in general appear more sensitive than their appointive counterparts to aggravating factors. When there were comparatively low numbers of aggravating factors, elected judges voted to reverse 24 percent of the time, while appointive judges voted to reverse 30 percent of the time. The most striking result concerns elective judges hearing cases with high aggravating circumstances. These judges voted to reverse in fewer than one in five cases, while their appointive counterparts facing comparable aggravating circumstances voted to reverse more than one in four times. The results concerning the differential effects of aggravating

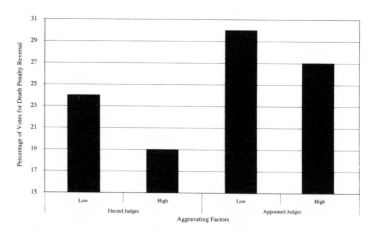

Fig. 10.6. Effect of aggravating factors on judges' votes in reversing capital punishment cases

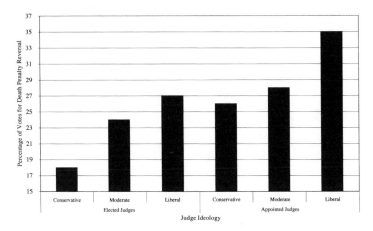

Fig. 10.7. Effect of judge ideology on judges' votes in reversing capital punishment cases

circumstances provides additional evidence that judicial elections are effecting judge voting in capital punishment cases.

The patterns presented thus far provide compelling if circumstantial evidence that state supreme court judges in capital punishment cases may vote with an eye toward the next election. These patterns would suggest that judicial elections mediate public opinion and alter judges' behavior on the bench. There is another way that elections might function to link public opinion to judicial outcomes, however. Elections might serve to recruit judges who have attitudes that are closer to the public's attitude. For example, judges with liberal attitudes in states with high public support for the death penalty might not run, or might not get elected, in those states. Instead, judges who share the public's sentiments about the death penalty would run and serve. This raises two related questions. First, does judge ideology predict how judges will vote in capital cases? Second, are judge ideologies correlated with the public's opinion on capital punishment?

The answer to the first question is a resounding yes, as illustrated in Figure 10.7.[38] As we would expect, conservative judges are less likely than moderate or liberal judges to reverse capital cases. These effects are heightened by elective selection, with elected liberals voting to reverse only slightly more regularly than appointed conservatives. The two extremes, however, illustrate the pattern most vividly. Elected conservative state supreme court judges voted to reverse capital cases 18 percent of the time, while liberal appointed judges voted to reverse 35 percent of the time. In

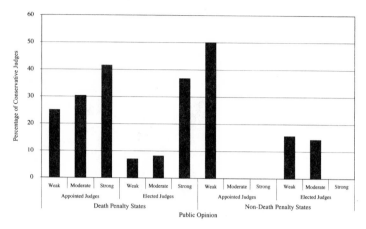

Fig. 10.8. Effect of public opinion on judge ideology

other words, elected conservatives were half as likely as appointed liberals to vote to reverse in capital cases.

Given the very striking effect of judge ideology, our next question is particularly apt. Do public preferences concerning the death penalty, operating through elections, serve to produce a more conservative bench? This is certainly not wild speculation. As noted at the outset, capital cases have turned some normally staid judicial elections into very heated contests. It could be that capital punishment as an issue gave otherwise disinterested and uninformed voters a litmus they could apply to candidates for state supreme court. When we look at the relationship between public support for the death penalty and judge ideology, an interesting pattern emerges (Figure 10.8).[39] Public support for the death penalty is associated with judge ideology in states with capital punishment and where they elect their state supreme court judges. The higher the public support, the more conservative are their state supreme court judges. This pattern also exists in death penalty states that appoint their state supreme court judges, yet comparison of all elected judges in death penalty states suggests that strong support for the death penalty uniquely encourages conservative judges unlike appointed states. It is also notable that patterns of conservative judge ideology are much different in states without the death penalty. There is no obvious relationship between conservative judge ideology and public support in states without the death penalty, whether appointed or elected. The overall pattern at least suggests that the issue of capital punishment operates in states with judicial elections to connect judges to the public by recruiting and electing judges that share their preferences.

Conclusions

When focusing on the states, one develops a strong impression that judges operate under quite different environments where the death penalty does or does not exist. Further affecting judges is the system of selection, or whether judges are elected and appointed. Of the patterns that exist within the state courts, few are as strong as the apparent linkage between the death penalty and the behavior of state supreme court judges. Most important, in elected states with strong public support for the death penalty, judges are much less likely to reverse the death penalty than in states with less support for capital punishment or within appointed courts. Patterns of judge behavior also suggest that a number of additional factors affect willingness to reverse capital cases. The timing and regulation of elections and judge ambitions to remain or retire all produce striking differences in the willingness of judges to reverse capital sentences and their sensitivity to the aggravating factors in cases.

Evidence presented in this chapter suggests that elections produce an indirect connection between public sentiment and judge voting in capital cases. In states that elect their judges, public support for the death penalty is related to the conservatism of their judges, and conservative judges are much less likely to reverse capital cases than their more liberal counterparts. In the end, the patterns revealed here indicate that judicial elections expose judges to public sentiment and, on this very salient issue at least, they respond by adjusting their voting in a manner that is consistent with public opinion. On this particular issue, too, elections serve to recruit judges who share the public's values. Elections thus function in a manner commonly valued in some democratic theories, producing elite responsiveness to mass opinions. When it comes to judicial elections, however, our findings may give pause to those who value judicial impartiality, particularly when it comes to a matter of life and death.

NOTES

1. For an insightful review of the development of our elected judiciary, see Hall, "Judiciary on Trial," and chapter 1 of this book. As of 1999, the period consid-

ered in this analysis, ten states used a partisan election format for the election of state supreme court justices, twelve states used a nonpartisan election format, three states used a legislative appointment format, nine states used an executive appointment format, and sixteen states used some form of the merit selection format (Council of State Governments, *Book of the States*).

2. Tocqueville, *Democracy in America*; Bryce, American Commonwealth; Pound, "Causes of Popular Dissatisfaction"; *Republican Party of Minnesota v. White*, 536 U.S. 765 (2002).

3. American Bar Association, *Model Code of Judicial Conduct, 1972*.

4. American Bar Association, *Model Code of Judicial Conduct, 1990*.

5. *White*, 536 U.S.

6. Ibid., p. 792.

7. Huber and Gordon, "Accountability and Coercion."

8. Baum, "Judicial Elections and Judicial Independence"; Hall, "Constituent Influence in State Supreme Courts."

9. Baum, "Judicial Elections and Judicial Independence."

10. Ibid., p. 35.

11. Huber and Gordon, "Accountability and Coercion."

12. Tabak, "Death of Fairness"; Case, "In Search of an Independent Judiciary"; Gibeaut, "Taking Aim"; Bright and Keenan, "Judges and the Politics of Death."

13. The effects of political pressures on death penalty decisions are analyzed in Blume and Eisenberg, "Judicial Politics, Death Penalty Appeals, and Case Selection"; Hall, "Constituent Influence in State Supreme Courts"; Hall, "Electoral Politics and Strategic Voting in State Supreme Courts"; and Hall, "Justices as Representatives." The argument that these pressures have a strong influence on judicial behavior is also presented by Bright and Keenan, "Judges and the Politics of Death."

14. Brace and Sims-Butler, "New Perspectives for the Comparative Study of the Judiciary."

15. Gallup Organization, *Gallup Poll*.

16. Liebman et al., "Capital Attrition."

17. Ibid.

18. Converse, "Nature of Belief Systems"; Zaller, *Nature and Origins of Belief Systems*.

19. Miller and Stokes, "Constituency Influence in Congress."

20. Achen, "Mass Political Attitudes and the Survey Response"; Achen, "Measuring Representation"; Erikson, "Constituency Opinion and Congressional Behavior"; Erikson et al., *Statehouse Democracy*; Page et al., "Constituency, Party, and Representation in Congress"; Bartels, "Constituency Opinion and Congressional Policy-Making."

21. Key, *Public Opinion and American Democracy*, p. 97.

22. Geer, *From Tea Leaves to Opinion Polls*.

23. Wlezien, "Public as Thermostat"; Wlezien, "Dynamics of Representation"; Wlezien, "Patterns of Representation"; Brace et al., "Public Opinion in the American States"; Johnson et al., "Public Opinion and Dynamic Representation."

24. Norrander, "Multi-Layered Impact of Public Opinion"; Brace et al., "Public Opinion in the American States."

25. Downs, *Economic Theory of Democracy*; Geer, *From Tea Leaves to Opinion Polls*; Jacobs and Shapiro, *Politicians Don't Pander*.

26. The research strategy for assessing how the U.S. Supreme Court responds to public opinion is longitudinal. The nature of over-time shifts in public opinion is compared with shifts in court output or judge voting in Mishler and Sheehan, "Supreme Court as a Countermajoritarian Institution?"; Flemming and Wood, "Public and the Supreme Court"; and McGuire and Stimson, "Least Dangerous Branch Revisited." Another way of judging opinion-policy responsiveness employs a cross-sectional research strategy and is most commonly found in cross-national and in state politics and policy research (e.g., Erikson et al., *Statehouse Democracy*). Here, interstate differences in policy are compared with interstate differences in public opinion. Given our interest in the effects of state opinion of state judges under differing selection mechanisms, this cross-sectional approach is ideally suited to our research questions.

27. Miller and Stokes, "Constituency Influence in Congress."

28. We dichotomize methods of selection into elective and appointive forms of judicial selection. While the states use a variety of elective and appointive forms of selection, there is limited evidence that dividing elective forms of selection into partisan and nonpartisan categories and appointive forms of selection into executive appointment, legislative appointment, and merit retention categories provides any discernable differences (e.g., Brace and Hall, "Interplay of Preferences, Case Facts, Context, and Rules"; Brace and Hall, "Studying Courts Comparatively"; and Hall and Brace, "Order in the Courts").

29. Texas uses partisan elections to select judges for the court of criminal appeals, the high court for criminal appeals within the state of Texas, and public support for the death penalty within Texas is higher than in most other states. New York, in contrast, uses executive appointments to select judges for the state court of appeals, the state high court. Public support for the death penalty within New York is lower than in most other states.

30. Using Brace et al.'s measure of state death penalty tolerance, support for the death penalty is divided into three categories of support: strong, moderate, and weak. States classified as having strong support for the death penalty represent the upper one-quarter of state death penalty tolerance scores. Moderate support likewise represents the middle one-half of death penalty tolerance scores. States with weak support for the death penalty occupy the lower one-quarter of death penalty tolerance scores among the states (Brace et al., "Public Opinion in the American States").

31. Scholars initially found minimal evidence of ideological shirking in Congress (Lott and Bronars, "Time Series Evidence on Shirking"; Poole and Romer, "Ideology, 'Shirking,' and Representation"; Poole and Rosenthal, *Congress*; Vanbeek, "Does the Decision to Retire"; Zupan, "Last Period Problem in Politics"). Other arguments have successfully made the counterpoint, however, with apparent ideological change for exiting members (Lott and Reed, "Shirking and Sorting in a Political Market"; Rothenberg and Sanders, "Severing the Electoral Connection"; Snyder and Ting, "Roll Calls, Party Labels, and Elections"; Tien, "Representation, Voluntary Retirement, and Shirking in the Last Term"). Lott and Reed argue that as congressional members near retirement, a "retirement effect" emerges that alleviates prior electoral constraint and allows politicians to maximize their utility more efficiently. This effect allows more sincere voting and overall decreased participation with greater participation in only those roll calls for which they feel most strongly. More recently, Rothenberg and Sanders suggest that ideological and participatory shirking exists. They find that exiting members dramatically modify their participation and modestly alter their ideological positions, especially among centrist representatives.

32. *Republican Party of Minnesota v. White*, 536 U.S. 765 (2002).

33. The following states have adopted the commit clause: Alaska, Arizona, Arkansas, California, Florida, Georgia, Illinois, Indiana, Kansas, Kentucky, Louisiana, Maine, Nebraska, Nevada, New Mexico, New York, North Dakota, Ohio, Oklahoma, Rhode Island, South Carolina, South Dakota, Tennessee, Vermont, Washington, West Virginia, and Wyoming.

34. Brief of the American Bar Association as amicus curiae in support of respondents in *Republican Party of Minnesota v. White*, 536 U.S. 765 (2002).

35. American Bar Association, *Model Code of Judicial Conduct, 1990*, Canon 5(A)(3)(d)(ii).

36. The reader may wonder why states with appointed judges have commit clauses. Several states appoint their high courts but elect some or all of their lower courts. Where judges were appointed, we would not expect campaign restrictions to influence their voting and, in fact, we find no difference.

37. Aggravating factors represent a range of thirty-one crimes present in state supreme court capital cases. Low aggravating factors represent cases with less than the mean number of additional crimes. High aggravating factors represent cases with more than the mean number of additional crimes present within state capital cases.

38. Judge ideology for state supreme court judges is determined using Brace et al.'s measure of judge preferences. This measure is used to create three categories of judge ideology: conservative, moderate, and liberal. Conservative judge preferences represent the lower one-quarter of judge ideology scores. Moderate judge preferences characterize the middle one-half of judge ideology scores. Liberal judge preferences are operationalized as the upper one-quarter of judge ideol-

ogy scores (Brace et al., "Measuring the Preferences of State Supreme Court Justices").

39. Like the relationship between public opinion and votes to reverse the death penalty reported in Figure 10.2, public support for the death penalty is separated into three categories: strong, moderate, and weak. These categories are determined by Brace et al.'s measure of state death penalty tolerance (Brace et al., "Public Opinion in the American States"). Similarly, as with the relationship between judge ideology and votes to reverse the death penalty reported in Figure 10.7, judge ideology is divided into three categories of ideology: conservative, moderate, and liberal. These categories are determined by Brace et al.'s measure of state supreme court judge ideology (Brace et al., "Measuring the Preferences of State Supreme Court Justices").

Chapter 11

Judicial Reform and the Future of Judicial Elections

Matthew J. Streb and Brian Frederick

As the preceding chapters clearly illustrate, debates over judicial selection are often heated. Arguments run the gamut from eliminating judicial elections entirely to allowing them to "look like" elections for other offices. It is not the contributors' intentions to engage in this debate here (although undoubtedly we all have our opinions on the best form of judicial selection). Instead, we have tried to provide empirical evidence about the judicial election process and will leave the normative debate about judicial elections to others.

Because of the controversy over judicial selection, reform movements are in full gear to attempt to limit what is seen by opponents of judicial elections as the corrupting process of the "new politics of judicial elections," especially as the courts seem to be moving in a direction that would allow judicial candidates to be subjected to the same rules as, say, a candidate for Congress. In this final chapter, we briefly address some of the strategies employed by the reformers and then comment on how they are likely to view the results of this book. Finally, we close by briefly discussing the future of judicial elections research.

Reform Efforts in the States

As Streb notes in chapter 1, discussion of judicial selection reform is as old as the process itself; it is certainly not a new phenomenon. However, recently reform advocates have seemed increasingly vocal, especially in the wake of the Supreme Court's decision in *Republican Party of Minnesota v.*

White.[1] In combination with the skyrocketing costs and the increasing bitterness of state judicial elections over the past decade, this decision has raised doubts among many legal observers about the character of the judicial system at the state and local levels. In addition, a wave of recent negative press coverage has called into question the impartiality and legitimacy of the judicial system.[2]

To counteract this image, numerous ideas have been advanced to restore confidence that justice can be administered fairly in the midst of such an allegedly unwieldy environment. In this section, we delineate some of the changes in judicial selection that have been proposed and, in some cases, enacted in recent years. These developments reveal that while monumental concerns are voiced about the perceived corrosive forces pervading state and local judicial systems, the steps actually taken to alter the status quo have been modest in character. Since the trends in this area are too numerous to cover exhaustively in a forum of this length, here we narrow the focus to five specific issues: (1) the perennial call for the elimination of contested judicial elections, (2) efforts to reform the financing of judicial campaigns, (3) the push for nonpartisan judicial elections, (4) the institution of judicial campaign conduct committees, and (5) the distribution of judicial voter guides. Some of the authors in this volume have touched on a few of these topics in their individual chapters (for example, Deborah Goldberg in chapter 5).

Elimination of Judicial Elections

For over seventy years, the American Bar Association (ABA) has been on record in favor of jettisoning judicial elections and replacing them with merit selection and retention, on the grounds that elections endanger the independence and impartiality of the judiciary.[3] The ABA is not alone in this belief, as many elected judges and politicians have also endorsed replacing judicial elections with a merit selection system relying on appointments. Former Republican governors John Engler of Michigan and Tom Ridge of Pennsylvania, and the chief justices of Texas, Ohio, and several other states, have been proponents of this idea as well.[4] Even in a strong party organization city like Philadelphia, local party leaders have warmed to the possibility of transitioning to a strictly appointive process. Philadelphia mayor John Street has referred to the present electoral system as "awful" and a "disincentive" to attracting qualified citizens to the bench.[5]

The belief that judicial elections compromise the fairness and integrity of the courts is apparently not shared by voters. When given the chance to forgo their right to an up or down vote on judges in contested elections, citizens have been unwilling to relinquish this responsibility. The South Dakota House and Senate overwhelmingly approved a constitutional amendment for consideration by the voters that would have done away with contested elections for trial court judges in the state and provided for appointment and retention following a merit screening. However, in November 2004, some 62 percent of the state's electorate decisively rejected this amendment.[6] In 2000, Florida voters were granted the same opportunity to decide on a circuit by circuit basis whether they wanted to transition from contested elections to appointment and retention; in all of the twenty circuits, this option was resoundingly rejected. In Michigan, a constitutional amendment to replace elections for the state's supreme court with gubernatorial appointment was introduced in the state senate in 2001, but it never made it out of committee. The Louisiana legislature considered constitutional amendments to provide for merit selection in 1997, 1999, and 2003; those proposed amendments never garnered enough support to reach the ballot.[7] These examples signify deep voter suspicion toward surrendering their right to have direct electoral control over the selection of judges. While the normative debate over whether judicial elections should exist will continue, because of the recent inability to eliminate judicial elections, reformers must seek out other alternatives.

Public Financing of Judicial Elections

Confronted with a landscape that does not spell the end of judicial elections any time in the foreseeable future, the ABA and other legal organizations have endorsed other measures to make sure that if contested elections are to happen, they do as little as possible to undercut the integrity of the judicial process. As Chris Bonneau mentions in chapter 4, one of the top agenda items for the ABA in furthering this aim is public campaign financing. In 2002 the ABA's Standing Committee on Judicial Independence published a report calling for states to adopt complete taxpayer funding of most judicial campaigns for all high court positions and some intermediate appellate judgeships.[8] The report found that this step was needed to curtail the escalating costs of judicial campaigns that often cause judges to take out loans to finance campaigns and to deflect charges that judicial decisions are influenced by campaign contributions. Also, according to the report, the need to raise money discourages qualified candidates who may be uncomfortable with soliciting donations.[9] The commission did not promote one specific policy prescription that each state should follow; instead, it outlined ten specific principles that ought to drive how such a plan should be implemented. These principles include sensitivity to the U.S. constitutional limits on campaign finance regulations, tailoring programs to meet the needs of the specific jurisdiction, full public funding at a level that is adequate to induce participation, restricting eligibility to serious candidates, conditioning participation on the willingness of candidates not to raise private contributions, and ensuring that stable revenue sources are available for maintenance of the program.[10]

Before 2002, Wisconsin was the only state with public financing of judicial elections. Under Wisconsin law, in operation since 1979, the state provides partial financial support to candidates in races for the supreme court, funded through a state tax return check-off. Nevertheless, as the ABA noted in its report urging public financing, this program has been plagued with a chronic shortfall of funds since its inception.[11] And, it is not clear that the law has kept candidates from spending large sums of money. For example, in 1999 Chief Justice Shirley Abrahamson accepted government funds, but her opponent did not. The two combined to spend $1.36 million on their campaigns.[12]

North Carolina is the only state that has enacted a public financing statute for judicial elections that is consistent with the ABA recommendations. On October 10, 2002, Governor Mike Easley signed into law the North Carolina Judicial Campaign Reform Act.[13] The bill established a voluntary program to supply public funding in the general election for candidates who run for a seat on an appellate court. To become eligible for the program, candidates are required to raise more than $10,000 of seed money in the year before the election, file a declaration of intention to participate with the North Carolina Board of Elections between January 1st and the date of the primary, collect a minimum of $33,000 but no more than $69,000 in contributions ranging between $10 and $500 from at least 350 North Carolina registered voters (none of which can be from political parties or political action committees), and finish first or second in the state's primary election, placing them on the ballot for the November general election.[14] Candidates who fulfill these criteria receive a lump sum payment of public funds that is 125 times the filing fee for a candidate for the North Carolina Court of Appeals and 175 times the filing fee for the North Carolina Supreme Court. In 2004, appeals court candidates were provided with $138,125 apiece, while supreme court candidates received

$201,775 each. There is also a provision that allocates additional funds to candidates if spending by nonparticipating candidates or independent groups exceeds the spending limit agreed to by the participating candidates.[15] Funding for the program is generated principally by a $3 check-off on individual state income tax forms and supplemented by $50 voluntary contributions from lawyers when they pay their privilege license tax, as well as contributions of any size from individuals, corporations, labor groups, and professional associations.

Supporters of public financing claim that the 2004 North Carolina elections were a success. Fourteen of the sixteen candidates who ran for the offices covered by the statute applied for funding, and twelve ended up meeting the requirements for disbursement of funds. Two candidates participating in the program won supreme court races, and two more participants won seats on the state court of appeals (another victorious appeals court candidate applied for funding but did not qualify). Since no candidate was outspent in the election, the matching funds provision was not triggered in any of the races. The winning candidates represented a wide spectrum of gender and racial and ideological diversity.[16] The actual cost of judicial campaigns declined as well, in contrast to most states in the rest of the nation where record after record for spending was eclipsed. In 2002 with six candidates competing for supreme court seats in North Carolina, candidates raised an average of $134,553 compared with 2004, where the candidate average was $126,745. In addition, the distribution of total contributions coming from lawyers plummeted from 40 percent in 2002 to 11 percent in 2004; for business interests, the corresponding figures were 12 percent in 2002 down to 4 percent in 2004.[17]

The outlook for North Carolina's experiment with public funding being replicated in a substantial number of other states is uncertain. When the electorates of Arizona, Maine, and Massachusetts have had the chance to vote on so-called Clean Elections Initiatives, creating programs to publicly fund legislative elections in these states, they have voted to do so. Further, in Illinois, which has been the scene of some of the most highly publicized state supreme court election battles, the state legislature is seriously considering a bill that would establish public financing for judicial campaigns.[18] Public interest groups in Florida, Georgia, Idaho, and Ohio have mobilized efforts to bring about this reform as well.[19] Notwithstanding these developments, there are many obstacles to exporting North Carolina's method of financing judicial campaigns to other states.

One challenge is the fiscal constraints with which most state and local governments must constantly grapple.[20] There are strong competing demands for taxpayer dollars to be used for popular services like health care, education, and transportation that take priority over reforming the way candidates are elected. Asking legislators to impose new fees or tax check-off schemes for this purpose is not a sure-fire vote getter. In fact, as Bonneau notes, only 7 percent of North Carolina taxpayers chose to allocate $3 of their taxes for the public funding of campaigns, an indication that, even if reformers are excited about the North Carolina model, citizens were less so.

Another barrier is the ideological opposition many conservatives feel toward using the public treasury to pay for the cost of campaigns that have traditionally been sponsored by private sources. Further, potential judicial candidates themselves are divided along party lines about whether this policy is advisable. One recent survey of judicial candidates found that 66 percent of Democrats thought that public financing would improve judicial campaigns and 19.1 percent thought it would make them worse, compared with 26.7 percent of Republicans who felt it would be an improvement and 57 percent who felt it would worsen campaigns.[21] These results portend a stark divide in who might participate in such programs were they enacted more broadly. They also undermine the unified front in the legal community that would be vital in leveraging the support behind public funding of judicial elections.

Nonpartisan Elections

With the expansion of public financing a questionable proposition at this juncture, advocates of reform have also highlighted the need to pursue other changes to judicial selection procedures, such as the adoption of nonpartisan elections. The ABA and other reform organizations have suggested that if judicial elections are to be conducted at all, they ought to be done on a nonpartisan basis. A report issued by the National Summit on Improving Judicial Selection, a working group of the National Center for State Courts, insisted that this change will lead to less-competitive elections, curtail the dependence of candidates on political parties and interest groups, and diminish the ideological polarization among candidates (all positives according to the group), even as they acknowledge that such a change may withhold the most important cue available to voters when evaluating judicial candidates.[22] North Carolina state legislators accepted this logic when they included switching to a nonpartisan ballot for judicial elections in the package of reforms passed in 2002. The initial trend toward nonpartisan elections dates back to the progressive era although, in modern times it has been Southern states who have led the way over the last thirty years, as Arkansas, Florida, Georgia, Kentucky, Louisiana, Mississippi, and North Carolina have all instituted nonpartisan judicial elections for some or all of their judges during this period.[23]

Apart from North Carolina, other contemporary examples of states shifting to nonpartisan elections include Arkansas, where in 2000 57 percent of voters approved an amendment to the state's constitution for this purpose, and Mississippi, which had partisan elections from 1910 until 1994 when the Nonpartisan Judicial Election Act was passed.[24] One case study assessing the move to nonpartisan judicial elections in Mississippi revealed that it did not have the effect anticipated by reformers. Spending by candidates for the state supreme court continues to set records, and any diminished role for political parties has been filled by closely aligned interest groups like the Chamber of Commerce, which has invested more heavily than ever before in the judicial election process.[25] And, as Streb finds in chapter 6, party activity has been far from eliminated in nonpartisan judicial contests.

Ending partisan judicial elections does not arouse controversy to the same extent as public financing, and, as the Arkansas example illustrates, there seems to be some public support for the idea. However, some political science research has questioned the wisdom of nonpartisan elections because they remove a cheap, generally reliable cue when voting.[26] Eliminating a candidate's party affiliation from the ballot may make it more difficult for people to cast informed votes, especially in low-information elections.

In spite of the trend toward nonpartisan judicial elections in the South, at least one governor has raised questions regarding the advisability of holding these elections. Georgia governor Sonny Perdue has said that, under certain conditions, he could envision himself supporting a constitutional amendment that would return Georgia to a system of partisan judicial elections. Perdue was willing to consider this change following a fiercely contested battle for the Georgia Supreme Court in 2004 between incumbent Leah Ward Sears, who was backed by many in the Democratic Party's establishment, and challenger Grant Brantley, who was supported by top Republicans, including the governor. In this supposedly nonpartisan race, representatives of both major parties were extremely active on behalf of their favored candidates, which ended in a victory by Sears. In response to the 2004 supreme court campaign, Perdue opined that "if the judiciary wants to keep their races as non-partisan, I think their candidates ought to act in a non-partisan fashion," declaring further that "if we are not able to take partisanship out of races . . . I think we ought to open it up."[27]

The outcome of the race frustrated Republican state legislators who sensed that nonpartisan ballots for judicial elections may stand as a barrier to the increasing GOP tide over the past few years. During the 2005 legislative session, Republican state representative Bill Hembree introduced a constitutional amendment that would mandate partisan judicial elections for all state courts. However, as of this writing, the bill has not advanced beyond the introduction stage, and the chances of it receiving the two-thirds vote of both houses of the Georgia legislature required to send an amendment to the voters seem slim.[28]

Campaign Conduct Committees

As Deborah Goldberg discusses in chapter 5, another area where judicial election reformers have turned their focus is the formation of judicial campaign conduct committees. Currently in place in at least ten states, these committees are designed to establish standards and ethical guidelines for judicial elections and monitor whether candidates comply with those practices. They employ public statements, negative publicity, and sometimes official sanctions, including fines, to help ensure that candidates campaign in an appropriate manner consistent with judicial canons.[29] One study identified three types of committees: (1) official committees, (2) quasi-official committees, and (3) unofficial committees.[30]

Official campaign conduct committees in operation in states such as Florida, Georgia, and Ohio since the 1990s have the official imprimatur of the government and are established by the court system or some other agency within the state or local jurisdiction. Quasi-official committees that have been used in states like Alabama, Michigan, and South Dakota typically consist of a group of private citizens appointed by a court system but lacking specific statutory authority. Unofficial committees are created by private legal organizations such as the ABA and function completely independent of government. One recent example of a successful unofficial committee was developed in Georgia. In April 2004, as a response to an appeals court decision in *Weaver v. Bonner*[31] that weakened Georgia's law governing campaign conduct, a group of community leaders came together to form the Committee for Ethical Judicial Conduct. This unofficial committee intervened in one court of appeals race, admonishing one candidate for sponsoring misleading television advertisements; the candidate ultimately lost the race.[32]

One of the most effective campaign conduct committees occurred in Alabama for the 1998 judicial elections.[33] Facing the fallout from extremely negative judicial election contests in the early 1990s, the supreme court created a campaign conduct committee to rein in perceived past abuses. According to one case study, the committee dealt with over 350 candidate inquiries about what constituted proper election conduct and was credited by members of the Alabama legal community interviewed for the study with the improvement in the tone and quality of the campaign that occurred in the 1998 and 2000 campaigns. However, due to a budget shortfall, no committee was created for the 2002 judicial election.[34]

Illinois also recently established a campaign conduct committee, although it had less success than the ones in Georgia and Alabama. With an expensive, bitterly partisan race anticipated for the Illinois Supreme Court in 2004, a statewide committee was launched; it called for misleading advertisements to be pulled from television in this race, but this declaration was ignored.[35]

Voter Information Guides

Finally, judicial voter guides are also a step judicial election reformers feel can counter the surging power of special interests they deem a threat to the integrity of the legal system. These guides often contain biographies, a listing of a candidate's legal experience and credentials, and a short, personal statement from the candidates offering an informative cue for voters who may be unaware of who is running for judge in their jurisdiction. Advocates of voter information guides contend that they "provide a clear, unfiltered means by which voters can receive quality information about those who are running, in an easily digestible, side-by-side format" and "do not need to provide a forum for announcing views on hot button issues; they just need to carry basic information about the candidates directly to the voters."[36]

Before 2004, Alaska, California, Oregon, Utah, and Washington mailed out voter guides that included information about judicial candidates, as well as candidates for other offices.[37] Ohio and Michigan have partnered with private groups to produce on-line voter guides. However, it is North

Carolina that pioneered the use of voter information guides in the 2004 election by mailing to every registered voter in the state a separate booklet focused exclusively on judicial candidates.[38]

The American public seems to believe that voter guides would be useful. A survey conducted by Zogby International for the judicial reform group Justice at Stake revealed that 67 percent of Americans would be more likely to vote in judicial elections if they received a judicial voter guide.[39] Polling by Washington State University following the 1996 election found that 71 percent of individuals who voted for judicial candidates felt the more general voter guide was an important source of information when they cast their ballots.[40]

To be sure, the quality of voter guides can vary considerably, making some more useful than others. For example, in the five contested California judicial races in Los Angeles County in 2004, only four of the ten candidates provided statements; in only one race did both candidates give a write-up. In that race, the candidates listed endorsements of a wide range of individuals and groups, but the information was of little help. They each received endorsements from law enforcement agencies and were rated "well qualified" by the Los Angeles County Bar. Both were backed by prominent Democrats. While Los Angeles County Sheriff Lee Baca endorsed one, he said about the other, "Judy Meyer has shown herself to be a person of honesty, integrity, and sound judgment." From the candidates' statements, it is extremely difficult to determine which candidate is more qualified and would do a better job.

Furthermore, objections to government-sponsored guides could once again come from conservatives who do not think it is the responsibility of government to commandeer a responsibility that rightfully belongs to the candidates themselves. Of course, state and local budget climates will also dictate whether this reform can spread to other states, unless nonpartisan organizations will step forward to foot the bill.

Judicial Election Advocates versus Judicial Election Reformers

The debate over whether judicial elections should exist, and, if so, over how they should be conducted will not subside any time soon. While there is little evidence that judicial elections will be abandoned, scholars and government leaders will continue the normative discussion. Advocates and reformers can point to many of the nonnormative findings of this book to bolster their normative arguments. What is most interesting, however, is that advocates and reformers will likely stress the *same* findings to make their claims.

The chapters by Melinda Gann Hall (chapter 9) and Paul Brace and Brent Boyea (chapter 10) best illustrate this point. Supporters of judicial elections will be pleased by Hall's findings that judicial elections do promote accountability, and Brace and Boyea's analysis that shows that judicial decisions may be influenced by the threat of reelection. These reasons, according to judicial election advocates, are exactly why judges should be elected. Judges should be accountable to the people, and public opinion should have some role in a judge's decision. Many supporters of judicial elections oppose retention elections because of the belief that they fail to hold judges as accountable as those who run in partisan or nonpartisan elections; Hall's findings confirm this view. Opponents of judicial elections will likely point out that the findings of these two chapters are *exactly the problem.* Judicial accountability threatens judicial independence, and the job of a judge is not to follow what could be momentary passions of a fickle public but to uphold and interpret the law. If we are forced to have judicial elections, opponents would argue, then we should have retention elections for exactly the reasons that supporters of judicial elections are less supportive of retention elections.

Advocates and reformers are likely to argue over whether the results of other chapters in the book are positive or negative as well. On the one hand, increased campaign spending and growing interest group and partisan activity (as documented by Bonneau [chapter 4], Goldberg [chapter 5], and Streb [chapter 6]) could be beneficial because voters will be more likely to obtain information. On the other hand, greater campaign spending requires judicial candidates to raise money, which can lead to a conflict of interest—perceived or otherwise. Interest group involvement can threaten judicial independence and change the tone of judicial campaigns. Partisan activity can embroil judges in politics, which can affect the public's perception as judges being impartial observers of the law.

Advocates and reformers may also argue over the positives and negatives of Rachel Caufield's findings (chapter 3). Advocates argue that recent court rulings, such as *White,* have the potential to allow voters to cast more informed votes by allowing candidates to speak more freely about issues. And, again, counter reformers, that is exactly the problem. Rulings such as *White* are likely to lead to nastier judicial campaigns where the qualifications of judges won't be paramount but, instead, their positions on issues such as abortion or the death penalty. Caufield's results show preliminary evidence that this could be the case. And, if Richard Hasen (chapter 2) is correct about the constitutional future of many judicial canons, this trend could only get worse.

Advocates and reformers will likely debate the pros and cons of Lawrence Baum and David Klein's findings (chapter 8) as well. "See," advocates will argue, "high-information campaigns will allow more people to participate in judicial elections." Judicial reformers will likely respond, "True, but the determinants of the vote changed little." In other words, voters don't appear to be any more informed even when additional information is available about the candidates.

It is not just a debate over whether judicial elections should exist; there is also controversy over what *kind* of judicial elections should exist. Supporters of nonpartisan elections might emphasize the Bonneau or Streb chapters to illustrate that nonpartisan elections can control campaign spending and partisan activity. Supporters of partisan elections would counter that we don't necessarily want these activities to be controlled, and, in any case, it doesn't appear that nonpartisan elections eliminate campaign spending and partisan activity as much as supporters of nonpartisan elections would like. Also, supporters of partisan elections would likely identify Brian Schaffner and Jennifer Segal Diascro's findings (chapter 7) as a reason to institute partisan elections instead of nonpartisan ones since partisan elections are more likely to receive press coverage, which may help people cast more-informed votes.

In sum, while the chapters in this book paint a much clearer picture of what is happening in judicial campaigns and how those campaigns affect judges once on the bench, they do little to settle the normative debate over whether judicial elections should exist and, if so, in what form they should exist.

Future of Judicial Elections Research

While the debate over judicial elections will no doubt continue, we hope that systematic research of judicial elections and their effects continue as well. Much good work has already been done, but many important questions remain, related to the fields of both law and political behavior. The future of judicial election research looks promising because the data-collection obstacles that once severely limited judicial election research are diminishing somewhat. Organizations, such as Justice at Stake, have a wealth of data related to state supreme court elections available on their website (particularly impressive is the data on campaign commercials that have been collected over the last few campaign cycles). Still, data on voting in judicial elections is scare since judicial elections are rarely included on preelection and postelection surveys.

There are two particular voids that we would like to see addressed. First, much more research is needed on the effects of judicial campaigns on turnout and voter decisionmaking, especially after *White*. What conditions lead to greater voter turnout (and less voter rolloff) in judicial elections? What effects do campaign advertisements in judicial elections have on voters? Do they stimulate turnout? Is negative advertising a positive in that it informs more people, which makes them more likely to vote, or damaging in that it makes people more cynical about the justice system? These are just a few of the many questions that we hope researchers will tackle in the future.

A second void in the study of judicial elections is research regarding trial court and intermediate appellate court elections. Most of the chapters in this book (and in the judicial elections research in general) analyze state supreme court elections. This is certainly understandable since state supreme courts are the "courts of last resort" and there are only a few races for which data must be collected each year. The number of judges serving on lower-level courts is enormous, making data collection more difficult. Still, questions about the quality of voting, the influence of campaigns, and whether elections can hold judges at these levels accountable remain to be explored.

Nevertheless, the future of judicial election research looks promising. Hopefully future research will continue to add to the debate over judicial elections and whether one should have to run for judge.

NOTES

1. *Republican Party of Minnesota v. White*, 536 U.S. 765 (2002).
2. Glaberson, "States Taking Steps to Rein in Excesses of Judicial Politicking"; Wilke, "Chamber of Commerce Targets State Races"; France and Woellert, "Battle over the Courts."
3. Streb, "Judicial Elections."
4. Glaberson, "States Taking Steps to Rein in Excesses of Judicial Politicking."

5. Quoted in Gelbart, "Even the Power Brokers Seek Appointed Judges."

6. Rottman and Schotland, "2004 Judicial Elections."

7. Edwards, *Judicial Selection in Southern States.*

8. American Bar Association Standing Committee on Judicial Independence, *Report of the Commission on Public Financing of Judicial Campaigns.*

9. Ibid., pp. 11–26.

10. Ibid., pp. 30–55.

11. Ibid., p. 27.

12. Kay, "Taxing Thought."

13. Bend, "North Carolina's Public Financing of Judicial Campaigns."

14. Goldberg et al., *New Politics of Judicial Elections 2004*, p. 38.

15. Bend, "North Carolina's Public Financing of Judicial Campaigns," pp. 600–602.

16. Goldberg et al., *New Politics of Judicial Elections 2004*, p. 39.

17. Ibid., p. 21.

18. Ewing, "Judicial Reform Proposal Calls for Public Funding of Elections in Illinois."

19. Thomas et al., "Interest Groups and State Court Elections."

20. Bend, "North Carolina's Public Financing of Judicial Campaigns," p. 607.

21. Abbe and Herrnson, "Public Financing for Judicial Elections?"

22. National Center for State Courts, *Call to Action*, p. 14.

23. Becker and Reddick, *Judicial Selection Reform*, p. 28.

24. Edwards, *Judicial Selection in Southern States*, p. 5.

25. Becker and Reddick, *Judicial Selection Reform*, pp. 27–33.

26. Schaffner et al., "Teams without Uniforms"; Schaffner and Streb, "Partisan Heuristic in Low-Information Elections."

27. Basinger, "Perdue Looks at Partisan Judicial Elections."

28. Ibid.

29. Goldberg et al., *New Politics of Judicial Elections 2004*, p. 41.

30. Reed and Schotland, "Judicial Campaign Conduct Committees."

31. *Weaver v. Bonner*, 309 F.3d 1312 (11th Cir. 2002).

32. Rottman and Schotland, "2004 Judicial Elections," p. 18.

33. Goldberg et al., *New Politics of Judicial Elections 2004*, p. 42.

34. Becker and Reddick, *Judicial Selection Reform*, pp. 11–16.

35. Rottman and Schotland, "2004 Judicial Elections," p. 18.

36. Goldberg et al., *New Politics of Judicial Elections 2004*, pp. 40–41.

37. Becker and Reddick, *Judicial Selection Reform*, p. 43.

38. Goldberg et al., *New Politics of Judicial Elections 2004*, p. 41.

39. Ibid., p. 40.

40. Becker and Reddick, *Judicial Selection Reform*, p. 46.

Bibliography

Articles and Books

2003 State Expenditure Report. Washington, D.C.: National Association of State Budget Officers, 2004.

Abbe, Owen G., and Paul S. Herrnson. "Public Financing for Judicial Elections? A Judicious Perspective on the ABA's Proposal for Campaign Finance Reform." *Polity* 35 (2003): 535–554.

Abramson, Paul R., John H. Aldrich, and David W. Rohde. *Change and Continuity in the 2004 Elections.* Washington, D.C.: CQ Press, 2006.

Achen, Christopher H. "Mass Political Attitudes and the Survey Response." *American Political Science Review* 69 (1975): 1218–1231.

———. "Measuring Representation." *American Journal of Political Science* 22 (1978): 475–510.

Administrative Office of Courts. "Candidate Free Speech Ruling Does Not Affect Mississippi Code of Judicial Conduct." Press Release, July 10, 2002.

Alabama Civil Justice Reform League. "Trial Lawyer Money." Advertisement storyboard. Available at http://www.brennancenter.org/programs/downloads/buying time_2004/stsupct_al_alcjr_trial_lawyer_money.pdf (accessed July 11, 2006).

Aldrich, John H. *Why Parties? The Origin and Transformation of Political Parties in America.* Chicago: University of Chicago Press, 1995.

American Bar Association. *Annotated Model Code of Judicial Conduct.* Chicago: Center for Professional Responsibility, 2004.

———. *Model Code of Judicial Conduct, 1972.* Chicago: American Bar Association, 1972.

———. *Model Code of Judicial Conduct, 1990.* Chicago: American Bar Association, 1990.

———. *Model Code of Judicial Conduct, 2003.* Chicago: American Bar Association, 2003.

American Bar Association Standing Committee on Judicial Independence. *Report of the Commission on Public Financing of Judicial Campaigns.* Chicago: American Bar Association, 2002.

American Judicature Society. *Judicial Selection in the States: Appellate and General Jurisdiction Courts.* N.d. Available at http://www.ajs.org/js/JudicialSelection Charts.pdf (accessed February 3, 2006).

American RadioWorks. *Justice for Sale?* January 2005. Available at http://american radioworks.publicradio.org/features/judges (accessed July 12, 2006).

Arnold, R. Douglas. *Congress, the Press and Political Accountability.* Princeton, N.J.: Princeton University Press, 2004.

Aspin, Larry T., and William K. Hall. "Retention Elections and Judicial Behavior." *Judicature* 77 (1994): 306–315.

Badertscher, Nancy. "Justice Candidates Trade Barbs on TV." *Atlanta Journal Constitution,* July 9, 2004: 2E.

Bagdikian, Ben H. *The Media Monopoly,* 5th ed. Boston: Beacon, 1987.

Baker, Kara. "Is Justice for Sale in Ohio? An Examination of Ohio Judicial Elections and Suggestions for Reform Focusing on the 2000 Race for the Supreme Court." *Akron Law Review* 35 (2001): 159–184.

Banks, Jeffrey S., and D. Roderick Kiewiet. "Explaining Patterns of Candidate Competition in Congressional Elections." *American Journal of Political Science* 33 (1989): 997–1015.

Barber, Kathleen L. "Judicial Politics in Ohio." In *Government and Politics in Ohio,* ed. Carl Lieberman. Lanham, Md.: University Press of America, 1984.

Bartels, Larry M. "Constituency Opinion and Congressional Policy-Making: The Reagan Defense Build Up." *American Political Science Review* 85 (1991): 457–474.

Basinger, Brian. "Perdue Looks at Partisan Judicial Races." *Augusta Chronicle,* May 23, 2005. Available at http://chronicle.augusta.com/stories/052405/met_4227612 .shtml (accessed July 12, 2006).

Baum, Lawrence. "Electing Judges." In *Contemplating Courts,* ed. Lee Epstein. Washington, D,C,: CQ Press, 1995: 18–43.

———. "The Electoral Fates of Incumbent Judges in the Ohio Court of Common Pleas." *Judicature* 66 (1983): 420–430.

———. "Explaining the Vote in Judicial Elections: The 1984 Supreme Court Elections." *Western Political Quarterly* 40 (1987): 361–371.

———. "Judicial Elections and Judicial Independence: The Voter's Perspective." *Ohio State Law Journal* 64 (2003): 13–41.

Bayne, William C. "Lynchard's Candidacy: Ads Putting Spice into Justice Race." *Commercial Appeal,* October 29, 2000: DS1.

Becker, Daniel, and Malia Reddick. *Judicial Selection Reform: Examples from Six States.* Des Moines, Iowa: American Judicature Society, 2003.

Behrens, Mark A., and Cary Silverman. "The Case for Adopting Appointive Judicial Selection Systems for State Court Judges." *Cornell Journal of Law and Public Policy* 11 (2002): 273–360.

Bend, Doug. "North Carolina's Public Financing of Judicial Campaigns: A Preliminary Analysis" *Georgetown Journal of Legal Ethics* 18 (2005): 597–609.

Berkowitz, Dan, and David Pritchard. "Political Knowledge and Communication Resources." *Journalism Quarterly* 66 (1989): 697–701.

Berkson, Larry C. "Judicial Selection in the United States: A Special Report." *Judicature* 64 (1980): 176–193.

Bischoff, Laura A. "Races for the Court Raised Millions." *Dayton Daily News,* March 4, 2003: B1.

Blume, John, and Theodore Eisenberg. "Judicial Politics, Death Penalty Appeals, and Case Selection: An Empirical Study." *Southern California Law Review* 72 (1999): 465–503.

Bond, Jon R., Richard Fleisher, and Jeffrey C. Talbert. "Partisan Differences in Candidate Quality in Open Seat House Races, 1976–1994." *Political Research Quarterly* 50 (1997): 281–299.

Bonneau, Chris W. "Electoral Verdicts: Incumbent Defeats in State Supreme Court Elections." *American Politics Research* 33 (2005): 818–841.

———. "Patterns of Campaign Spending and Electoral Competition in State Supreme Court Elections." *Justice System Journal* 25 (2004): 21–38.

———. "What Price Justice(s)? Understanding Campaign Spending in State Supreme Court Elections." *State Politics and Policy Quarterly* 5 (2005): 107–125.

Bonneau, Chris W., and Melinda Gann Hall. "Mobilizing Interest: Money, Quality, and Ballot Rolloff in State Supreme Court Elections." Paper presented at the Annual Meeting of the Midwest Political Science Association, Chicago, April 20–23, 2006.

———. "Predicting Challengers in State Supreme Court Elections: Context and the Politics of Institutional Design." *Political Research Quarterly* 56 (2003): 337–349.

———. "The Wisconsin Judiciary." In *Wisconsin Government and Politics,* 8th ed., ed. Ronald E. Weber. Boston: McGraw-Hill, 2004: 171–196.

Bosworth, Matthew H. *Courts as Catalysts: State Supreme Courts and Public School Finance Equity.* Albany: State University of New York Press, 2001.

Brace, Paul, and Melinda Gann Hall. "The Interplay of Preferences, Case Facts, Context, and Rules in the Politics of Judicial Choice." *Journal of Politics* 59 (1997): 1206–1231.

Brace, Paul, and Kellie Sims-Butler. "New Perspectives for the Comparative Study of the Judiciary: The State Supreme Court Project." *Justice Systems Journal* 22 (2002): 243–262.

———. "Studying Courts Comparatively: The View from the American States." *Political Research Quarterly* 48 (1995): 5–29.

Brace, Paul, Melinda Gann Hall. and Laura Langer. "Judicial Choice and the Politics of Abortion: Institutions, Context, and the Autonomy of Courts." *Albany Law Review* 62 (1999): 1265–1303.

———. "Measuring the Preferences of State Supreme Court Justices." *Journal of Politics* 62 (2000): 387–413.

Brace, Paul, Kellie Sims-Butler, Kevin T. Arceneaux, and Martin Johnson. "Public Opinion in the American States: New Perspectives Using National Survey Data." *American Journal of Political Science* 46 (2002): 173–189.

Bradshaw, James. "Special-Interest Money Dominates O'Donnell-Resnick Race." *Columbus Dispatch,* October 8, 2000: D5.

Brady, Henry E., and Paul M. Sniderman. "Attitude Attribution: A Group Basis for Political Reasoning." *American Political Science Review* 79 (1985): 1061–1078.

Brennan Center for Justice. *Advice, Consent and Advertising: Television Advertising on Nominations to the U.S. Supreme Court.* Available at http://www.brennan center.org/programs/scnominations/robertsnomination.html (accessed July 12, 2006).

——. Republican Party of Minnesota v. White: *What Does the Decision Mean for the Future of State Judicial Elections?* Available at http://www.brennancenter .org/programs/dem_fc_lit_white_kellymemo.html (accessed July 10, 2006).

——. *Buying Time 2004: Final Reports.* Available at http://brennancenter.org/ programs/buyingtime_2004/finaldata_2004.html (accessed July 7, 2006).

Briffault, Richard. "Judicial Campaign Codes after *Republican Party of Minnesota v. White.*" *University of Pennsylvania Law Review* 153 (2004): 181–238.

Bright, Stephen B., and Patrick J. Keenan. "Judges and the Politics of Death: Deciding between the Bill of Rights and the Next Election in Capital Cases." *Boston University Law Review* 75 (1995): 759–835.

Brody, Richard A., and Benjamin I. Page. "The Assessment of Policy Voting." *American Political Science Review* 66 (1972): 450–458.

Brooks, Richard R. W., and Steven Raphael. "Life Terms or Death Sentences: The Uneasy Relationship between Judicial Elections and Capital Punishment." *Journal of Criminal Law and Criminology* 92 (2002): 609–639.

Bryce, James. *The American Commonwealth.* New York: Macmillan, 1914.

Bundy, Jennifer. "Judge Dismisses Former Justice's Libel Lawsuit." *WVEC.com,* July 26, 2005. Available at http://www.wvec.com/sharedcontent/APStories/stories/ D8BIPHI04.html (accessed July 12, 2006).

Byrne, Gary C., and J. Kristian Pueschel. "But Who Should I Vote for For County Coroner?" *Journal of Politics* 36 (1974): 778–784.

"Campaign Trail." *Olympian,* September 25, 2002: 4B.

Campbell, Angus, Phillip E. Converse, Warren E. Miller, and Donald Stokes. *The American Voter.* New York: Wiley, 1960.

Cann, Damon M. "Campaign Contributions and Judicial Behavior." *American Review of Politics* 23 (2002): 261–274

Carp, Robert A., and Ronald Stidham. *Judicial Process in America,* 5th ed. Washington, D.C.: CQ Press, 2001.

Case, David W. "In Search of an Independent Judiciary: Alternatives to Judicial Elections in Mississippi." *Mississippi College Law Review* 13 (1992): 1–36.

Caufield, Rachel Paine. "In the Wake of *White:* How States Are Responding to *Republican Party of Minnesota v. White* and How Judicial Elections Are Changing." *Akron Law Review* 38 (2005): 625–647.

Champagne, Anthony. "Access to Justice: Can Business Coexist with the Civil Justice System?" *Loyola of Los Angeles Law Review* 38 (2005): 1483–1515.

————. "Interest Groups and Judicial Elections," *Loyola of Los Angeles Law Review* 34 (2001): 1391–1404.

————. "Political Parties and Judicial Elections." *Loyola of Los Angeles Law Review* 34 (2001): 1411–1427.

————. "The Politics of Judicial Selection." *Policy Studies Journal* 31 (2003): 413–419.

Champagne, Anthony, and Judith Haydel. *Judicial Reform in the States.* Lanham, Md.: University Press of America, 1993.

Cheek, Kyle, and Anthony Champagne. *Judicial Politics in Texas: Partisanship, Money, and Politics in State Supreme Courts.* New York: Peter Lang, 2005.

————. "Political Party Affiliation in Partisan and Nonpartisan Judicial Elections: Partisan Judicial Elections?Lessons from a Bellwether State." *Willamette Law Review* 39 (2003): 1357–1383.

"Cheers and Jeers." *Cleveland Plain Dealer,* November 8, 2002: B8.

Citizens for a Strong Ohio. "O'Donnell Lanzinger Safety." Advertisement storyboard. Available at http://www.brennancenter.org/programs/downloads/buying time_2004/stsupct_oh_cfsoh_odonnell_lanzinger_safety.pdf (accessed July 11, 2006).

Clark, John A., and Charles L Prysby. "Studying Southern Political Party Activists," In *Southern Political Party Activists: Patterns of Conflict and Change, 1991–2001,* ed. John A. Clark and Charles L. Prysby. Lexington: University Press of Kentucky, 2004: 1–12.

Clarke, Peter. and Susan H. Evans. *Covering Campaigns: Journalism in Congressional Elections.* Stanford, Calif.: Stanford University Press, 1983.

Converse, Phillip E. "The Nature of Belief Systems in Mass Publics." In *Ideology and Discontent,* ed. David Apter. Glencoe, Ill.: Free Press, 1964: 206–231.

Cook, Timothy E. *Governing the News: The News Media as a Political Institution.* Chicago: University of Chicago Press, 2005.

Cotter, Cornelius P., James L. Gibson, John F. Bibby, and Robert J. Huckshorn. *Party Organizations in American Politics.* New York: Praeger, 1984.

Council of State Governments. *The Book of the States.* Lexington, Ky.: Council of State Governments, 1998–1999.

Coyle, Marcia. "It Won't Be Long: Supreme Court Took a Narrow View in Ruling on Judicial Candidates Talking on the Issues, so Lawsuits Are Expected Soon." *Broward Daily Business Review,* July 17, 2002: A8.

Craig, Jon. "O'Neill Seeks to Unseat Appointee O'Donnell." *Columbus Dispatch,* October 31, 2004: B5.

————. "Other Ad Campaigns." *Columbus Dispatch,* October 29, 2002: B9.

Croley, Steven P. "The Majoritarian Difficulty: Elective Judiciaries and the Rule of Law." *University of Chicago Law Review* 62 (1995): 689–714.

Crosson, Scott. *Impact of the 2004 North Carolina Judicial Voter Guide.* Raleigh: North Carolina Center for Voter Education and Justice at Stake Campaign, 2005.

Dao, James. "In a Rare Battle, Justices Are Fighting for Their Seats." *New York Times,* November 6, 2005: 25.

Davies, Janet. "Supreme Court Has One Contested Seat." *Statesman Journal,* October 16, 2000: 1A.

Davis, Richard. *Decisions and Images: The Supreme Court and the Press.* Englewood Cliffs, N.J.: Prentice Hall, 1994.

DeFleur, Melvin L., Lucinda Davenport, Mary Cronin, and Margaret DeFleur. "Audience Recall of News Stories Presented by Newspaper, Computer, Television, and Radio." *Journalism Quarterly* 71 (1992): 443–456.

Delli Carpini, Michael X., and Scott Keeter. *What Americans Know about Politics and Why It Matters.* New Haven, Conn.: Yale University Press, 1996.

Demers, David. "Corporate Newspaper Bashing: Is It Justified?" *Newspaper Research Journal* 20 (1999): 83–97.

Democracy North Carolina. *Judicial Campaign Reform Successes, By the Numbers.* 2005. Available at http://www.democracync.org/nc/judicialcampaignreform/JCRAsuccess.pdf (accessed July 12, 2006).

Dimino, Michael R. "Judicial Elections versus Merit Selection: The Futile Quest for a System of Judicial 'Merit' Selection." *Albany Law Review* 67 (2004): 803–819.

Downs, Anthony. *An Economic Theory of Democracy.* New York: Harper, 1957.

Dreiling, Geri L. "Supreme Fight: Special Interests Are Turning the Race for a Seat on Illinois' High Court into a Battle over Legal Reform." *Illinois Times,* May 27, 2004. Available at http://illinois.gyrosite.com/gyrobase/Content?oid=3205 (accessed July 12, 2006).

Dubois, Philip L. *From Ballot to the Bench: Judicial Elections and the Quest for Accountability.* Austin: University of Texas Press, 1980.

———. "Voter Turnout in State Judicial Elections: An Analysis of the Tail on the Electoral Kite." *Journal of Politics* 41 (1979): 865–887.

———. "Voting Cues in Nonpartisan Trial Court Elections: A Multivariate Assessment." *Law and Society Review* 18 (1984): 395–436.

Edwards, Todd. *Judicial Selection in Southern States.* Atlanta: Council of State Governments, 2004.

Eisenstein, James. "Financing Pennsylvania's Supreme Court Candidates." *Judicature* 84 (2000): 10–19.

Epstein, Lee, Jack Knight, and Olga Shvetsova. "Selecting Selection Systems." In *Judicial Independence at the Crossroads: An Interdisciplinary Approach,* ed. Stephen B. Burbank and Barry Friedman. Thousand Oaks, Calif.: Sage, 2002: 191–226.

Erikson, Robert S. "Constituency Opinion and Congressional Behavior: A Reexamination of the Miller-Stokes Representation Data." *American Journal of Political Science* 22 (1978): 511–535.

Erikson, Robert S., Gerald C. Wright, and John P. McIver. *Statehouse Democracy: Public Opinion and Policy in the American States.* New York: Cambridge University Press, 1993.

Ewing, Phillip. "Judicial Reform Proposal Calls for Public Funding of Elections in Illinois." *St. Louis Post-Dispatch,* February 2, 2006: B7.

Flanigan, William H., and Nancy H. Zingale. *Political Behavior of the American Electorate,* 11th ed. Washington: CQ Press, 2006.

Flemming, Roy B., and B. Dan Wood. "The Public and the Supreme Court: Individual Justice Responsiveness to American Policy Moods." *American Journal of Political Science* 41 (1997): 468–498.

France, Mike, and Lorraine Woellert. "The Battle over the Courts: How Politics, Ideology and Interests Are Compromising the U.S. Justice System." *Business Week,* September 27, 2004. Available at http://www.businessweek.com/magazine/content/04_39/b3901001_m2001.htm?campaign-id=search (accessed July 12, 2006).

Francia, Peter L., Paul S. Herrnson, John P. Frendreis, and Alan R. Gitelson. "The Battle for the Legislature: Party Campaigning in State House and State Senate Elections." In *The State of the Parties: The Changing Role of Contemporary American Parties,* 4th ed., ed. John C. Green and Rick Farmer. Lanham, Md.: Rowman and Littlefield, 2003: 171–189.

Franz, Michael, and Kenneth Goldstein. "Following the (Soft) Money: Party Advertisements in American Elections." In *The Parties Respond: Changes in American Parties and Campaigns,* 4th ed., ed. L. Sandy Maisel. Boulder, Colo.: Westview Press, 2002: 139–162.

Frendreis, John, and Alan R. Gitelson. "Local Parties in the 1990s: Spokes in a Candidate-Centered Wheel." In *The State of the Parties,* 3rd ed., ed. John C. Green and Daniel M. Shea. Lanham, Md.: Rowman and Littlefield, 1999: 135–153.

Frendreis, John P., James L. Gibson, and Laura L. Vertz. "The Electoral Relevance of Local Party Organizations." *American Political Science Review* 84 (1990): 225–235.

Frendreis, John, Alan R. Gitelson, Gregory Flemming, and Anne Layzell. "Local Political Parties and Legislative Races in 1992." In *The State of the Parties: The Changing Role of Contemporary American Parties,* ed. Daniel M. Shea and John C. Green. Lanham, Md.: Rowman and Littlefield, 1994: 149–162.

Frontline. *Justice for Sale.* Available at http://www.pbs.org/wgbh/pages/frontline/shows/justice/ (accessed July 12, 2006).

Gallagher, Eileen. "Judicial Ethics and the First Amendment: A Survey of States." *Judges' Journal* (Spring 2003): 26–28.

Gallup Organization, Inc. *The Gallup Poll [Online].* March 2, 2001. Available at http:/www.gallup.com/poll/releases/pr010302.asp (accessed July 12, 2006).

Geer, John. *From Tea Leaves to Opinion Polls.* New York: Columbia University Press, 1996.

Gelbart, Marcia. "Even the Power Brokers Seek Appointed Judges" *Philadelphia Inquirer*, April 17, 2005: A1.

Geyh, Charles Gardner. "Publicly Funded Judicial Elections: An Overview." *Loyola of Los Angeles Law Review* 34 (2001): 1467–1487.

———. "Why Judicial Elections Stink." *Ohio State Law Journal* 64 (2003): 43–79.

Gibeaut, John, "Taking Aim." *American Bar Association Journal* 82 (1996): 50–55.

Gibson, James L., John P. Frendreis, and Laura L. Vertz. "Party Dynamics in the 1980s: Change in County Party Organizational Strength, 1980–1984." *American Journal of Political Science* 33 (1989): 67–90.

Gibson, James L., Cornelius P. Cotter, John F. Bibby, and Robert J. Huckshorn. "Whither the Local Parties? A Cross-Sectional and Longitudinal Analysis of the Strength of Party Organizations." *American Journal of Political Science* 29 (1985): 139–160.

Glaberson, William. "A Spirited Campaign for Ohio Court Puts Judges on New Terrain." *New York Times*, July 7, 2000: A11.

———. "States Taking Steps to Rein in Excesses of Judicial Politicking" *New York Times*, June 15, 2001: A1.

Goldberg, Deborah. *Public Funding of Judicial Elections: Financing Campaigns for Fair and Independent Courts.* New York: Brennan Center for Justice, 2002.

Goldberg, Deborah, and Samantha Sanchez. *The New Politics of Judicial Elections 2002: How the Threat to Fair and Impartial Courts Spread to More States in 2002.* Washington, D.C.: Justice at Stake, 2003. Available at http://faircourts.org/files/newpoliticsreport2002.pdf (accessed July 8, 2006).

Goldberg, Deborah, Craig Holman, and Samantha Sanchez. *The New Politics of Judicial Elections: How 2000 Was a Watershed Year for Big Money, Special Interest Pressure, and TV Advertising in State Supreme Court Campaigns.* Washington, D.C.: Justice at Stake, 2002.

Goldberg, Deborah, Sarah Samis, Edwin Bender, and Rachel Weiss. *The New Politics of Judicial Elections 2004: How Special Interest Pressure on Our Courts Has Reached a 'Tipping Point'—and How to Keep Our Courts Fair and Impartial.* Washington, D.C.: Justice at Stake, 2005. Available at http://www.justiceatstake.org/files/newpoliticsreport2004.pdf (accessed July 12, 2006).

Goldberger, David. "The Power of Special Interest Groups to Overwhelm Judicial Election Campaigns: The Troublesome Interaction between the Code of Judicial Conduct, Campaign Finance Laws, and the First Amendment." *University of Cincinnati Law Review* 72 (2003): 1–43.

Goldenberg, Edie N., and Michael W. Traugott. "Mass Media in Legislative Campaigns." *Legislative Studies Quarterly* 12 (1987): 317–339.

Gordon, Tom. "Amendments, Court Races Lead State Ballot," *Birmingham News*, November 5, 2000.

Graber, Doris A. *Mass Media and American Politics.*, 7th ed. Washington, DC: CQ Press, 2006.

Gray, Cynthia. *Developments following* Republican Party of Minnesota v. White, *536 U.S. 765 (2002).* 2006. Available at http://www.ajs.org/ethics/pdfs/development afterwhite.pdf (accessed July 8, 2006).

———. "The States' Response to *Republican Party of Minnesota v. White.*" *Judicature* (2002): 163–164.

Gustin, Georgina. "Candidates Are Asked to Pull Ads." *St. Louis Post-Dispatch,* October 21, 2004: E01.

Hall, Kermit. "The Judiciary on Trial: State Constitutional Reform and the Rise of an Elected Judiciary." *Historian* 46 (1983): 337–354.

Hall, Melinda Gann. "Ballot Roll-off in Judicial Elections: Contextual and Institutional Influences on Voter Participation in the American States." Paper presented at the Annual Meeting of the American Political Science Association, Atlanta, Ga., September 2–5, 1999.

———. "Constituent Influence in State Supreme Courts: Conceptual Notes and Case Study." *Journal of Politics* 49 (1987): 1117–1124.

———. "Electoral Politics and Strategic Voting in State Supreme Courts." *Journal of Politics* 54 (1992): 427–446.

———. "Justices as Representatives: Elections and Judicial Politics in the American States." *American Politics Quarterly* 23 (1995): 485–503.

———. "Mobilizing Voters in State Supreme Court Elections: Competition and Other Contextual Forces as Democratic Incentives." Unpublished ms., Michigan State University, East Lansing, n.d.

———. "State Judicial Politics: Rules, Structures, and the Political Game." In *American State and Local Politics: Directions for the 21st Century,* ed. Ronald E. Weber and Paul Brace. New York: Chatham House, 1999: 114–138.

———. "State Supreme Courts in American Democracy: Probing the Myths of Judicial Reform." *American Political Science Review* 95 (2001): 315–330.

———. "Voluntary Retirements from State Supreme Courts: Assessing Democratic Pressures to Relinquish the Bench." *Journal of Politics* 63 (2001): 1112–1140.

Hall, Melinda Gann, and Chris W. Bonneau. "Does Quality Matter? Challengers in State Supreme Court Elections." *American Journal of Political Science* 50 (2006): 20–33.

Hall, Melinda Gann, and Paul Brace. "Order in the Courts: A Neo-Institutional Approach to Judicial Consensus." *Western Political Quarterly* 42 (1989): 391–407.

Hampel, Paul. "Big-Money Race Sets Record for a U.S. Judicial Contest." *St. Louis Post-Dispatch,* October 31, 2004: A1.

Hansen, Mark. "The High Cost of Judging." *ABA Journal* 77 (1991): 44.

Hasen, Richard L. *The Supreme Court and Election Law: Judging Equality from* Baker v. Carr *to* Bush v. Gore. New York: New York University Press, 2003.

Haynes, Evan. *The Selection and Tenure of Judges.* Newark, N.J.: National Conference on Judicial Councils, 1944.

Herrnson, Paul. "Do Parties Make a Difference? The Role of Party Organizations in Congressional Elections." *Journal of Politics* 48 (1986): 589–615.

Hill, Kim Quaile, and Jan E. Leighley. "Party Ideology, Organization, and Competitiveness as Mobilizing Forces in Gubernatorial Elections." *American Journal of Political Science* 37 (1993): 1158–1178.

Hogan, Robert E. "Party Activists in Election Campaigns." In *Southern Political Party Activists: Patterns of Conflict and Change, 1991–2001,* ed. John A. Clark and Charles L. Prysby. Lexington: University Press of Kentucky, 2004: 171–184.

Hojnacki, Marie, and Lawrence Baum. "Choosing Judicial Candidates: How Voters Explain Their Decisions." *Judicature* 75 (1992): 300–309.

Hoover, Tim. "Conservative Groups Take Aim at Missouri Judge." *Kansas City Star,* October 28, 2004: B3.

Howard, Trisha. "Chamber Backs Judicial Candidate." *St. Louis Post-Dispatch,* June 9, 2004. Available at http://www.stltoday.com/stltoday/news/stories.nsf/News/Metro+East/BD8756721C6AF3940penDocument&Headline=Illinois+Chamber+of+Commerce+endorses+Judge+Karmeier (accessed July 12, 2006).

Huber, Gregory A., and Sanford C. Gordon. "Accountability and Coercion: Is Justice Blind When It Runs for Office?" *American Journal of Political Science.* 48 (2004): 247–263.

Illinois Lawsuit Abuse Watch and Illinois Civil Justice League. *Justice for Sale: The Judges of Madison County.* Arlington Heights: Illinois Lawsuit Abuse Watch and Illinois Civil Justice League 2002.

———. *Justice for Sale II: Half-Million Form Five Trial Lawyers Flood Campaign Coffers.* Arlington Heights: Illinois Lawsuit Abuse Watch and Illinois Civil Justice League, 2004.

"Institute Backs GOP Candidates for High Court." *Birmingham News.,* October 20, 2000. Available at http://www.bhamnews.com/archives/ with Article ID 0010270321 (accessed July 12, 2006).

Institute on Money in State Politics. *State at a Glance: Alabama 2002.* Available at http://www.followthemoney.org (accessed July 12, 2006).

———. *State at a Glance: Mississippi 2002.* Available at http://www.followthemoney.org (accessed July 12, 2006).

———. *State at a Glance: Ohio 2002.* Available at http://www.followthemoney.org (accessed July 12, 2006).

Iyengar, Shanto. "The Effects of Media-Based Campaigns on Candidate and Voter Behavior: Implications for Judicial Elections." *Indiana Law Review* 35 (2001): 691–700.

Jackson, Donald W., and James W. Riddlesperger. "Money and Politics in Judicial Elections: The 1988 Election of the Chief Justice of the Texas Supreme Court." *Judicature* 74 (1991): 184–189.

Jackson, John E. "Issues, Party Choices, and Presidential Votes." *American Journal of Political Science* 19 (1975): 161–185.

Jacobs, Lawrence R., and Robert Y. Shapiro. *Politicians Don't Pander: Political Manipulation and the Loss of Democratic Responsiveness.* Chicago: University of Chicago Press, 2000.

Jacobson, Gary C. *The Politics of Congressional Elections,* 4th ed. New York: Longman, 1997.

Johnson, Martin, Paul Brace, and Kevin T. Arceneaux. "Public Opinion and Dynamic Representation: The Case of Environmental Attitudes." *Social Science Quarterly* 86 (2005): 87–108.

Johnson, Rick A. "Judicial Campaign Speech in Kentucky after *Republican Party of Minnesota v. White.*" *Northern Kentucky Law Review* 30 (2003): 347–413.

Just, Marion, Rosalind Levine, and Todd Belt. "Thinner, Cheaper, Longer." *Columbia Journalism Review* November/December (2001): 12.

Justice at Stake Campaign. *Justice at Stake Frequency Questionnaire.* 2001. Available at http://www.justiceatstake.org/files/JASNationalSurveyResults (accessed January 8, 2006).

———. *Poll of American Voters.* Conducted by Greenberg, Quinlan, Rosner Research Inc. October 30–November 7, 2001. Available at http://www.justiceatstake .org (accessed July 12, 2006).

Justice for All PAC. "Who Is Behind Karmeier?" Advertisement storyboard. Available at http://www.brennancenter.org/programs/downloads/buyingtime_2004/ stsupct_il_jfapac_who_is_behind_karmeier.pdf (accessed July 11, 2006).

Kaniss, Phyllis. *Making Local News.* Chicago: University of Chicago Press, 1991.

Kay, Julie. "A Taxing Thought: Move Afoot in South Florida to Have Public Money Fund Judicial Elections Throughout the State." *Palm Beach Daily Business,* July 17, 2002: A1.

Kearney, Joseph D., and Howard B. Eisenberg. "The Print Media and Judicial Elections: Some Case Studies from Wisconsin." *Marquette Law Review* 85 (2002): 593–778.

Kenworthy, Bill. *Judicial Campaign Speech.* Available at http://www.fac.org/speech/ campaignfinance/topic.aspx?topic=judicial_speech (accessed December 1, 2004).

Key, V. O., Jr. *Public Opinion and American Democracy.* New York: Knopf, 1961.

King, Gary, Michael Tomz, and Jason Wittenberg. "Making the Most of Statistical Analyses: Improving Interpretation and Presentation." *American Journal of Political Science* 44 (2000): 347–361.

Klein, David, and Lawrence Baum. "Ballot Information and Voting Decisions in Judicial Elections." *Political Research Quarterly* 54 (2001): 709–728.

Langer, Laura. *Judicial Review in State Supreme Courts: A Comparative Study.* Albany: State University of New York Press, 2002.

Lawson, Kay, Gerald Pomper, and Maureen Moakley. "Local Party Activists and Electoral Linkage: Middlesex County, NJ." *American Politics Quarterly* 14 (1986): 345–375.

Leighley, Jan E., and Jonathan Nagler. "Socioeconomic Class Bias in Turnout,

1964–1988: The Voters Remain the Same." *American Political Science Review* 86 (1992): 725–736.

Lhotka, William C. "High Court Judge Faces Ouster." *St. Louis Post Dispatch*, October 27, 2004: D1.

Lieb, David A. "Missouri Ruling Lets Candidates for Judge Speak Out." *St. Louis Post-Dispatch*, July 19, 2002: B1.

Liebman, James S., Jeffrey Fagan, Valerie West, and Jonathan Lloyd. "Capital Attrition: Error Rates in Capital Cases, 1973–1995. *Texas Law Review* 78 (2000): 1839–1865.

Link, Bradley. "Had Enough in Ohio? Time to Reform Ohio's Judicial Selection Process." *Cleveland State University Law Review* 51 (2004): 123–152.

Lott, John R., Jr., and Stephen G. Bronars. "Time Series Evidence on Shirking in the United States House of Representatives." *Public Choice* 76 (1993): 125–149.

Lott, John R., Jr., and W. Robert Reed. "Shirking and Sorting in a Political Market with Finite-Lived Politicians." *Public Choice* 61 (1989): 75–96.

Lovrich, Nicholas P., John C. Pierce, and Charles H. Sheldon. "Citizen Knowledge and Voting in Judicial Elections." *Judicature* 73 (1989): 28–33.

Lowenstein, Daniel Hays, and Richard L. Hasen. *Election Law: Cases and Materials,* 3d ed. Durham, N.C.: Carolina Academic Press, 2004.

Mabin, Butch. "North Platte Man Seeks Judges' Ouster." *Lincoln Journal Star,* April 1, 2006. Available at http://www.journalstar.com/articles/2006/04/01/local/doc442ddd9703a96928813339.txt (accessed July 12, 2006).

Manheim, Jarol B. "The News Shapers: Strategic Communication as a Third Force in News Making." In *The Politics of News: The News of Politics,* ed. Doris Graber, Dennis McQuail, and Pippa Norris. Washington, D.C.: Congressional Quarterly Press, 1998: 94–109.

Margolies, Dan. "Ruling Throws a Wrench into the Missouri Plan." *Kansas City Star,* July 16, 2002: D18.

Markus, Gregory B., and Phillip E. Converse. "A Dynamic Simultaneous Equation Model of Electoral Choice." *American Political Science Review* 73 (1979): 1055–1070.

McDermott, Monika L. "Candidate Occupations and Voter Information Shortcuts." *Journal of Politics* 67 (2005): 201–219.

———. "Voting Cues in Low-Information Elections: Candidate Gender as a Social Information Variable in Contemporary United States Elections." *American Journal of Political Science* 41 (1997): 270–283

McElhinny, Brad. "McGraw Campaign Cries Foul." *Charleston Daily Mail,* September 22, 2004: 1A.

McGuire, Kevin T., and James A. Stimson. "The Least Dangerous Branch Revisited: New Evidence on Supreme Court Responsiveness to Public Preferences." *Journal of Politics* 66 (2004): 1018–1035.

Menefee-Libey, David. *The Triumph of Campaign-Centered Politics.* New York: Chatham House, 2000.

Miller, Warren E., and Donald E. Stokes. "Constituency Influence in Congress." *American Political Science Review* 57 (1963): 45–56.

Mishler, William, and Reginald S. Sheehan. "The Supreme Court as a Countermajoritarian Institution? The Impact of Public Opinion on Supreme Court Decisions." *American Political Science Review* 87 (1993): 87–101.

Moerke, Katherine A.. "Must More Speech Be the Solution to Harmful Speech? Judicial Elections after *Republican Party of Minnesota v. White.*" *South Dakota Law Review* 48 (2003): 262–326.

Mondak, Jeffrey J. "Newspapers and Political Awareness." *American Journal of Political Science* 39 (1995): 513–527.

Morello, Carol. "W.Va. Supreme Court Justice Defeated in Rancorous Contest." *Washington Post,* November 4, 2004: A15.

Morris, Brian. "Free Speech in Judicial Elections: Recent U.S. Supreme Court Decision May Affect Montana." *Montana Lawyer,* August 2002. Available at http://www.montanabar.org/montanalawyer/august2002/freespeech.html (accessed July 12, 2006).

Mueller, John E. "Choosing among 133 Candidates." *Public Opinion Quarterly* 34 (1970): 395–402.

Nagel, Stuart. "Political Party Affiliation and Judges' Decisions." *American Political Science Review* 55 (1961): 843–850.

National Ad Hoc Advisory Committee on Judicial Campaign Conduct. *Effective Judicial Campaign Conduct Committees: A How-to Handbook.* Williamsburg, Va.: National Center for State Courts, 2004. Available at http://www.judicial campaignconduct.org/Handbook.pdf (accessed July 12, 2006).

National Center for State Courts. *Call to Action: Statement of the National Summit on Improving Judicial Selection.* Williamsburg, Va.: National Center for State Courts, 2002.

———. *How the Public Views the State Courts: A 1999 National Survey.* Williamsburg, Va.: National Center for State Courts, 1999.

Noe, Glenn C. "Alabama Judicial Selection Reform: A Skunk in Tort Hell." *Cumberland Law Review* 28 (1998): 215–244.

Norrander, Barbara. "The Multi-layered Impact of Public Opinion on Capital Punishment Implementation in the American States." *Political Research Quarterly* 53 (2000): 771–793.

Office of the Administrator of the Courts. *How the Public Views the Courts: A 1999 Washington Statewide Survey Compared to a 1999 National Survey.* Bellevue, Wash.: GMA Research Corporation, 1999. Available at http://www.courts.wa .gov/ (accessed July 11, 2006).

Ohio Political Survey, November 1986. The poll of 988 Ohio voting age residents was conducted during November 1986 and was obtained from the Odum Institute for Research in Social Science, University of North Carolina (NNSPOH 001).

Ohio Political Survey, December 1988. The poll of 652 Ohio voting age residents was conducted during December 1988 and was obtained from the odum Institute for Research in Social Science, University of North Carolina (NNSPOH 003).

Ohio Secretary of State. *Ohio Election Statistics.* Available at http://sos.state.oh.us/ (accessed July 12, 2006).

O'Reilly, James T. "Tort Reform and Term Limits: The 2004 Ohio Experience." *Capital University Law Review* 33 (2005): 529–548.

———. "Writing Checks or Righting Wrongs: Election Funding and the Tort Decisions of the Ohio Supreme Court." *Cleveland State Law Review* 51 (2004): 643–658.

Page, Benjamin I., Robert Y. Shapiro, Paul W. Gronke, and Robert M. Rosenberg. "Constituency, Party, and Representation in Congress." *Public Opinion Quarterly* 48 (1984): 741–756.

Patterson, Thomas E. *The Mass Media Election: How Americans Choose Their President.* New York: Praeger, 1980.

Patterson, Thomas E., and Robert D. McClure. *The Unseeing Eye: The Myth of Television Power in National Politics.* New York: Putnam, 1976.

Pennsylvanians for Modern Courts. *As Pennsylvania Goes, So Goes the Nation: A Case Study of a Supreme Court election in the Post-White Era.* Available at http://www.pmconline.org/pagoesthenation.htm (accessed July 12, 2006).

Poole, Keith T., and Thomas Romer. "Ideology, 'Shirking,' and Representation." *Public Choice* 77 (1993): 185–196.

Poole, Keith T., and Howard Rosenthal. *Congress: A Political-Economic History of Roll Call Voting.* New York: Oxford University Press, 1997.

Popkin, Samuel. *The Reasoning Voter: Communication and Persuasion in Presidential Campaigns.* Chicago: University of Chicago Press, 1991.

Pound, Roscoe. "The Causes of Popular Dissatisfaction with the Administration of Justice." *Journal of the American Judicature Society* 45 (1962): 55–66.

Price, Polly J. "Selection of State Court Judges." In *State Judiciaries and Impartiality: Judging the Judges,* ed. Theodore J. Boutrous et al. Washington, D.C.: National Legal Center for the Public Interest, 1996: 9–19.

Rankin, Bill. "Bernes Wins Judicial Election; Appeals Court Race Long, Costly." *Atlanta Journal-Constitution,* November 24, 2004: D1.

———. "Divisive Supreme Court Fight Ends in Victory for Sears." *Atlanta Journal-Constitution,* July 21, 2004: D1.

Rapp, Christopher. "The Will of the People, the Independence of the Judiciary, and Free Speech in Judicial Elections after *Republican Party of Minnesota v. White.*" *Journal of Law and Politics* 21 (2005): 103–145.

"Recent Cases: State Tort Reform—Ohio Supreme Court Strikes Down State General Assembly's Tort Reform Initiative.—*State Ex Rel. Ohio Academy of Trial Lawyers v. Sheward* 715 N.E.2d 1062 (Ohio 1999)." *Harvard Law Review* 113 (2000): 804–809.

Reed, Barbara, and Roy A. Schotland. "Judicial Campaign Conduct Committees." *Indiana Law Review* 35 (2002): 781–805.

Reid, Traciel V. "The Politicization of Judicial Retention Elections: The Defeat of Justices Lanphier and White." *Research on Judicial Selection 1999*. Chicago: American Judicature Society, 2000: 41–72.

Richey, Diane. "GOP: Justice Race TV Ad 'Misleading.'" *Dayton Daily News*, October 20, 2002: B1.

Rizzo, Katherine. "Chamber Ads Failed in Ohio, Worked Elsewhere." *Associated Press*, November 8, 2000.

Robinson, John P., and Dennis K. Davis. "Television News and the Informed Public: An Information-Processing Approach." *Journal of Communication* 40 (1990): 106–119.

Rothenberg, Lawrence S., and Mitchell S. Sanders. "Severing the Electoral Connection: Shirking in the Contemporary Congress." *American Journal of Political Science* 44 (2000): 316–325.

Rottman, David B., and Roy A. Schotland. "2004 Judicial Elections." *Spectrum* 78 (2005): 17–19.

———. "What Makes Judicial Elections Unique?" *Loyola of Los Angeles Law Review* 34 (2001): 1369–1373.

Schaffner, Brian F., and Patrick J. Sellers. 2003. "The Structural Determinants of Local Congressional News Coverage." *Political Communication* 20 (2003): 41–57.

Schaffner, Brian F., and Matthew J. Streb. "The Partisan Heuristic in Low-Information Elections." *Public Opinion Quarterly* 66 (2002): 559–581.

Schaffner, Brian F., and Michael W. Wagner. "Buy One Get One Free? The Impact of Advertising on Senate Campaign Coverage." Paper presented at the Annual Meeting of the Midwest Political Science Association, Chicago, April 7–10, 2005.

Schaffner, Brian F., Matthew Streb, and Gerald Wright. "Teams without Uniforms: The Nonpartisan Ballot in State and Local Elections." *Political Research Quarterly* 54 (2001): 7–30.

Schotland, Roy A. "Comment: Judicial Independence and Accountability." *Law and Contemporary Problems* 61 (1998): 149–155.

———. "Elective Judges' Campaign Financing: Are State Judges' Robes the Emperor's Clothes of American Democracy?" *Journal of Law and Politics* 2 (1985): 57–167.

———. "Financing Judicial Elections, 2000: Change and Challenge." *Detroit College of Law at Michigan State University Law Review* (2001): 849–898.

———. "Myth, Reality, Past and Present, and Judicial Elections." *Indiana Law Review* 35 (2002): 659–667.

Schotland, Roy A. "Should Judges Be More Like Politicians?" *Court Review* 39 (2002): 8–11.

———. "To the Endangered Species List, Add: Nonpartisan Judicial Elections." *Willamette Law Review* 39 (2003): 1397–1424.

Seely, Christopher. " 'Activist' Judges Targeted." *Southern Voice,* June 11, 2004. Available at http://www.sovo.com/2004/6-11/news/localnews/judge.cfm (accessed July 12, 2006).

Sheldon, Charles H., and Linda S. Maule. *Choosing Justice: The Recruitment of State and Federal Judges.* Pullman: Washington State University Press, 1997.

Shepard, Randall T. "Campaign Speech: Restraint and Liberty in Judicial Ethics." *Georgetown Journal of Legal Ethics* 9 (1996): 1059–1089.

Shields, Tood D., and Robert K. Goidel. "Participation Rates, Socioeconomic Class Biases, and Congressional Elections: A Crossvalidation." *American Journal of Political Science* 41 (1997): 683–691.

Slotnick, Elliot E., and Jennifer A. Segal. *Television News and the Supreme Court: All the News That's Fit to Air?* New York: Cambridge University Press, 1998.

Sniderman, Paul M., Michael G. Hagen, Philip E. Tetlock, and Henry E. Brady. "Reasoning Chains: Causal Models of Policy Reasoning in Mass Publics." *British Journal of Political Science* 16 (1986): 405–430.

Sniderman, Paul M., Richard A. Brody, and Phillip E. Tetlock. *Reasoning and Choice: Explanations in Political Psychology.* New York: Cambridge University Press, 1991.

Snyder, James M., Jr., and Michael M. Ting. "Roll Calls, Party Labels, and Elections." *Political Analysis* 11 (2003): 419–444.

Solimine, Michael E. "The False Promise of Judicial Elections in Ohio." *Capital University Law Review* 30 (2002): 559–582.

Squire, Peverill, and Eric R.A.N. Smith. "The Effect of Partisan Information on Voters in Nonpartisan Elections." *Journal of Politics* 50 (1988): 169–179.

Streb, Matthew J. "Judicial Elections: A Different Standard for the Rulemakers?" in *Law and Election Politics: The Rules of the Game,* ed. Matthew J. Streb. Boulder, Colo.: Lynne Rienner, 2005: 251–276.

Symposium, "Judicial Professionalism in a New Era of Judicial Selection Transcript—Session Three: Improving the Election of Judges, Part II." *Mercer Law Review* 56 (2005): 859–884.

Tabak, Ronald J. "The Death of Fairness: The Arbitrary and Capricious Imposition of the Death Penalty in the 1980s." *New York University Review of Law and Social Change* 14 (1986): 797–847.

Tabarrok, Alexander, and Eric Helland. "Court Politics: The Political Economy of Tort Awards." *Journal of Law and Economics* 42 (1999): 157–187.

Tarr, G. Alan, and Mary Cornelia Aldis Porter. *State Supreme Courts in State and Nation.* New Haven, Conn.: Yale University Press, 1988.

Thomas, Clive S., Michael L. Boyer, and Ronald J. Hrebenar. "Interest Groups and State Court Elections." *Judicature* 87 (2003): 135–149.

Thornton, Kim. *Judicial Campaign Ethics.* King County Bar Association. Available at http://www.kcba.org/barbulletin/0410/article2.html (accessed March 20, 2005).

Tien, Charles. "Representation, Voluntary Retirement, and Shirking in the Last Term." *Public Choice* 106 (2001): 117–130.

Timpone, Richard J. "Ties That Bind: Measurement, Demographics, and Social Connectedness." *Political Behavior* 20 (1998): 53–77.

Tocqueville, Alexis de. 1831. *Democracy in America,* ed. Phillips Bradley. New York: Vintage, 1945.

Uelmen, Gerald F. "Crocodiles in the Bathtub: Maintaining the Independence of State Supreme Courts in an Era of Judicial Politicization." *Notre Dame Law Review* 72 (1997): 1133–1154.

Vanbeek, James R. "Does the Decision to Retire Increase the Amount of Political Shirking?" *Public Finance Review* 19 (1991): 444–456.

Visser, Penny S., Jon A. Krosnick, Jesse Marquette, and Michael Curtain. "Mail Surveys for Election Forecasting? An Evaluation of the Columbus Dispatch Poll." *Public Opinion Quarterly* 60 (1996): 181–227.

Walsh Commission. *The People Shall Judge: Restoring Citizen Control to Judicial Selection.* Olympia, Wash.: Walsh Commission, 1996.

Wattenberg, Martin P. *The Rise of Candidate-Centered Politics: Presidential Elections in the 1980s.* Cambridge, Mass.: Harvard University Press, 1991.

Wattenberg, Martin P., Ian McAllister, and Anthony Salvanto. "How Voting Is Like Taking an SAT Test: An Analysis of American Voter Rolloff." *American Politics Quarterly* 28 (2000): 234–250.

Weaver, David, and Dan Drew. "Voter Learning in the 1990 Off-Year Election: Did the Media Matter?" *Journalism Quarterly* 70 (1993): 356–368.

Weber, Ronald E., Harvey J. Tucker, and Paul Brace. "Vanishing Marginals in State Legislative Elections." *Legislative Studies Quarterly* 16 (1991): 29–47.

Weisberg, Herbert F. *The Total Survey Error Approach: A Guide to the New Science of Survey Research.* Chicago: University of Chicago Press, 2005.

Weiss, Rachel. *Fringe Tactics: Special Interests Target Judicial Races.* Helena, Mont.: Institute on Money in State Politics, 2005.

West Virginia Consumers for Justice. "Out of State Interests." Advertisement storyboard. Available at http://www.brennancenter.org/programs/downloads/buying time_2004/stsupct_wv_wvcj_out_of_state_interests.pdf (accessed July 11, 2006).

Whitcover, Jules. *No Way to Pick a President: How Money and Hired Guns Have Debased American Elections.* New York: Farrar, Straus Giroux, 1999.

Wielhouwer, Peter W., and Brad Lockerbie. "Party Contacting and Political Participation, 1952–1990." *American Journal of Political Science* 38 (1994): 211–229.

Wilke, John. "Chamber of Commerce Targets State Races: Money Pours into Ads Challenging Candidates Who Are Seen as Anti-Business." *Wall Street Journal,* September 16, 2004.

Williams, Jason E. "*Republican Party of Minnesota v. White* Threatens Judicial Impartiality in Texas." *Houston Law Review* 41 (2004): 201–235.

Wlezien, Christopher. "Dynamics of Representation: The Case of U.S. Spending on Defense." *British Journal of Political Science* 26 (1996): 81–103.

———. "Patterns of Representation: Dynamics of Public Preferences and Policy." *Journal of Politics* 66 (2004): 1–24.

———. "The Public as Thermostat: Dynamics of Preferences for Spending." *American Journal of Political Science* 39 (1995): 981–1000.

Wold, John T., and John H. Culver. "The Defeat of the California Justices: The Campaign, the Electorate, and the Issue of Judicial Accountability." *Judicature* 70 (1987): 348–355.

Woodbury, Richard. "Is Texas Justice for Sale?" *Time,* January 11, 1988: 74.

Yeric, Jerry L. *Mass Media and the Politics of Change.* Itasca, Ill.: F. E Peacock, 2001.

Zaccari, Laura. "Judicial Elections: Recent Developments, Historical Perspective, and Continued Viability." *Richmond Journal of Law and the Public Interest* 3 (2004). Available at http://law.richmond.edu/rjolpi/past_issues.html (accessed July 12, 2006).

Zaller, John R. *The Nature and Origins of Belief Systems.* New York: Cambridge University Press, 1992.

Zupan, Mark A. "The Last Period Problem in Politics: Do Congressional Representatives Not Subject to Reelection Constraint Alter Their Voting Behavior?" *Public Choice* 65 (1990): 167–180.

Court Cases

Brown v. Hartlage, 456 U.S. 45 (1982).

Buckley v. Valeo, 424 U.S. 1 (1976).

Chamber of Commerce v. Moore, 288 F.3d 187 (5th Cir. 2002).

DeRolph v. State, 728 N.E.2d 993 (Ohio 2000).

Dimick v. Republican Party of Minnesota, No. 05-566, Petition for Writ of Certiorari.

Eu v. San Francisco County Democratic Central Committee, 489 U.S. 214 (1989).

Family Trust Foundation v. Kentucky Judicial Conduct Commission, 388 F.3d 224 (6th Cir. 2004).

In re Raab, 793 N.E.2d 1287, 1291 (NY 2003).

In re Watson, 100 N.Y.2d 290, 302 (2003).

Lopez-Torres v. New York State Bd. of Elections, F. Supp. 2d, 2006 WL 213955 (E.D.N.Y. Jan. 27), *appeal filed* (2d Cir. Feb. 8, 2006)

McConnell v. FEC, 540 U.S. 93 (2003).

North Dakota Family Alliance, Inc., v. Bader, 361 F. Supp. 2d 1021 (D.N.D. 2005)

Republican Party of Minnesota v. White, 536 U.S. 765 (2002).

Republican Party v. Kelly, 247 F.3d 854 (8th Cir. 2001).

Republican Party v. White, 416 F.3d 738 (8th Cir. 2005) (en banc). [*White II*]

Spargo v. NY Commission on Judicial Conduct, 351 F.3d 65 (2d Cir. 2003).

State ex rel. Ohio Academy of Trial Lawyers v. Sheward, 715 N.E.2d 1062 (Ohio 1999).

U.S. Civil Serv. Commission v. Nat'l Ass'n of Letter Carriers, 413 U.S. 548 (1973).

Weaver v. Bonner, 309 F.3d 1312 (11th Cir. 2002).

Wells v. Edwards, 409 U.S. 1095 (1973).

About the Contributors

Matthew J. Streb is Assistant Professor of Political Science at Northern Illinois University. He is the author, editor, or co-editor of five books, including *The New Electoral Politics of Race* (2002) and *Academic Freedom at the Dawn of a New Century* (2006), and has published articles in journals, including *Political Research Quarterly, Public Opinion Quarterly, Social Science Quarterly, Election Law Journal,* and *Politics and Policy.*

Lawrence Baum is Professor of Political Science at The Ohio State University. He is the author of *The Puzzle of Judicial Behavior* (1998), *The Supreme Court* (2004), and *American Courts* (2002), and has published in journals such as the *American Political Science Review,* the *American Journal of Political Science,* and the *Journal of Politics.* He has been chair of the Law, Courts, and Judicial Process section of the American Political Science Association and has been a member of several editorial boards, including the *American Political Science Review* and the *American Journal of Political Science.* He has received the Alumni Award for Distinguished Teaching and the University Distinguished Scholar Award.

Chris W. Bonneau is Assistant Professor of Political Science at the University of Pittsburgh. His work on judicial elections has been funded by the National Science Foundation and has appeared in such journals as the *American Journal of Political Science, Political Research Quarterly,* and *American Politics Research.* He is also coauthor of *Strategic Behavior and Policy Choice on the U.S. Supreme Court* (2005).

Brent D. Boyea is Assistant Professor of Political Science at the University of Texas at Arlington. He received the Best Paper Award presented by the *State Politics and Policy Quarterly* for a paper delivered at the 2004 American Political Science Association annual meeting (with Paul Brace), and the Best Graduate Student Paper Award, presented by the Southwestern Political Science Association for a paper delivered at the 2003 Southwestern Political Science Association annual meeting.

Paul Brace is Clarence L. Carter Professor of Political Science at Rice University. He has published in the *American Political Science Review, American Journal of Political Science, Journal of Politics, Political Research Quarterly, Polity, Social Science Quarterly, American Politics Quarterly, Legislative Studies Quarterly,* and numerous other journals. He is coauthor of *Follow the Leader: Opinion Polls and the Modern Presidents* (1992), author of *State Government and Economic Performance* (1993), and coeditor of *The Presidency in American Politics* (NYU Press, 1989) and *American State and Local Politics* (1999). His current research on strategic behavior in state supreme courts is funded by the National Science Foundation.

Rachel P. Caufield is Assistant Professor of Political Science at Drake University. She has published an article in the *Akron Law Review,* and has served as a Visiting Fellow at The Brookings Institution in Washington, D.C. She also currently serves as research and program consultant to the Hunter Center for Judicial Selection at the American Judicature Society.

Jennifer Segal Diascro is Assistant Professor of Government at American University. She is coauthor of *Television News and the Supreme Court: All the News That's Fit to Air?* (1998) and co-editor of *Inside the Judicial Process: A Contemporary Reader in Law, Politics, and the Courts* (2006) and has published her research in *Political Research Quarterly, Judicature, American Review of Politics,* and the *Federal Sentencing Reporter.*

Brian Frederick is a Ph.D. candidate in political science at Northern Illinois University.

Deborah Goldberg is the Democracy Program Director of the Brennan Center for Justice at NYU School of Law. She has written or coauthored several publications on judicial elections, including the 2000, 2002, and 2004 editions of *The New Politics of Judicial Elections* and *Public Funding of Judicial Elections: The Roles of Judges and the Rules of Campaign Finance.* She clerked for Hon. Stephen G. Breyer, then on the U.S. Court of Appeals for the First Circuit, and the late Hon. Constance Baker Motley of the U.S. District Court for the Southern District of New York.

Melinda Gann Hall is Professor of Political Science at Michigan State University. Her research has appeared in the *American Political Science Re-*

view, American Journal of Political Science, Journal of Politics, Political Research Quarterly, Social Science Quarterly, American Politics Quarterly, Judicature, and a variety of other scholarly journals, law reviews, and edited volumes. She has received both the American Judicature Society Award and the McGraw-Hill Award from the Law and Courts Section of the American Political Science Association for her research on judicial elections. She is serving, or has served, on numerous editorial boards, including the *American Journal of Political Science, Journal of Politics, Political Research Quarterly, American Politics Quarterly,* and *State Politics and Policy Quarterly,* and on a wide variety of committees and executive councils of professional associations. Currently she is President of the State Politics and Policy Section of the American Political Science Association and Vice President of the Midwest Political Science Association.

Richard L. Hasen is the William H. Hannon Distinguished Professor of Law at Loyola Law School in Los Angeles. He is a nationally recognized expert in election law and campaign finance regulation, coauthor of a leading casebook on election law, and coeditor of the quarterly peer-reviewed publication, *Election Law Journal.* His most recent book is *The Supreme Court and Election Law: Judging Equality from* Baker v. Carr *to* Bush v. Gore (NYU Press, 2003). Hasen also writes the widely read "Election Law Blog."

David Klein is Associate Professor of Politics at the University of Virginia. He is the author of *Making Law in the United States Courts of Appeals* (2002), and has published articles in *Political Research Quarterly, Law and Society Review,* and *Journal of Legal Studies.*

Brian F. Schaffner is Assistant Professor of Government and a research fellow at the Center for Congressional and Presidential Studies at American University. He has published articles in several journals, including the *American Political Science Review, American Journal of Political Science, Political Research Quarterly, Public Opinion Quarterly, Legislative Studies Quarterly,* and *Political Communication.*

Index